ON ROCK OR SAND?

Firm foundations for Britain's future

Edited by
John Sentamu

First published in Great Britain in 2015

Society for Promoting Christian Knowledge
36 Causton Street
London SW1P 4ST
www.spckpublishing.co.uk

British Library Cataloguing-in-Publication Data
A catalogue record for this book is available from the British Library

ISBN 978–0–281–07174–6
eBook ISBN 978–0–281–07175–3

Typeset by Graphicraft Limited, Hong Kong
Manufacture managed by Jellyfish
First printed in Great Britain by CPI
Subsequently digitally printed in Great Britain

eBook by Graphicraft Limited, Hong Kong

Produced on paper from sustainable forests

For hard-pressed families
on poverty wages

Grateful thanks

I am grateful to the many people whose spirit of generosity has inspired and shaped the work of the Bishopthorpe symposia. I would like to thank the outstanding contributors to this book and, in particular, Sir Philip Mawer for his expert guidance in chairing the symposia and in coordinating this project.

Contents

Contents

Contributors

Andrew Adonis

Lord Adonis has been a member of the House of Lords since 2005. He served for twelve years in government as a minister and special adviser. He was Secretary of State for Transport, Minister for Schools, Head of the No. 10 Policy Unit and senior No. 10 adviser on education, public services and constitutional reform. He has pioneered key public service reforms, including the Academy programme, which established over 200 independent state schools to replace failing secondary schools, and the university tuition fees and grants reform of 2004. He is a Trustee of Teach First.

Kersten England

Kersten England has been Chief Executive in York since 2009. In addition to over twenty-five years in local government, Kersten's career has included work in the voluntary sector, higher education and central government. She is passionate about community capacity building, diversity and equality, supporting civic leadership and sustainable urban growth.

Ruth Fox

Dr Ruth Fox is Director and Head of Research of the Hansard Society. She regularly contributes to current affairs programmes on radio and television, commentating on parliamentary process and political reform. She has also served as an independent member of the Northern Ireland Assembly's Committee Review Group, and worked as historical adviser at the Public Record

Office (now the National Archives) after being awarded a PhD in political history from the University of Leeds.

Philip Mawer

Sir Philip Mawer was the Secretary General of the General Synod and subsequently the Parliamentary Commissioner for Standards and the Prime Minister's Independent Adviser on Ministers' Interests. He is currently Chairman of Allchurches Trust Limited (the charitable owner of the Ecclesiastical Insurance Group).

Oliver O'Donovan

Oliver O'Donovan was until recently Professor of Christian Ethics and Practical Theology at the University of Edinburgh. He has served the Church of England as a member of the Board for Social Responsibility, the Doctrine Commission, the Faith and Order Advisory Group and the General Synod.

John Sentamu

The Most Revd and Rt Hon. Dr John Sentamu has been Archbishop of York since 2005. Prior to that, he was appointed Bishop for Stepney in 1996 and Bishop for Birmingham in 2002. He is Primate of England and Metropolitan, a member of the House of Lords and a Privy Councillor.

Andrew Sentance

Dr Andrew Sentance was formerly an external member of the Monetary Policy Committee of the Bank of England (2006–11). He is currently Senior Economic Adviser to PwC (Pricewaterhouse Coopers, a multinational professional services network) and Professor at Warwick Business School. Earlier in his career, he held senior economic positions at British Airways, the Confederation of British Industry and London Business School.

Julia Unwin

Julia Unwin CBE is Chief Executive of the Joseph Rowntree Foundation and the Joseph Rowntree Housing Trust. She was a member of the Housing Corporation Board for ten years and a Charity Commissioner from 1998 to 2003. Julia has researched and written extensively on the role, governance and funding of the voluntary sector.

Justin Welby

The Most Revd and Rt Hon. Justin Welby has been Archbishop of Canterbury since 2013. Prior to that, he was Bishop of Durham from 2012. He is Primate of All England and Metropolitan, a member of the House of Lords and a Privy Councillor. Before ordination, he worked in the oil industry at a senior level. An expert on the politics and histories of Kenya and Nigeria, he has lectured on reconciliation at the US State Department. In the summer of 2012, he was asked to serve on the Parliamentary Commission on Banking Standards.

James Woodward

The Revd Dr James Woodward is a Canon of St George's Chapel, Windsor. Until 2009 he was founding director of the Leveson Centre for the Study of Ageing, Spirituality and Social Policy, an interdisciplinary forum for developing the theory and practice of care for older people through conferences, research and publications. He continues to research, write and teach in this area.

Abbreviations

AAS	*Acta Apostolicae Sedis*
CBI	Confederation of British Industry
CCGs	Clinical Commissioning Groups
ESV	English Standard Version
GDP	Gross Domestic Product
GLA	Greater London Authority
GPs	General Practitioners
HMRC	Her Majesty's Revenue and Customs
IFS	Institute for Fiscal Studies
JRF	Joseph Rowntree Foundation
LIBOR	London Interbank Offered Rate
LW	Living Wage
KJV	King James Version
MHA	Methodist Homes for the Aged
MPC	Monetary Policy Committee
NASB	New American Standard Bible
NEETs	Young People Not in Education, Employment or Training
NHS	National Health Service
NMW	National Minimum Wage
NPNF	Nicene and Post-Nicene Fathers
NRSV	New Revised Standard Version
OECD	Organisation for Economic Co-operation and Development
PPI	payment protection insurance
SCOP	Spiritual Care for Older People
SMEs	small and medium-sized enterprises

List of abbreviations

SNA	System of National Accounts
TUC	Trades Union Congress
UN	United Nations
UNFCCC	United Nations Framework Convention on Climate Change
VAT	value added tax

Preface

JOHN SENTAMU

———— •◦• ————

At the beginning of this decade the impact of the financial crisis was being felt not only by business but also by individuals, families and communities across Britain.

In April 2010, in the context of this financial depression, and with the prospect of a general election, I considered that it was vital that a dynamic and accessible common language be found to articulate the challenges and to look for paths of hope.

In times of shock and confusion, we need people who have depth of understanding, practical experience and a broad and hopeful imagination to help us see beyond our present turmoil.

I therefore invited a group of academics and practitioners to come together to take stock, not only of the policies by which our society and our economy should be governed but also of the underlying virtues and principles of which that society and economy are an expression.

Over the past four years, this group has met regularly to discuss how the structures and foundations of our public life are affected by government policies and financial pressures, and to consider how the virtues of global justice, mutual responsibility, and hope for the future could be nurtured. Our approach was truly 'bifocal': our quest was for a 'big vision', both moral and practical.

We explored the challenges raised by the economic crisis, poverty, education, provision of healthcare, work, ageing, children and young people, and the Welfare State. These are all issues which affect every citizen at some time in their life, and the Church has a duty not only of care for those affected by changes and uncertainty but also of offering challenge and critical friendship to those in positions of responsibility.

In the wake of the Second World War, Archbishop William Temple had called together just such a symposium, the result of which was his book, *Christianity and Social Order*. This provided the Christian undergirding of the Beveridge Report that sought to slay the 'five giant evils' of Want, Disease, Ignorance, Squalor and Idleness.

When the Welfare Act was passed by Parliament, Archbishop William Temple said, 'This is the first time anybody had set out to embody the whole spirit of the Christian ethic in an Act of Parliament.'[1]

Now, as we approach the next general election, some of our symposia members have drawn together some of our thinking and discussions in this book of essays.[2] Britain needs a thorough and holistic health check to discover whether she has firm foundations on which to build for the future. Are these on rock or sand?

---

[1] Correlli Barnett, *The Audit of War: The Illusion and Reality of Britain as a Great Nation* (London: Pan, 2001), pp. 26–7.

[2] See more at <http://www.archbishopofyork.org/pages/the-archbishops-symposium.html>, accessed 13 October 2014.

1

Introduction: Hope today for a brighter tomorrow

JOHN SENTAMU

———◆·◆·◆———

'His money won't work! How will he survive?' Olivia, the grand-daughter of the Bishop of Edmonton, asked, when I was visiting Canada some time ago. Olivia was relieved to hear that I wouldn't be needing my British currency since her grandparents were taking care of my wife and me. But her question made me consider how we help people in our own communities whose money, what little they have, doesn't work, who have to make hard choices, for example between heating and eating. How will *they* survive? They will survive, I think, only if we stop thinking about 'my money' and start thinking about 'our money' and how we can make our money work for all of us.

A few weeks after visiting Canada, I went to Egypt to see how the diocese is serving the very poorest in their communities. One image stayed with me: the picture of a small child and the caption, 'My name is "Today": today I need to eat, today I need to play, today I need care, today I need love. Give me hope today for a brighter tomorrow.'

How do we nourish and nurture care and compassion like that of Olivia – she was then three and a half years of age? How do we rise to the challenge to meet all the needs of 'Today'? Are the well-springs of solidarity still overflowing, or have

1

they run dry, leaving us all in a dry pit where there is no water?[1] Have we 'forsaken the fountain of living water and dug out cisterns for [ourselves], cracked cisterns that can hold no water'?[2]

What I want to do in this introductory chapter is to give us hope today for a brighter tomorrow, building on firm foundations centred on God's free gift of life in Jesus Christ, offering humankind a transforming vision for our 'Common Profit'.[3] That is: the well-being and wholeness of every human being flowing out from the loving purposes of God made visible in the face of Jesus Christ.

The need to build

In April 2010, just before the General Election, the first meeting of the Bishopthorpe symposia was held.

This was a gathering of economists, social thinkers, contemporary historians and theologians whom I had invited to reflect on some of the pressing challenges of the day. It seemed to be an opportune time to take stock not only of the policies by which our society and our economy should be governed but also of the underlying values, virtues and principles of which our society and economy are an expression.

Such a gathering had been in my plans for some four years, but its formation was given added impetus by the signs of increasing dysfunction in the country, and the distress and disaffection among people in the wake of the Financial Crisis and the Credit Crunch.

---

[1] Jer. 14.3.

[2] Jer. 2.13 (NRSV).

[3] Common Profit, a phrase borrowed from John Chrysostom, Homily XXV, *Homilies on the Epistles of Paul to the Corinthians*, NPNF. I shall return to this theme later in the chapter.

Can we achieve a common vision?
Religion and the public debate

How were we to recover confidence in our society and its direction? Was the answer to be found in politics alone? Would the particular colour or leaning of a political party be the golden bullet that would shatter the old and outdated order, and usher in a fresh vision for the governance of Britain? But what was our responsibility – as individuals, as communities?

During the years in which we have been meeting, there have been calls, from all sections of society, for a rebirth of civic values and virtues. The experience of growing inequalities in Britain, the loss of hope for the future among many of our young people, the financial struggle faced by individuals and families, the threat to health and welfare provision, etc. have been a catalyst for this.

In reflecting on achieving a common vision, we have been drawn back repeatedly to the language of 'the common good' (i.e. the universal well-being and good of all); to questions about the real meaning of wealth and what makes for a good society; to the need for a robust vision of what is due to all human beings to enable their flourishing. We have recognised our need to rediscover our fundamental values and virtues, and to be clear about what we may hope for as citizens of Great Britain.

It has seemed clear to us that politics alone is not able to provide a complete answer to contemporary problems. The growing apathy and cynicism about politics and politicians has undermined their ability either to convince the electorate of or even to articulate clearly their vision for the country in an effective way. Jim Wallis, writing in an American context, explains why. He says, in his book *On God's Side*:

It's time to find a better vision for our life together. Politics is failing to solve most of the biggest problems our world now faces – and the disillusionment with elections and politicians has gone global.

Politicians continue to focus on blame instead of solutions, winning instead of governing, ideology instead of civility.[4]

That doesn't mean, however, that a Christian vision of our future will readily be received.

For example, Dame Mary Warnock, a philosopher who has made a prominent contribution to the public debates about ethical issues, in her book, *Dishonest to God*, is concerned with 'what part Christianity should continue to play in legislation and politics and what influence it has and should continue to have in Parliament, whose responsibility is to Christian and non-Christian alike'.[5] From where she stands, religion and morality must be prised apart, however close they may both have been in the past.

I am a considerable admirer of the contribution Lady Warnock has made to public life but on this I cannot accept her argument. This is false prophecy, and potentially fatal to our social fabric. It is false because morality is or should increasingly be a matter of public concern and not just a private matter. It is false because there is a danger that societies in which the expression of belief is weakened may become societies which cannot articulate a common vision. It is false because, unless informed by a conception of the Divine, moral principles are always in danger of fading away into moral relativism.

---

[4] Jim Wallis, *On God's Side: What Religion Forgets and Politics Hasn't Learned about Serving the Common Good* (Oxford: Lion Books, 2013), p. xi. See also Jim Wallis, *The (Un)Common Good: How the Gospel Brings Hope to a World Divided* (Grand Rapids, Mich.: Brazos Press, 2013), p. xii, which 'focuses even more on how we can restore our better values'.

[5] Mary Warnock, *Dishonest to God* (London: Continuum, 2010), p. 1.

In his book *The Idea of Human Rights: Four Inquiries*, Michael Perry throws down the gauntlet that to speak, as so many claim to do, of 'human rights' from a purely secular perspective may well not make any sense.

In the first of these inquiries, R. H. Tawney is quoted as saying in his diary:

> The essence of all morality is this: to believe that every human being is of infinite importance, and therefore that no consideration of expediency can justify the oppression of one by another. But to believe this it is necessary to believe in God.[6]

Three days earlier, Tawney had quoted in his diary the words of T. W. Price, Midland Secretary of the Workers Educational Association, and lecturer at Birmingham University:

> Unless a man believes in spiritual things – in God – altruism is absurd. What is the sense of it? Why should a man recognise any obligation to his neighbour, unless he believes that he has been put in the world for a special purpose and has a special work to perform in it? A man's relations to his neighbours become meaningless unless there is some higher power above them both.[7]

But secularists are not the only people who say that 'the Church should get out and stay out of politics'. Some religious people would also argue that the Church should stay clear of politics. For them, the call to seek first the kingdom of God and the salvation of souls does not encompass a social dimension.

I would argue, however, that Christians are impelled to speak into the public discussion of social issues – not only as involved

---

[6] Michael J. Perry, *The Idea of Human Rights: Four Inquiries* (Oxford: Oxford University Press, 2000), p. 11.

[7] Perry, *Idea of Human Rights*, p. 109n.1 (from R. H. Tawney, *R. H. Tawney's Commonplace Book*, ed. J. M. Winter and D. M. Joslin (London: Cambridge University Press, 1972), p. 67, diary entry of 13 August 1913).

citizens but also because of the Christian understanding of what a just and sustainable society looks like. For we are created by God as fellow-humans, and that is why the Christian calling implies involvement in the needs and well-being of humankind wherever they may be met.

Like the Old Testament prophets, I suggest, it is essential for religion to speak truth to power. And so speaking up for the poor, the widow and the orphan flows from what the Church is and what it's for. And it's important for power to hear this religious voice, even if what is said is uncomfortable to hear.

Of course the Church cannot assume a right to be heard and must establish that right not only by its demonstrable commitment to the universal well-being and the good of all but also by the competence of the contributions it makes.

If the Church is to do that, it has to begin by ensuring that it properly understands the nature of the challenges confronting our society. This was the task our symposia undertook over the past five years at Bishopthorpe, drawing on the broad experience and expertise of the participants.[8]

A number of themes have become clear in our symposia. The first is the need for a more honest, informed and measured style of public debate on the weighty matters of the day. It is understandable that politicians on all sides will want to present their case as persuasively as they can. Sections of the media appear to believe that stories written in stark terms are more likely to attract attention and therefore readers and hearers. But if public debate is constantly conducted in soundbites, the public can end up frustrated, confused and alienated. The Church needs to stand among those who represent the 'still, small voice of calm' as the debate swirls around us.

---

[8] The fruit of some of those conversations can be found on <http://www.archbishopofyork.org/pages/the-archbishops-symposium.html>, accessed 8 October 2014.

The second is the urgent task of focusing on and affirming reiteratively the essentials of the gospel which should underpin our social understanding:

- that all human beings are of equal worth in God's sight;
- that both children and adults will flourish only in the context of a well-ordered society, and a society is well-ordered only as it offers all its members ways of flourishing;
- that flourishing requires both a measure of security in the face of typical human needs, and a measure of openness to the emergence of individual creativity and initiative;
- that work is not merely a means to secure what we need to consume, but a form of communication with other people which dignifies us as individuals and draws us together in community.

The gospel call for social justice

Our society needs to come to a common understanding of and desire for the common good of all. We must turn away from the frenetic seeking after individual satisfaction and individual personal gain, and help one another make real progress together for our 'common profit'. Why 'common profit'?

Suffice it to say here that 'common good' might convey no more than the static idea of an economic reserve, the benefits of which are to be shared fairly within the community. We need to think of how we make real progress together ('profit') and how we may help each other make that progress.

Jesus' first recorded proclamation in the synagogue in Nazareth[9] (after he had read from the prophet Isaiah (61.1–2a)), makes it clear that the Good News of God's kingdom (which he came to proclaim and demonstrate), is for the poor, those who are

---

[9] Luke 4.16–19.

held captive by the oppressive chains of poverty, blindness and enslavement. Concern for a society that addresses problems of poverty and other injustices in society flows out of an evangelism that has the promise of God's kingdom at its centre.

Jesus went on to say to his hearers, 'I must proclaim the good news of the kingdom of God to the other cities also; for I was sent for this purpose' (NRSV). So says Jesus of Nazareth in Luke 4.43, when the people of Capernaum try to detain him.

Jesus' priority was to let the movement of the Holy Spirit bring about a movement of human participation in the reign of God. This is the purpose that all who are called to follow him must adopt as their own.

Having rejected the temptation of the Evil One, to settle for less – whether it was a sort of *humanitarianism*, through which stones could be turned into bread to feed the hungry, or a sort of *supernaturalism* by which a spectacular demonstration of power could attract followers, or a sort of *secularisation* which would accord him worldly power, without the necessity of God – he set out a more radical mission of God.

This holistic and healing mission was committed to the right sort of humanitarian aid, which involved God's action in bringing healing and hope; to the right sort of supernatural powers, which called for the reality of God's kingdom on earth; and to the right kind of social engagement with the world. His mission did not rely on the application of sticking-plaster solutions, but depended on deep change in people's hearts, attitudes and aspirations by the life-giving Holy Spirit.

Jesus was calling people to a universal movement of forgiveness, reconciliation and freedom. And this movement is one which we, as his Body, the Church, are called to participate in and proclaim. The Church is to be both a sign and a servant of the kingdom.

Does evangelism come first, or social action? Jesus demands both: he refuses the 'either/or'.

The question concerns both who people are and what they do. Jesus is concerned both with change of heart and with change of physical conditions. As his teaching about the good tree bearing good fruit makes clear,[10] he leads people to a life of radical transformation and discipleship – continually learning, being renewed and serving others.

We are created for fellowship, mutual responsibility, community and mutuality. The test for social and political parties is whether they advance this.

This vision of mutuality is at the centre of Jesus' own conception of ethical reflection, of moral decision making, since, clearly, every community has neighbours.

> Just then a lawyer stood up to test Jesus. 'Teacher,' he said, 'what must I do to inherit eternal life?' He said to him, 'What is written in the law? What do you read there?' He answered, 'You shall love the Lord your God with all your heart, and with all your soul, and with all your strength, and with all your mind; and your neighbour as yourself.' And he said to him, 'You have given the right answer; do this, and you will live.'[11]

The lawyer in this Gospel story, having answered his own question of what he had to do to inherit eternal life – total love for God and total love for neighbour – goes on to justify himself by asking, 'And who is my neighbour?'

Jesus answers the lawyer by way of a parable: the story of 'The neighbourly Samaritan',[12] who – in contrast to the Priest and the Levite – showed mercy to the man who fell among robbers who stripped him, beat him and left him half dead.

---

[10] Matt. 7.16–18.

[11] Luke 10.25–28 (NRSV).

[12] Jesus never called the Samaritan '*The good* Samaritan'. For Jesus, 'only God is good' (Mark 10.18).

'And who is my neighbour?' In telling that story, Jesus tells the lawyer to put into practice what he already knows, and to stop avoiding the challenge of neighbourly love, which extends to everyone, even those to whom one would give no regard. Love must be practical and not merely consist in sentiment.[13]

In the context of our present argument, we need to recognise that injury can be caused by individuals not only doing personal physical violence to one another but also embracing choices which deprive others of the means of financial security, work, housing, education, healthcare, or dignity in old age.

The parable Jesus of Nazareth told the lawyer is not a case of a singular goodness but of never-ending neighbourly love. If our neighbours' needs are to be met, we must meet them because we are God's agents of transformation, and he depends upon us to do his work.

Jesus of Nazareth can be seen either as the neighbourly Samaritan ministering to humanity who lie wounded and dying by the wayside and bringing them healing, hope, health, and wholeness; or as himself the victim, wounded for our transgressions and suffering with all who suffer. In tending to their needs we are tending to his. 'I was hungry and you gave me food, I was thirsty and you gave me something to drink, I was a stranger and you welcomed me, I was naked and you gave me clothing, I was sick and you took care of me, I was in prison and you visited me.'[14]

In fact Jesus Christ is both the neighbourly Samaritan and the wounded traveller by the roadside. Our relationship to the hungry, the thirsty, the stranger, the naked, the sick, those in prison, shows forth our relationship to God, his relationship to us in Christ, his relationship to us as the neighbourly Samaritan and as the wounded traveller on the roadside.

---

[13] No doubt the Priest and the Levite felt a pang of pity for the wounded man, but they did nothing. Compassion, to be real, must issue in deeds.

[14] Matt. 25.35 (NRSV).

We must be prepared to help anyone who has been hurt by others: anyone from any nation, tribe and language, who is in need, is our neighbour. Our help must be as wide as the love of God.

The role of the Church in the well-being of society

The Church cannot be about God if it is not about the welfare, or, better, as I argue below, the well-being, of all God's children. For in Jesus' summary of the law, the first commandment to love God and the second to love your neighbour as yourself are not independent commandments, where you can satisfy one but not the other, but rather two interdependent commandments, where to do one you must already do the other. So being in the God-business, as the Church surely is, must also mean that the Church is in the well-being business.

But they aren't the same business. They are two sides of the same coin. We can see this in what another of my predecessors in York, Archbishop Michael Ramsey, said of the double orientation of the Church, namely, towards God and the world:

> It lives towards God and towards the world. Towards God it worships; towards the world, it preaches the Gospel, it brings people into fellowship with God, it infects the world with righteousness, it speaks of divine principles on which the life of humanity is ordered.[15]

So, the Church is oriented both towards God, in worship, and towards the world, in preaching and bringing people into fellowship with God.

To do this, the Church must present a vision for the ordering of our social life, a political vision. Therefore, to be faithful, the Church must be fully engaged in the public deliberations of how to organise and to govern a society where everyone

---

[15] A. M. Ramsey, *Introducing the Christian Faith* (London: SCM Press, 1961), p. 72.

lives to the full stature of what it is to be human, which is what we find in Jesus of Nazareth.

Such an understanding of the Church has its roots not only in Jesus' preaching and teaching but also in the Church Fathers' understanding of who Jesus is and what he means to those who put their trust in him.

In commenting on 1 Corinthians 11.1, John Chrysostom writes,

> 'Be ye imitators of me, even as I also am of Christ.'[16]
>
> This is a rule of the most perfect Christianity, this is a landmark exactly laid down, this is the point that stands highest of all; viz. the seeking those things which are for the common profit: which also Paul himself declared, by adding, 'even as I also am of Christ.'
>
> For nothing can so make a man an imitator of Christ as caring for his neighbours. Nay, though you should fast, though you should lie upon the ground, and even strangle yourself, but take no thought for your neighbour; you have wrought nothing great, but still standest far from this Image, while so doing.[17]

Thus, according to Chrysostom, loving one's neighbours consists in seeking the 'Common Profit', which is central to the Christian life and faith. But what is the Common Profit? It is, I think, the *eudaimonia* of the community.[18]

In commenting on the origins of the Church, Rowan Williams writes,

---

[16] 1 Cor. 11.1.

[17] John Chrysostom, Homily XXV, *Homilies on 1 Corinthians 11*, p. 258.

[18] *Eudaimonia* is a term of ancient Greek moral philosophy. It can be translated variously as 'flourishing', 'happiness' or 'well-being'. None of these translations are adequate, though, on their own, since plants and animals can flourish but only rational beings can have *eudaimonia*; 'happiness' tends to connote subjective satisfaction but *eudaimonia* is an objective matter, and well-being, on at least some accounts, is hedonistic, which *eudaimonia* is not. 'Blessedness' may come closer, because this word lacks the randomness of 'happiness' (*hap = chance*). Consequently, I will leave the term untranslated.

The Christian Church began as a reconstructed version of the notion of God's people – a community called by God to make God known to the world in and through the forms of law-governed common life – the 'law' being, in the Christian case, the model of action and suffering revealed in Jesus Christ. It claimed to make real a pattern of common life lived in the fullest possible accord with the nature and will of God – a life in which each member's flourishing [*eudaimonia*] depended closely and strictly on the flourishing [*eudaimonia*] of every other . . .

So Christian identity is irreducibly political in the sense that it defines a *politeia*, a kind of citizenship (Philippians 3:20); yet its existence and integrity are not bound to a successful realisation of this citizenship within history. There does not have to be final and sacred political order created in order for the integrity of the Church to survive.[19]

Just as it was then, at the origins of the Church, it is now the task of the Church to articulate a vision of what the Common Profit, the *eudaimonia* of the community, looks like and how to realise it in our own time.

A vision in which each member's flourishing depends on that of others is a theme further developed in Justin Welby's contribution to this collection of essays.

The Church of God is called by its creation, foundation and mission to speak God's word of justice. The prophet Micah announced to all humanity what is required: 'He has told you, O mortal, what is good; and what does the Lord require of you: only to do justice, and to love goodness, and to walk modestly with your God; then your name will achieve wisdom.'[20]

---

[19] Rowan Williams, *Faith in the Public Square* (London: Bloomsbury, 2012), pp. 28–9.

[20] Mic. 6.8–9, *Jewish Study Bible*, ed. Adele Berlin and Marc Zvi Brettler, consulting editor Michael Fishbane, Jewish Publication Society, Tanakh Translation (Oxford: Oxford University Press, 2004), p. 1215.

Law, religion and morals

The Church has a particular responsibility to speak to power with a prophetic voice for justice and freedom.

For me, justice goes beyond the simple administration of laws. Justice is only possible when law, religion and morals are intermingled.

Lord Denning wrote in 1953,

> The severance of these ideas – of law from morality, and of religion from law – belongs very distinctly to the later stages of the evolution of modern thought. This severance has gone a great way. Many people now think that religion and law have nothing in common.
>
> The law, they say, governs our dealings with our fellows, whereas religion concerns our dealings with God. Likewise, they hold that law has nothing to do with morality. Law lays down rigid rules which must be obeyed without questioning whether they are right or wrong. Its function is to keep order, not to do justice.
>
> The severance has, I think, gone much too far. Although religion, law and morals can be separated, they are nevertheless still very much dependent on one another. Without religion, there can be no morality, there can be no law.[21]

That was written more than sixty years ago, but I am of the view that what he wrote still holds true.

Religion concerns the spirit in humanity, whereby we are able to recognise what is truth and what is justice; whereas law is only the application, often imperfectly, of truth and justice in our everyday affairs.

The common law of England has been moulded for centuries by lawyers and judges who have been brought up in the Judaeo-

---

[21] Right Honourable Sir Alfred Denning, *The Changing Law* (London: Stevens, 1953).

Christian Religion. The precepts of religion, consciously or unconsciously, have been their guide in the administration of justice. 'If religion perishes in the land, truth and justice will also. We have already strayed too far from the faith of our forebears. Let us return to it, for it is the only thing that can save us.'[22] So said Lord Denning.

This position is enshrined in the governance of our country: the Queen in Parliament under God. Think of the Coronation Service for our Queen, and for future kings and queens. The service is not just a meaningless pageant for 'The Coronation Service is where the Divine Law is placed before the law of the State, acknowledged and reverenced. It reminds us of the source of all our law, in truth and in justice.'[23]

As a thirteenth-century lawyer, Henry of Bracton, rightly said, the King or Queen 'must not be under man but under God and the law, for the law makes the king'.[24]

In forcing King John to sign the Magna Carta, 800 years ago this year, were the barons not insisting that he observed this principle and his coronation oath?[25]

It is interesting to note, however, that Chapters 39 and 40 of the Magna Carta, 1215, echo the Law and the Prophets of the Hebrew Scriptures:

39. No free man shall be seized or imprisoned or stripped of his rights or possessions, or outlawed or exiled, or deprived of

---

[22] Right Honourable Sir Alfred Denning, *The Influence of Religion on Law* (Gwent: Sterling Press, 1989), pp. 33–4.

[23] L. L. Blake, *The Royal Law: Source of Our Freedom Today* (London: Shepheard-Walwyn, 2000), p. 15.

[24] Blake, *Royal Law*, p. 15.

[25] To 'love the holy Church, and the ordained of it and would preserve it indemnified from the Incursions of the Malignant; and that the perverse Laws being destroyed, he would substitute good ones, and would exercise right Justice in England' (Nathaniel Johnston, *The Excellency of Monarchical Government, Especially of the English Monarchy Wherein Is Largely Treated of the Several Benefits of Kingly Government* (1686).

his standing in any other way, nor will we proceed with force against him, or send others to do so, except by the lawful judgement of his equals or by the law of the land.

40. To no one will we sell, to no one deny or delay right or justice.[26]

The Judaeo-Christian wisdom is in Britain's veins, whether recognised or not. Her laws, her language and many of her values were formed by that Religion and virtue. It is enshrined in our Constitution – namely, in the Coronation Service, the Magna Carta and the Rule of Law.

We must therefore guard against the tendency for the laws and structures of our government to become regarded purely as an instrument for regulating our personal affairs – completely severed from morality and religion. Like Lord Denning, I believe that this separation has gone too far.

My analysis chimes in with Lord Bingham's examination of the meaning of the Rule of Law, in which he makes it clear that the Rule of Law is not an arid legal doctrine but is the foundation of a fair and just society, a guarantee of responsible government, and an important contribution to economic growth, as well as offering the best means yet devised for securing peace and co-operation.

He advocates eight conditions which capture its essence as understood in Western democracies today:

1 The law must be accessible and, so far as possible, be intelligible, clear and predictable;
2 Questions of legal right and liability should ordinarily be resolved by application of the law and not by the exercise of discretion;

---

[26] Translated from the Latin: Tom Bingham, *The Rule of Law* (London: Allen Lane, 2010), p. 10.

3 The law should apply equally to all, except to the extent that objective differences justify differentiation;

4 The law must afford adequate protection of human rights;

5 Means must be provided for resolving, without prohibitive cost or inordinate delay, bona fide civil disputes which the parties themselves are unable to resolve;

6 Ministers and public officers at all levels must exercise the powers conferred on them reasonably, in good faith, for the purpose for which the powers were conferred, and without exceeding the limits of such powers;

7 Judicial and other adjudicative procedures must be fair and independent;

8 There must be compliance by the State with its International Law obligations.

He ends by saying that,

> The rule of law is one of the greatest unifying factors, perhaps the greatest, the nearest we are likely to approach to a universal secular religion. It remains an ideal, but an ideal worth striving for, in the interests of good government and peace, at home and in the world at large.[27]

As a liberal democracy, we have good reason to encourage citizens to participate in political discussion, to offer justifications for their views, and to support the passing of laws they believe to be morally appropriate. So, if citizens holding religious faith are to participate in a liberal democracy, they must be able to support the political views they hold and advocate the laws they believe to be morally appropriate using religious reasons.

Given that there are some secularists for whom questions of faith do not arise and some religious citizens for whom faith is central to their conception of the good and the right, how

---

[27] Bingham, *Rule of Law*, p. 174.

are we to deliberate together on creating a vision for Britain's future? We must do this by trying to see the world from the other's point of view, such that the other is no longer 'the other'. By trying to learn each other's grammar, to understand from the inside why we hold the many and various views we do on how to organise and to govern society.

Properly functioning public discourse in a society with different religions present, and a diversity of cultures, requires empathy and gracious magnanimity – meeting each other half way and with a genuine desire to promote the Common Profit, the *eudaimonia* of the community. Without that desire, there is no point in politics.

But we live in fractious and worrying times, in which the role of the Church, like other elements in the social fabric, is constantly questioned and often attacked. What then is the particular contribution the Church can make at such a time as this, and how should its members go about making it?

First, they must remind themselves and others of the value and importance of the contribution that trust in God makes to our national life. Believers in God and the communities they create are part of the glue which holds our society together.

Of course, religious faith can be a source of division in society, but so can many other differences in human understanding and allegiance. The fact is that all our communities benefit from the contribution of those who adhere to the worship of God, expressed in a life of service to their fellow human beings.

Second, the Church has a particular calling to the task of building up the wellsprings of solidarity in our society.

On the occasion of her Diamond Jubilee, the Queen, speaking specifically about the Church of England, recognised this role in a speech to all religious leaders at Lambeth Palace on 15 February 2012. She said,

The concept of our established Church is occasionally misunderstood and, I believe, commonly underappreciated. Its role is not to defend Anglicanism to the exclusion of other religions. Instead, the Church has a duty to protect the free practice of all faiths in this country.

The Church is woven into the fabric of this country, and has helped to build a better society. It has created an environment for other faith communities and indeed people of no faith to live freely.

Building on our history: The inheritance of Church involvement in social justice

The greatest privilege the Church has in Great Britain is also its greatest responsibility, namely, that of living alongside and ministering to every community, large and small, up and down Britain.

Part of that responsibility is to hold up the mirror to contemporary society to see clearly whether it reflects what a healthy and hopeful society should look like. The Church does this by calling on the resources of centuries of moral thinking that our religious traditions have in their storehouses.

And we need one another, religious and secularist citizen alike, if politics is not to be myopic, at best, or blind, at worst: it must make use of these resources. To adapt Kant's pithy phrase about intuitions and concepts,[28] 'Religion without politics is empty; politics without religion is blind.'[29]

We must use, and not cut ourselves off from, the wisdom of the past.

---

[28] Immanuel Kant, *Critique of Pure Reason*, trans. Paul Guyer and Alan Wood (Cambridge: Cambridge University Press, 1990 (1781/1787)), A51/B76.

[29] By 'politics' I mean not party politics but rather the public deliberation of how to organise and govern society.

That is the task which members of my symposia have undertaken in our meetings over the past four years, and in the writing of this series of essays. I have already mentioned that one of my predecessors, Archbishop William Temple, undertook a similar exercise after the Second World War. He played a crucial part in forming the shared moral as well as political understanding that led to the development of the Welfare State after 1945.

Forty years before, three young men had first met at Balliol College, Oxford. Between them, they were to develop and realise a major vision for Britain. In addition to Temple, they were Richard Tawney and William Beveridge.

One man in particular had a major influence over the whole Balliol student community at that time. He was the Master of the College, the eminent Scottish philosopher Edward Caird. Deeply influenced by the poverty he had witnessed in his native Glasgow, he had campaigned for social reform. At Balliol he encouraged his undergraduates to become involved with the university settlements in the East End of London – in Bethnal Green and Whitechapel – and in Bermondsey in South London.

At Oxford the three young men were challenged to go to the East End of London to 'find friends among the poor, as well as finding out what poverty is and what can be done about it'.[30] In the East End their consciences were pricked by poverty: visible, audible, and smellable.

The experience in the East End of London had a lasting impact, opening their eyes to the often grim realities of life for many of their fellow citizens. All three went on to seek radical reform – each in his own way was to help build a new vision for Britain.

William Temple was both deeply affected by that experience and increasingly troubled by the poverty and deprivation he

---

[30] Norman Dennis and A. H. Halsey, *English Ethical Socialism: Thomas More to R. H. Tawney*, (Oxford: Clarendon Press, 1988), p. 153.

had later witnessed as Bishop of Manchester and, latterly, as Archbishop of York and then of Canterbury. In his seminal work *Christianity and Social Order* (1942), he called on the government to set themselves six objectives to address the crisis.

These were: (1) proper housing for children; (2) decent education; (3) a proper income for workers and the unemployed; (4) opportunities for workers to have a voice in the running of their firms; (5) adequate leisure; and (6) liberty.

Many of the reforms which William Temple had called for were realised in Beveridge's Report in 1942. The subsequent implementation of these reforms by the newly elected Clement Attlee Government led to the creation of what came to be known as the Welfare State.

The recommendations of the report were based on three guiding principles:

1 That any proposals for the future should not be restricted by consideration of sectional interests.
2 That the proposals should be part of a comprehensive policy on social progress. The welfare reforms tackled the evil of Want, but Beveridge also identified four other giant evils: Disease, Ignorance, Squalor and Idleness. All these should be part of social reconstruction.
3 That social security should be achieved by co-operation between the State and the individual which should leave room and encouragement for incentive, opportunity and responsibility.

When the report was turned into law, Archbishop Temple wrote, 'This is the first time anybody had set out to embody the whole spirit of the Christian ethic in an Act of Parliament.'[31]

---

[31] Correlli Barnett, *The Audit of War: The Illusion and Reality of Britain as a Great Nation* (London: Pan, 2001), p. 29.

The reforms which Tawney, Temple and Beveridge achieved in the 1940s represented the apogee of a shared vision for Britain in the last century. Britain achieved a National Health Service which became a model for Europe and the rest of the world. Moreover, the United Kingdom in the Welfare State has provided income and support to those who are sick, unemployed or incapacitated in many other ways. And we have developed an educational system to provide a free and full education for all primary and secondary school pupils.

Have we lost this vision? For me, and I'm sure for many others, a major concern is the extent to which the social compact which the Welfare State represented is now under threat.

Regaining the vision

There is an urgent need for the Church once more to rise to the challenge and to provide reflection on how the social compact can be refashioned in ways that make sense in the light of today's serious social and economic realities.

The context in which we find ourselves is easily, if depressingly, stated. It is one of economic uncertainty, and of worrying failure of all governments to create a climate in which full employment can happen, and where we no longer see the devastating effects of unemployment on the young. Meanwhile the gulf continues to widen between those who have plenty and those who are struggling to make ends meet with the misery of fiscal deficit and deep cuts in public expenditure, of rising levels of student and trade union unease, and of low levels of trust between elected representatives and those whom they govern. Our economic situation is well explored by Andrew Sentance in his contribution to this collection of essays, where he considers questions of economic growth and what counts as good growth.

The solidaristic vision of Britain, the vision of Tawney, Temple and Beveridge, following the Second World War has given way to an individualist and consumerist vision, with public goods such as health, as explored by Kersten England in her contribution, and education, as explored by Andrew Adonis, increasingly becoming privatised, where society has become a market society, with everything going to the highest bidder and the poor being left behind in the unceasing drive to increase the nation's Gross Domestic Product.

This cannot be right. As Temple writes, 'Maximum output is not a true end of human enterprise; the end is fullness of personality in community; nothing economic is a true end.'[32]

Indeed, as Richard Wilkinson and Kate Pickett argue, 'further improvements in the quality of life no longer depend on further economic growth: the issue is now community and how we relate to each other.'[33] While many have benefited from the economic progress of past decades, the consequences of this rampant consumerism and individualism – both economic and social – have been to eradicate the glue that holds communities together.

Astonishingly, this disintegrative process is then expressed in what it means to live a good life. In previous generations, a good life was one defined by making a positive difference to one's community, nation and even the world. This was expressed in lives of service and solidarity with one's neighbours. But that idea has given way to an individualist and consumerist conception of the good life characterised by the management of individual pleasure.

As Miroslav Volf writes,

---

[32] William Temple, *Social Witness and Evangelism* (London: Epworth Press, 1942), p. 12.
[33] Richard Wilkinson and Kate Pickett, *The Spirit Level: Why Equality Is Better for Everyone* (London: Penguin Books, 2010), p. 254.

The idea of flourishing as a human being has shrivelled to meaning no more than leading an experientially satisfying life. The sources of satisfaction may vary: power, possessions, love, religion, sex, food, and drugs – whatever. What matters most is not the *source* of satisfaction but the *experience* of it – *my* satisfaction. Our satisfied self is our best hope.

Not only is this petty, but a dark shadow of disappointment stubbornly follows our obsession with personal satisfaction. We are meant for something larger than our own satisfied selves. Petty hopes generate self-subverting, melancholy experiences.[34]

A further effect of individualism and consumerism is the dehumanisation of many members of society, particularly the poor. When your life revolves only around you and what you can acquire, when society itself becomes 'the acquisitive society', to use Tawney's (1920) phrase, people become instruments and those who have no use become invisible.

But the poor in this 'age of austerity' experience what I call a 'new poverty', where many of the 'new poor' are in work. Once upon a time, you couldn't really be living in poverty if you had regular wages. You could find yourself on a low income, but not living in poverty. That is no longer so.

You can be in work and still live in poverty, and the work these people have is not 'good work', a concept explored by Oliver O'Donovan in his essay.

Politicians often refer to 'hard-working families'. They should speak instead of 'hard-pressed families'. Yet we are an advanced economy, a first-world country and we have been one for longer than most. Nevertheless, we suffer from blight – increasing poverty in a land of plenty, as Julia Unwin explores in her contribution.

---

[34] Miroslav Volf, *A Public Faith: How Followers of Christ Should Serve the Common Good* (Grand Rapids, Mich.: Brazos Press, 2011), pp. 99–100.

We are a developed economy and a first-world country, so how can it be that in this day and age we are seeing malnutrition, food poverty and energy poverty at such levels in our country?

Building on firm foundations

This question and others that follow from it were all questions which posed themselves to us as members of the symposia. Where do we go from here? How can we build in a way which affirms and reflects the unique value of each individual, created and loved by God? How can we rediscover the wellsprings of solidarity? What particular contribution can the Church make in such a time? How should it go about making it?

In the Gospels of Matthew and Luke,[35] Jesus concludes his Sermon on the Mount by telling a story of two house builders, one of whom took the trouble to study the terrain and put in the effort of digging deep down to lay foundations on the shelf of the rock below.

The other saw the tempting and attractive level ground of the smoothed-over sand, ready for a quick-build and immediate satisfaction. The rain poured down, the rivers flooded over, and the winds blew against both houses. The one on the rock did not fall; but the one on the sand did – and what a terrible fall that was!

Both builders wanted to build; both no doubt built well – houses that looked good and sturdy in themselves. But only the house whose foundations were firm could withstand the storms of life. I shall return to this question of Foundations: Rock or Sand? in my Conclusion.

It is clear that the ground beneath us today is shifting and uncertain. Many are being swept away in the storms of poverty

---

[35] Matt. 7.24–27; Luke 6.46–49.

and deprivation; others, relying on the apparent good life of experiential satisfaction of individualism and consumerism, are losing contact with the virtues which sustain us.

The task we set ourselves in our symposia discussions was to survey the terrain and the foundations of our society's structures and to discover the virtues and values which will provide the firm foundation for the future.

In order to build something which can withstand the storms, we have to identify both our foundational values and virtues, and our common purpose. We must embrace the Common Profit that comes from recognising each other's worth and from caring for one another.

What stability is offered by our financial institutions, our education, our health and welfare provision? In the essays that follow, we shall explore the moral foundations of our society in the hope that we may build more firmly and securely so that all its members may weather the storms together.

2

Building the common good

JUSTIN WELBY

━━━━━◆◆◆━━━━━

At the time of writing (May 2014) the UK economy has just recovered to its level immediately before the Great Recession which began in 2008. About six years have passed, a longer period below the previous peak than in the Great Depression of 1929–32. It may well be another ten years before the consequences of the crisis are out of the system. The mood today is rightly upbeat and optimistic. That is a cause for celebration. At the same time it is a good moment to ask how the renewed economic life of the nation may be more sustainable and more equitably distributed than in the period before 2008. This is not a question about economics, let alone party politics; it is a question of the moral basis of our prosperity.

Jesus tells a parable of the workers in the vineyard: 'And about five o'clock he went out and found others standing around; and he said to them, "Why are you standing here idle all day?" They said to him, "Because no one has hired us." He said to them, "You also go into the vineyard."'[1]

Introduction

Stability and hope are linked to purpose and productivity. While they may be found in other ways, for most people the major

---

[1] Matt. 20.6–7 (NRSV).

source of stability and hope is found from engagement in a worthwhile occupation. This gives self-respect in enabling people to earn a living and provide for those around them. It broadens the network of acquaintances who may become friends. It gives a place where, for some who wish it, there may be the possibility of advancement and developing knowledge and skills, or of fulfilment for others who choose the predictability of doing something worthwhile day by day. Let us not be utopian: most people have Monday morning blues, but the blues are a great deal worse when they are seven days a week. Many people have boring work, or work that they don't enjoy. But no work is almost invariably even worse.

The parable of the workers in the vineyard is rich in meaning, but early on it almost casually expresses the sense of lostness in those seeking to be productive who find the economy does not offer them the opportunity to work in the first place. The economy does not offer them stability or hope. This circumstance, presupposed by the parable, stands in contradiction to God's expressed desire (indeed, you might say God's command!) for humanity to have dominion over the earth and to enjoy its fruits (Gen. 1.28–29). The extent to which humanity does not have access to stability and hope is the extent to which humanity is in crisis. When God created us, he intended us to work, not to be idle. Alas, in many ways the circumstance of the parable of the workers in the vineyard is the circumstance of today. There are many individuals throughout our country who, like those waiting outside the vineyard, long for employment but for reasons beyond their control cannot find a way over the wall. Stability and hope are beyond their grasp.

But, in another sense, the economic realities of today are even more complex than in the biblical parable. There are entire towns and regions of our country that are being left 'outside the vineyard', as it were, trapped in an apparently inescapable economic downward spiral. Reasons for this are complex (under-productivity, globalising markets, outsourcing of labour, etc.), but the reality remains the same: we are a people in crisis. And I believe we have a responsibility to try to turn the tide. We must seek to cultivate a vineyard with room for everyone to work – and not only that, but for everyone to live with stability and hope. This will only come through a mass conversion of our hearts and minds to a gratuitous[2] and widespread commitment to solidarity – of a society built and lives lived on the principles of the inherent dignity of the person, outside and beyond any economic value, and of the commonality of the human journey. The good of our society, on every level, depends on precisely such a transformation.

All in it together? The shape of the economic crisis

The extent of the problem we face is manifested starkly in figures published in the *Financial Times* in 2012.[3] Its report showed that London is the only region in England where economic output per capita was growing. According to its research, London's economic output grew by 3.7 per cent between 2007 and 2010, while all other regions (except Scotland) saw output fall. Growing levels of insolvency and the 'greatest household financial stress', found in the North East, contrast with reports of a steadily improving situation in London and the South East. More recent figures show that the UK now has the largest variation in living standards between regions in the

---

[2] 'Gratuitous' in this sense is used as a theological concept implying 'freely given'. It is rooted in Catholic Social Teaching of the gratuitous love of God for us, whereby God freely confers being and life on everything which exists without obligation.

[3] B. Groom, 'London widens gap with regions', *Financial Times* (3 January 2012) <http://www.ft.com/cms/s/0/b91d7d4c-2cb9-11e1-8cca-00144feabdc0.html?siteedition=uk#axzz2sGT5UfL4>, accessed 2 September 2014.

European Union, with the nation's capital accounting for over 22 per cent of UK gross value added.[4] The output of ten of the twelve regions that make up the UK is below the national average, with only London and South East England above it.[5]

London's output is close to being twice the national average, while in the past twenty years at the time of writing, there has been stagnation, and even a shrinking of output, in other regions such as Wales and the North East. Added to this is more recent research about population movements, such as that done by the think tank Centre for Cities, which indicates that growing numbers of young people are moving from the regions to London.[6] Increasingly people do not see the regions as places in which either to put down roots or to invest in the economy – but as places to leave behind.

In 2007, the think tank Policy Exchange published a report called *Cities Unlimited: Making Urban Regeneration Work*.[7] It offered a wide-ranging examination of the problems facing many cities and towns around the country where there were signs of long-term decline (with particular attention to cities on the coast). The report made for sobering reading. It argued that for some towns and cities, which may once have been

---

[4] Gross value added is the value of output less the value of intermediate consumption; it is a measure of the contribution to Gross Domestic Product (GDP) made by an individual producer, industry or sector; gross value added is the source from which the primary incomes of the System of National Accounts (SNA) are generated and is therefore carried forward into the primary distribution of income account. Source: OECD, *Glossary of Statistical Terms* from <https://stats.oecd.org/glossary/detail.asp?ID=1184>, accessed 28 April 2014.

[5] J. Pickford, 'Recovery likely to widen wealth gap between London and regions', *Financial Times* (19 January 2014) <http://www.ft.com/cms/s/0/1412c032-80f4-11e3-95aa-00144feab7de.html#axzz2uSNqJmn7>, accessed 2 September 2014.

[6] Centre for Cities, *Cities Outlook 2014*, 15–17 <http://www.centreforcities.org/assets/files/2014/Cities_Outlook_2014.pdf>, accessed 2 September 2014.

[7] T. Leunig and J. Swaffield, *Cities Unlimited: Making Urban Regeneration Work* (London: Policy Exchange, 2007).

vital components of British economic and social life, 'regeneration, in the sense of convergence, will not happen, because it is not possible'.[8] Is that really the case, or can we imagine new possibilities?

The hard truth is that many of these cities are in what appear to be lose–lose situations. Already in decline, the road towards recovery and growth is made even more difficult. There are now fewer readily available government resources able to support economic development in these regions; and also, since the 1980s, the banking system has become more and more London-concentrated and consequently out of touch with local needs. As businesses gravitate towards more prosperous areas, more and more parts of the country find themselves facing significant financial exclusion.

Areas away from London, even when they grow economically, do so less quickly than London and the South East generally. Lending too – whether in the form of mortgages, small business loans or personal loans – is concentrated overwhelmingly in London and the South East, with areas in the north largely out of the loop. The economic gap between London and the South East and the rest of the country does not seem likely to shrink at any point in the near future.

As the South East grows, many cities are left feeling abandoned and hopeless. They are in dire need of economic rejuvenation, and they have the fewest resources with which to accomplish it. It is a vicious circle of decline. And while some excellent pieces of research have made recommendations on how to tackle this vicious circle – notably Lord Heseltine's report *No Stone Unturned: In Pursuit of Growth*[9] – their conclusions

---

[8] Leunig and Swaffield, *Cities Unlimited*, p. 62.
[9] M. Heseltine, *No Stone Unturned: In Pursuit of Growth* (London: Department for Business, Innovation and Skills, 2012).

have not been taken as seriously as they should have been and remain, in large part, ignored.

Much of England is experiencing economic crisis. Our economy appears to be, in one sense, a tale of two cities – one being a growing and constantly improving London (and the South East generally), and the other being most, but not all, other cities, alike in that they are each trapped in apparently inevitable decline.

Of course, London has many economic problems of its own. While on a national level entire cities are being cast aside and left to their own devices, one cannot walk the streets of London for long before realising that this national trend is happening at an individual level in this massive city. There is poverty around the corner from every multi-million and multi-billion pound industry – individuals and families similarly trapped in apparently inescapable circles of despair.

This sketch of our current plight will not come as news to many. It is the reality we experience and see on a daily basis. I believe that many of the prescribed remedies that so often accompany this diagnosis are deeply flawed. In fact, questioning these prescriptions is, I think, the first step towards cultivating a vineyard in which everyone has the chance to achieve stability and hope.

What we have tried and what has not worked

There have been numerous and varied attempts by our governments to rescue cities in decline. There were significant efforts in economic planning in the 1960s, followed by the market-based trickle-down strategy of the 1980s and 1990s. More recently, governments and planners have tried ideas such as regeneration-from-the-centre projects (known as the 'doughnut effect'), investment in public transport networks, and investing in new housing and house-building. One thing all these strategies have in common is that none has experienced the success which was hoped for, or which was predicted. Nothing has really worked so far.

One example of the regeneration-from-the-centre approach is found in Liverpool, which I saw first-hand during my time as Dean of Liverpool Cathedral. The idea is that if one injects enough cash into local economies the resulting economic production will have a ripple effect from the centre out to the outskirts of the city. In Liverpool, the Liverpool ONE development resulted in investments of over £1 billion in central Liverpool,[10] and yet six years later the nearest boroughs of the city – just a twenty-minute walk away – remain untransformed by the project's impact.

The lack of success heralded by this approach, and the gap between highly affluent 'centres' and the forgotten 'inner suburbs', can be seen most starkly in our capital city. Take the relationship between two of the most affluent and economically productive parts of London – the City of London and Canary Wharf – and the boroughs around them which include some of the most hard-pressed parts of the city. In the shadows of some of our most successful businesses, the boroughs of Tower Hamlets, Hackney and Newham see few of the benefits that the City and Canary Wharf offer the economy. According to official statistics,[11] around three-quarters of these areas are amongst the 20 per cent most deprived in the country. An article in *The Economist*, written as far back as 2002, vividly captured the failure of this theory when it described the 'British doughnut' as 'a lump of indifferent carbohydrate with jam in

---

[10] <http://www.rudi.net/node/21921>, accessed 2 September 2014.
[11] Department for Communities and Local Government, *English Indices of Deprivation 2010* (2011), https://www.gov.uk/government/publications/english-indices-of-deprivation-2010>, accessed 2 September 2014.

the middle . . . rich inner-city development surrounded by acres of gloom'.[12]

Other approaches have been proposed by academics, planners, think tanks and politicians, and they appear to be becoming more radical in their suggested remedies for the decline of our cities. One view is that the demands of the changing marketplace cannot, ultimately, be resisted and so the remedy is to plan for continued growth in London and the South East while the rest of the country, especially the northern cities, declines and stagnates. This is economic determinism at its extreme. Many of these cities have been world leaders in industry for decades – whether trade in Liverpool, textiles in Manchester and the surrounding towns, or mining and other heavy industry in the cities of the North East – and such an approach writes off the possibility that we can achieve the leap of imagination that will transform these places into economic hubs once again.

We are not alone in trying (and failing) to find solutions to the problem of urban regeneration and more general economic malaise. It is equally hard to find examples of other countries where economic problems are solved with purely economic solutions. France continues to struggle despite increases in government spending and taxation. The south of Europe remains in many cases mired in deep depression, with the threat of deflation, and economists throughout the Continent are voicing despair as to whether the current situation will ever change.

There is one factor that unites those engaged in the debate. They all assume that the value of a given community is founded solely on its economic output. This is *the* fundamental sin of our economic rescue missions. We have convinced ourselves that economic problems can be solved with economic solutions alone.

---

[12] 'The doughnut effect', *The Economist* (17 January 2002), <http://www.economist.com/node/940671>, accessed 2 September 2014.

Economics is not an exact science – because it deals with the aggregate of human decisions. Economists are sometimes accused of treating selfishness as *the* characteristic human trait, but the economist's job is to make generalisations that help predict how people will behave in response to various stimuli. On aggregate, an assumption that people follow their own interests seems to be true. But that does not make it a truth for every person all the time. If people decide to behave altruistically, as many have done over the issue of Fair Trade, for example, the economic models will reflect that fact. In other words, we are not controlled by economic models – economic models reflect our collective choices.

So while it is true, for example, that many of the cities studied in the *Cities Unlimited* report have continued down the path of decline and despair, a small number have experienced radical and unpredicted renewal, and are now flourishing and growing. For example, according to a 2013 report by the Confederation of British Industry (CBI),[13] Leeds – one of those cities 'pre-destined for failure' – has flourished in a way that other cities have not. The report identifies local choices like the creation of new office space for professional services as the driving force behind its regeneration, and, while policies like this are not a panacea for every struggling city, the example gives hope that the problems we are facing today can be addressed. Recent developments in Manchester, both encouraged by and driving an ability to attract young entrepreneurs and innovators from across the globe, are also noteworthy and offer signs of hope. The decision to move a large part of the BBC's structures to and the development of 'Media City' in Salford have already shown a positive impact on the regeneration of areas outside

---

[13] CBI, *Locally Grown: Unlocking Business Potential through Regeneration* (London: CBI, 2013), p. 7.

the centre of Manchester, as have developments around the City of Manchester Stadium in Eastlands and rapid expansion of the tram system. These positive examples of urban regeneration highlight that there is no 'one-size-fits-all' approach to regeneration, and that it is vital for holistic and specifically local responses to be supported and developed.

Elsewhere there are also signs of hope, with the Church acting as catalyst and convenor (a subject that I turn to in more detail in the next section). Across the country, we are beginning to see the development of well-structured and researched local initiatives focused on improving social inclusion, particularly in major cities. These initiatives have brought together the facts of unacceptable inequalities and identified integrated responses from the widest range of statutory, local authority, business, third sector and faith organisations and their leaders.

One excellent example of such an initiative is the National Social Inclusion Network, which drew together seventeen cities and boroughs to sign the Birmingham Declaration in March 2014.[14] The Network, which includes leaders from many of the cities mentioned in this chapter, was convened by the Rt Revd David Urquhart, the Bishop of Birmingham, with a spirit of fresh determination to promote social inclusion and ask the Government to release resources to allow local leaders to get on with the job of improving social inclusion at the local level – a call that echoes the central recommendations of Lord Heseltine's report, cited previously.

While I am delighted that these efforts appear to be making progress in tackling the problems found in modern cities in England, we cannot be satisfied with solutions based entirely on economic determinism. Nor can governments *by themselves*

---

[14] National Social Inclusion Network, 'Birmingham Declaration' (2014), <http://fairnessnetwork.wordpress.com/>, accessed 2 September 2014.

solve the problem. More dependency on cash injected on the basis of some grand plan or strategy, or dependency on the collateral benefits of a free market, are not sufficient answers. Our economic crisis is not fundamentally an economic problem. We must dig deeper. Our economic crisis is a theological problem.

It's not just about economics

The Church would describe an economic landscape in which there are not only poor individuals but also poor cities, which feel that they have been abandoned and left to their own devices, as a society that lacks 'solidarity'. The concept of solidarity has a deeply theological heritage, but today, unfairly it seems to me, the word is far more closely associated with political ideology than with its Christian foundations. Reclaiming the Christian definition of solidarity for the common good is vital if we are to reimagine our economic landscape so that individuals and communities are no longer left behind. Christian solidarity is concerned with how we value people and communities. That is, it values people not according to their economic output or capacity but in and of themselves. Any economic policy that truly has the potential to help *everyone* must be rooted in this conviction. It is a key to cultivating a vineyard with room for everybody to work so that everyone can have stability and hope.

Of course, many in society will ask why they should listen when the Church speaks, echoing William Temple's[15] famous question: 'What right has the church to interfere?'[16] And it is true that the Church has no automatic right to intervene, nor

---

[15] Archbishop of Canterbury 1942–4.
[16] W. Temple, *Christianity and Social Order* (London: Shepheard-Walwyn, 1942), p. 7.

can it assume one, no matter how long it has been speaking out in favour of the common good and solidarity. But the Church is committed to mutual flourishing and desires a society in which no one is left behind. Over the centuries it has very often been the Church, whether through its monasteries or later through its commitment to social reform, that has spoken up for a society of solidarity. We often see this in places where the Church is one of the few remaining institutions engaged in the local community. The Church expresses its 'core business' of worshipping God and calling people to Christ by trying to exemplify God's desire for solidarity throughout his creation. So you will find the Church offering debt advice courses, feeding and housing the homeless and vulnerable, standing with those who are sick or face injustice.

Archbishop Temple was writing during the Second World War, and the differences between then and now are telling. By the time he died in 1944, the economies of Europe were bankrupt or destroyed; every sinew had been strained for nearly five years in order to achieve a victory against the Nazi regime and its allies. The effects of this would last for decades in the economies of Europe. In all countries across the Continent, however, there was found a new, invigorated sense of purpose, a sense of the need to create a new world from the ashes of the old. In such extreme moments, imagination is liberated by inspired leaders across whole regions, and the post-war period saw energy and imagination blossoming all over Europe and in the United States. The greatest gestures of solidarity were seen in the Marshall Plan, and in the creation of what has become the European Union. In Britain the National Health Service was founded and the Welfare State began its work. It was a moment of great change and, indeed, solidarity.

At that time, the foundations of Christian belief were still of significance in the general life of the nation. Certainly, churchgoing was even then a minority occupation, but Christian principles were largely unchallengeable in the public sector. There is no denying, for example, that the belief in the intrinsic value of human beings – an explicitly Christian principle – was the driving conviction behind many significant social changes over the past two hundred years. In the nineteenth century it drove the abolition of the slave trade as well as the various social reforms of working conditions and in the treatment of children; it powered the establishment of universal education as well as moves towards pensions and a health service. In the twentieth and twenty-first centuries we see it as the motivation behind international movements such as those that seek reconciliation to end war, to defeat human trafficking, to care for those caught up in oppressive regimes or mass movements of peaceful protestors responding to civil disorder.

Some people in Temple's time already saw the abyss of secularism ahead. Writing between the two great wars of the last century, John Maynard Keynes could assert that his was the lucky generation, inheriting the social benefits of a societally shared faith from their parents, but not yet having reached the inevitable decadence that would be the consequences of the abandonment of that faith.[17]

But whereas this previous generation that Archbishop Temple was writing to and for had a common vision for the future based on Christian principles (and therefore the motivation to get there), our greatly secularised society seems to agree on only one, quite un-Christian principle: that it's every person for themselves. Social Darwinism (itself a misunderstanding of

---

[17] R. Skidelsky, *Keynes: The Return of the Master* (London: Penguin Books, 2009) (Kindle Edition), p. 151. See also, Virginia Woolf, *The Diary of Virginia Woolf*, ed. A. O. Bell, asst. A. McNeillie (Harmondsworth: Penguin Books, 1982), iv, 1931–5, p. 208 (19 April 1934); and J. M. Keynes, 'Economic Possibilities for Our Grandchildren' (1930), *Essays in Persuasion* (New York: W. W. Norton, 1963), pp. 358–73.

Darwin) may have become a core dogma of the twenty-first century. This is a major obstacle in establishing a widespread commitment to solidarity once again. Today there is no commonly held story about what is right and good and what makes for a society of mutual flourishing.

Solidarity may not be a popular virtue in the twenty-first century but that is not to say that it is absent from the public imagination altogether. We catch glimpses of its enduring flame, usually in the aftermath of moments of crisis. Following the riots during the summer of 2011, and more recently in response to the devastating flooding that has affected huge swathes of the country, we have seen communities bind themselves together for the good of those who have suffered. After the riots, we saw large groups of people assist in the clean-up of affected areas, or raise money to assist those who lost their livelihoods. In the wake of the floods, there were similar responses. This is solidarity in action.

And while responses to these crises came from all parts of society, it was very often the *local church* which acted as the catalyst and convenor for these responses – acting as the 'first responders', housing those who lost their homes to the floods, drawing strained communities together through powerful peace vigils in response to rioting. The Church is capable of inspiring solidarity in our society, when it engages it in a way that highlights the positive impact that a commitment to the common good can have. The problem we are now facing is that this flame of solidarity is not something that we are able to take for granted in our society any more. Society today displays a crisis of solidarity. Instead, we face our problems with resignation or wilful blindness.

There is a general social assumption that the economy has the power to dictate what is and is not possible for human beings. We believe that if we can fix the economy, the fixing of human beings will automatically follow. That is a lie. It is a lie because it is a narrative that casts money, rather than humanity, as the protagonist of God's story. The human person is not just one of God's creations in the long list of other things God has made. The human person is unique in God's creation because humanity bears God's own image (Gen. 1.27), and therefore 'the human creature [is] at the centre and summit of the created order'.[18] This *imago dei* establishes humanity's position in the world, on three particular fronts: in relation to God, in relation to one another, and in relation to the creation. Digging deeper into these theological roots will help us see more clearly the Church's stake in cultivating a society of solidarity.

Humanity's unique relationship to God is simple: made in God's image, we were created to be in relationship with him. Since we have been made in God's image, the human being has an inherent dignity. Individuals are therefore not to be valued according to their economic output or capacity (the famous *homo economicus* was originally a way of looking at certain aspects of behaviour, not an all-encompassing definition of the human creature).[19] They are to be valued in and of themselves, as God's image-bearers, created and loved by him. The principle of the intrinsic value of each human being has its foundation here. We are all equal.

Humanity's relationship with one another, before it is anything else, is *common*. As God created a companion for the first

---

[18] Pontifical Council for Justice and Peace, *Compendium of the Social Doctrine of the Church* (London: Burns & Oates, 2005 (2004)), p. 62. Published at the request of Pope John Paul II.

[19] While the exact origins of the term *homo economicus*, or the 'economic man', are not clear, and the ideas it puts forward are found in the theories of many classical economic theorists, many scholars ascribe the term's development, and subsequent criticism, to the work of John Stuart Mill, particularly his essay 'On the Definition of Political Economy; and on the Method of Investigation Proper to It' (1836).

human, so we too are created to be in relationship with one another. We are inherently social, not solitary, beings, and dependence on one another is as significant to our humanity as our autonomy as individuals. Our human journey is not a journey of individuals, it is a journey held in common, and no individual can safely be left behind. The principle of the common good and human flourishing finds its foundation here. We really are all in it together.

Humanity's relationship to creation has already been described: we are to have dominion over the earth as God's stewards. We are to subdue and enjoy it. However, the manner in which we are stewards over God's creation is to be subjected to these previous two relationships – with God and with one another. In other words, we cannot be stewards over creation in ways that impede our relationship with God, violate the inherent dignity of any individual human being, or ignore the commonality of our human journey. (An automatic consequence of abiding by these rules is that one would also be taking good care of creation itself.) Therefore the flourishing of the whole human community ought to be the end towards which society is ordered. Human beings do not exist to be instruments of the economy; rather, all social life, including the economy, exists to facilitate our common journey towards God.

Solidarity as a theological concept is the combination of the inherent dignity of each person with the commonality of the human journey. This combination is perfectly embodied in Jesus Christ – solidarity *par excellence*. Through his Incarnation Jesus became God-with-us, showing us God's unyielding and unwavering commitment to humanity. Jesus would not forsake his solidarity with humanity even to the point of death. Solidarity in Jesus looks like generosity, forgiveness and reconciliation. It looks like being friends with the poor and standing up to power for the sake of those on the margins of society.

Jesus helps us see that solidarity, in the words of Pope John Paul II, is not a

> feeling of vague compassion or shallow distress at the misfortunes of so many people, both near and far. On the contrary, it is a firm and persevering determination to commit oneself to the common good. That is to say to the good of all and of each individual, because we are all really responsible for all.[20]

Jesus' solidarity entails establishing stability and the giving of hope. Stability and hope are fundamental components of the common good; that is, individuals must have stability and hope if they are to have the opportunity to flourish. The idea of stability in this theological sense goes back to the Rule of St Benedict, written in the early sixth century. At its heart it means that an individual knows what their role is – that they are respected not for what they do but as a human being, and they have a well-established purpose. Stability is shown in a life well led. It is founded not only on loving and being loved but also on a sense of contributing and being remembered. I recall as a parish priest taking a funeral for a man who had no friends or relatives. There were no mourners and this so shocked the funeral directors that their staff turned out to mourn and to ensure that nobody went alone to a grave. Stories like this are, movingly, increasingly prevalent – one example being a Second World War veteran with no immediate family whose funeral was attended by hundreds of strangers thanks to the story being picked up on social media.[21]

Stability is based on the stability of God, who does not change. He knows us and enables us to know him. Stability is

---

[20] John Paul II, *Sollicitudo Rei Socialis*, 38: *AAS* 80 (1988), 565–6.

[21] 'Hundreds attend war veteran's funeral after newspaper ad', BBC News (11 November 2013), <http://www.bbc.co.uk/news/uk-england-london-24889924>, accessed 2 September 2014.

not stasis – God calls us to change and be changed. But a life of feverish change that destroys the possibility of stability is unendurable. In St Paul's letter to the Ephesians Paul comments that God has established good works for us to do from before the beginning of time. There is a purpose for every human being. Through the life, death and resurrection of Jesus the way is open for us to find that purpose.

Hope is also founded in the love and call of God. We already know how history turns out: Jesus returns, all wrongs are set right, and we will spend eternity as God's companions. Hope is the idea that all of life is a progression towards this end. Problems are solvable. Even if one is defeated by them, even when one dies, that is not the end of all things. Hope is a strong safety net that does not take away from us our freedom of choice and self-will.

A good society in Christian terms does not leave people behind, alone or abandoned, and does not consider them to be mere instruments within an economic system. One does not need to be a Christian to agree that an economy founded on human solidarity is a sign of a good society. One does not need to be a Christian to see the suffering of cities and individuals who are isolated from aid. One does not need to be a Christian to recognise that an idea with Christian roots works. As the former Chief Rabbi, Jonathan Sacks, noted in *The Home We Build Together*, 'We will have to work together on this with men and women of goodwill in every faith and none', to 'renew the much-worn, almost threadbare, concept of the common good'.[22] Solidarity is not a reality unless all areas have an opportunity to prosper from recovery and to deliver opportunities for human flourishing. Solidarity cannot depend on one group within

---

[22] J. Sacks, *The Home We Build Together: Recreating Society* (London, Continuum, 2007), p. 11.

society but has to be created together to make something that stays together. Unless all are building, what is constructed will not stand.

Solidarity in economics

Of course, it is all well and good to say that our economic policies must be rooted in a principle of solidarity and not to say anything about what that might actually look like once someone tries to translate that into economic policy. I said that our current economic crisis is not *fundamentally* an economic problem, but that does not mean that there are not manifold economic problems that are part of it. We still need good economists and imaginative policy-makers. I believe that an economic programme based on solidarity has four essential building blocks: a living wage, good housing, excellent education and training, and greater financial access. I will look at each of these in slightly greater detail.

The Living Wage (LW) is a concept which has grown up recently. Its essential aim is to remove a hand-to-mouth existence: to make work pay, to remove sufficient of the anxiety that bare subsistence generates and to allow people a capacity for joy through work. It does not provide for luxury but avoids penury. It is encouraging that, in a relatively short space of time, the idea of a living wage has gained so much support – and significantly, across much of the political spectrum. Since London Citizens launched its living wage campaign in 2001, we have seen businesses, charities, religious institutions and parts of the public sector buying in and signing up to this idea, and becoming 'Living Wage Employers'.

The Living Wage Commission, chaired by the Archbishop of York, has now published its first set of findings and recommendations on how we move from the living wage being an exception to becoming the mainstream – an acceptable level of pay that promotes human flourishing, dignity and economic prosperity which, in words on the Commission's website, 'can now become a reality for the many, not the few'.[23] The findings of the report not only highlight the moral and economic arguments for paying a living wage but also describe a number of possible ways in which paying the LW could have a positive multiplier effect in other aspects of life – including in educational attainment, health and family stability – all of which can strengthen the idea of solidarity in our society. Ensuring that work pays is an important marker for a society where our economic policies are led and governed by our values, and not vice versa.

The principle of the LW is a reminder that, whatever the advantages of a market economy (and the market is an extraordinarily efficient mechanism of distribution in a complex society), it requires a moral framework around it if it is to function as markets should. The market is a brilliant self-correcting mechanism – but its cycles can be very long. As Keynes noted, in the long run, we are all dead – so if we value people for their humanity, and not just as cogs on a wheel, there must be mechanisms, outside the market structure itself, which allow them to survive and flourish in the bottom of the economic cycle. A good economic case can be made for the LW. But the ultimate case is a moral one.

Good and affordable housing is widely recognised as necessary for generating economic prosperity. Reducing the burden of housing costs for those on low incomes reduces dependency on housing benefits and other associated support which the state must provide if people are not to be homeless. Beyond

---

[23] Living Wage Commission, 'About the Living Wage', <http://livingwagecommission. org.uk/about/>, accessed 2 September 2014.

this, and far more importantly, good and well-designed housing provides the opportunity for stable households. People begin to put down roots and invest in the well-being of their community, generating a renewed sense of solidarity. Many of the failures of the 1960s and 1970s arose in new building that destroyed communities rather than renewing them. Planners lacked the imagination to understand the importance of community structures which they themselves may never have needed or valued. A commitment to house-building – recognised by all the main political parties as a high priority – must not come at the expense of community, and new and innovative approaches to planning must recognise and sustain the idea of solidarity.

This sort of work is manifest in the housing association movement. Up and down the country, these organisations are tackling deprivation and homelessness, and are leading the attempt to regenerate communities in both rural and urban areas. There has been a long and fruitful relationship between housing associations and churches, and this coming together of institutions will strengthen our society and, I hope, show that solutions to intractable economic problems may be found in this idea of solidarity.

Education and training – whether in schools and universities, or through apprenticeships and vocational training – are too often seen as no more than preparation for economic activity. The education system is often criticised for not producing work-ready employees. But no one has ever been entirely prepared for work on leaving formal education. The dependency culture, which many fear is embedded in our society, has affected companies as much as individuals, where employers often expect their new employees to come ready-made. The loss of the 'job for life' has made it even more vital that people are equipped, not only with skills, but also with the character to adapt, to go on learning and yet to retain their integrity as a person through decades of change. The renewed interest and investment in apprenticeships is a welcome step, and it should continue to be a priority to ensure that young people are able to be trained in work that is both economically and socially useful and that will bring purpose, stability and hope to all young people as they begin their adult lives.

Financial access means ending what has become known as the poverty premium, by ensuring that everyone has access to financial services that can help them integrate into the economy, and provide for a more stable life. Progress has been made in recent years, initially through the Post Office and more recently in our high-street banks, to provide basic bank accounts that enable people to access their wages or social security payments without exposing them to unsupportable financial risk if they overdraw or make simple errors. Opening up savings opportunities to all is vital in an economic system that sees too many forced to live from one pay-cheque to the next without anything to fall back on in times of crisis save the siren-like appeal of a slick advertisement for a payday loan.

The Church has started to make its own contribution here, through direct and indirect support for credit unions – a model of banking which is based on the 'common bond' – thereby expressing in a very tangible way the significance of solidarity in serving people's financial needs. Credit unions make loans and promote savings – an integrated approach to people's needs which contrasts sharply with the one-way street of the payday lenders. I said, when we started this venture, that I wanted to see the payday lenders competed out of the market-place. The temptation to call on government to pass laws to abolish everything that is bad in society is seductive but needs to be resisted. I know from my work on the Parliamentary Commission for Banking Standards that regulation has its place in every functional market. But the financial crash which has caused so much havoc, and let the most vulnerable communities of our nation down so badly, was caused by market failure in the banking sector. Good markets require open competition but tend towards cartels and monopolies if we are not careful. The Church's long-term commitment to strengthening the credit union sector reflects a belief that markets can be made to serve people better if they are recognised as human beings with lives, loves, and bonds between them. The principle of solidarity could help revolutionise our financial markets.

All these areas need reform and radical imagination. We cannot rely solely on the invisible hand of the market to restore justice, for the market has no sense of value other than net-present value. Nor can we rely on hand-outs from governments with financial constraints of their own and locked in a five-year election cycle. Reliance on the one or the other, as if either alone represented the good society, has manifestly failed. The change, if there is going to be one, must happen first in our hearts and minds. Solidarity by its very definition cannot be delegated; it has to do with everyone's concern about everyone.

In his encyclical *Caritas in Veritate*, Pope Benedict XVI argues that a 'principle of gratuitousness' needs to be integrated into our normal economic activity.[24] The principle of gratuity is an aspect of Catholic Social Teaching which faces up to the difficulties of defining the common good and calls for solidarity and grace, not patronage from wealth or the myopia of wealth. In this remarkable encyclical there is all the radicality of the work of the Holy Spirit, the simplicity of the self-emptying of the Son and the grace and love of the Father. To demonstrate it, the Church must truly identify across society, especially with the poor.

Pope Benedict argued that unadulterated commercial logic, and the 'commutative justice' of the market that measures the

---

[24] Benedict XVI, *Caritas in Veritate* (2009), para. 34.

economic exchange of goods and services according to equal value, is not good enough to sustain mutual human flourishing. The rules of those systems misunderstand the kind of creature the human being truly is. The modern man, who believes 'he is the sole author of himself, his life and society', is mistaken,[25] because both our lives and society are, in fact, gratuitous gifts from God. More specifically, our gifted lives are shaped to receive the gift of Jesus Christ, given to a world in need. If 'economy' and 'market' are really abbreviations for the interactions of human beings, then our expectations for those interactions must go beyond the bare minimum of 'individual rights' and the exchange of 'equal-value goods'. We must include that principle upon which we were created: gratuitous love. Only an economy that takes into account a principle of gratuitousness will take the true nature of humanity seriously, because 'the human being is made for gift'.[26] Society should, as Professor Paul Dembinski summarises, act 'by putting some giving in generosity into the heart of economic practice (not aside of it) which means by going beyond the strict (and sterile) equivalence of exchange in order to write in a surplus, a dimension of giving'.[27]

In an economy without gratuity, one gives only out of duty. Gratuity invites humanity to give because of love. Gift cultivates relationship; relationship in turn cultivates solidarity; and solidarity will create an economy in which no one is left behind. Solidarity is gratuity in action. It reflects precisely the kind of gratuitous love poured out for us by Jesus on the cross. Gratuity is what makes a company spend on training, a church serve the

---

[25] Benedict XVI, *Caritas in Veritate*, para. 34.

[26] Benedict XVI, *Caritas in Veritate*, para. 34.

[27] P. Dembinski, *Encyclical Letter 'Caritas in Veritate': An Economist's Reading*, Working Papers SES 422 (Fribourg, Switzerland: Faculty of Economics and Social Sciences, University of Fribourg, 2011), p. 3.

poor of its area, a credit union invest in a system that will benefit small depositors and borrowers. It makes society respect the weak, not out of charity but solidarity, alongside whom the rich have received blessing. All wealth is gift and responsibility.

Conclusion

The workers are waiting, and the task of calling them to the vineyard to find their call from the Lord of the Harvest (who ends by treating all equally in the parable) is one for the Church to play in a society that will not make such a call by default.

Although the Church may call, there is a need for a new coalition of all agencies in the voluntary and statutory sectors – and the private sector too. There is also a need to show a sense of locality, and renew a sense of local history. Local culture and history provide the foundations for local renewal, and that regeneration is always expressed locally even when assisted by funds provided centrally.

None of this can be achieved at the local level alone. Without a common vision and solidarity of purpose that covers the whole country, no momentum is created to achieve what can be truly called the 'common' good. But without recognition of the uniqueness of each locality, and the gifts and challenges that its history have moulded, a top-down imposition of policy will never gain the community ownership – or common bond – that is needed to deliver the practicalities of a society demanding solidarity.

All this brings us back to stability and hope. Stability is not found in arrival at the end of the journey – that is, once everyone has been 'brought into the vineyard' – but through the journey itself, a journey that is taken together. All involved – whether vineyard owner, manager, labourer, support staff or their households – are invested in the value of the journey, in the knowledge that we are travelling together to that treasured destination we may call 'regeneration'. This destination – the vineyard – is where we find the vast disparity of prospects within our society reduced to the point where solidarity becomes truly real and tangible. As we journey together, stability becomes more apparent, for it is found in the respect that the travellers inspire in each other along the way, guiding one another to find help and support when it is required, and ensuring no one is left outside the vineyard. Above all, the parable calls us to recognise that solidarity springs from the Lord of the Vineyard, God, and is experienced and tangible in the person of Jesus Christ, who breaks all barriers between human beings.

3

The way ahead for the British economy

ANDREW SENTANCE

We are living through a time of economic upheaval. The Global Financial Crisis of 2008–9 was a major shock to the UK and other economies throughout the world. The British economy and other major economies are only slowly recovering from the crisis and the recession it created.

But that is not the only major economic challenge we are currently facing. We live in a world economy which is being reshaped by technology and the forces of globalisation. The internet, mobile phones and new media developments have accelerated the pace of change in business and in our personal lives, creating both opportunities and challenges. Meanwhile, the growth of China, India and other emerging market economies is having a major impact on the size and shape of the world economy and the UK's position within it.

This new world economic order has created many opportunities for trade, investment, social interaction and economic growth. Globalisation has allowed many poorer economies to access world markets and develop their economies as a result – including China and India. China is now the second largest economy in the world and India has moved into the top ten. Average living standards for the majority of the world's population living in Asia, Africa and Latin America have improved significantly, and the numbers living in extreme poverty have fallen. According to the World Bank, the percentage of people in the developing world living in extreme poverty ($1.25 or less a day at 2005 prices) has fallen to 21 per cent in 2010, compared with 43 per cent in 1990 and 52 per cent in 1981.[1]

But there have also been downsides from these developments in the global economy. The pressure on natural resources and the environment is creating new problems, including global warming. The benefits of economic growth have not been spread evenly across society – with income inequality rising in many countries, including the UK. Less-skilled workers have been especially vulnerable to the way in which low-cost competition has held down wages and reduced employment prospects. This has added to income insecurity and increased the problems young people have faced in getting into the world of work. The squeeze on poorer households has also been aggravated by rising food and energy prices – which have been pushed up in a world where strong demand has been outstripping available supplies.

This is the background against which we need to chart the way forward for the UK economy in the years ahead. What are the policies and practical steps needed to maintain a successful and harmonious society in this changing and challenging world? And how can our approach be informed by Christian principles and values? These are the questions which this chapter aims to address.

The chapter starts with a more detailed analysis of the issues facing the UK economy, in the aftermath of the financial crisis and in a world shaped by the forces of globalisation. We appear to be in a 'New Normal' economy, in which we cannot expect

---

[1] <http://www.worldbank.org/en/topic/poverty/overview>, accessed 4 September 2014.

a return to the type of growth we saw before the financial crisis. The disappointing outlook for economic growth is compounding other problems which appeared more manageable in better economic times – the control of public finances, the challenges facing low-paid workers and others on low incomes, and the barriers to employment facing young people with limited skills and experience. In contrast, the UK economy does have some strengths which do not always come out so clearly in the public economic debate. Our economy is very international, with leading positions in key services industries and a number of areas of high-value manufacturing. The UK's flexible labour market has helped avoid the high rates of unemployment we have seen following earlier recessions and which some other economies are now experiencing. And we have a tradition of being open and attractive to the rest of the world as a location for business, trade and investment – helped by the advantages of British culture and pragmatism and the English language. In the UK, we should be aiming to build on these strengths while addressing the challenges facing our economy in the 'New Normal' post-crisis world.

Christian values can shape our approach to managing the economy and operating within it. We cannot hope to hold back the big global tides which are shaping our economy. But we can seek to mould the way in which our economy is responding to them. In the second section of the chapter, I set out three key principles which should guide our approach to charting the way ahead for the economy: sustainable growth; shared prosperity; and responsible business.

These principles can inform our thinking on both policy and the way in which we contribute to the economy as individuals and within our churches and communities. This is the subject of the third section of the chapter. In the policy domain, I highlight some key areas where we need to focus attention in

the years ahead in order to address the challenges our economy currently faces: economic and financial stability; skills,
education and employment; reform of the tax system; and
environmental sustainability. But in addition to these important
policy areas, our economy and society is ultimately shaped by
the actions of individuals. Consistent with the Christian calling
to be the 'salt of the earth', members of the Church and of other
faith communities can have an important influence on the way
ahead for the economy through their individual contribution
to the organisations they work for and the communities where
they live.

The 'New Normal' – the UK economy after the crisis

It is clear that the UK economy[2] – like many other economies
around the world – is not returning to the pattern of economic
growth which we saw before the financial crisis. The year 2008
was a watershed for the economies of the Western world of the
sort we rarely see in peacetime. Looking back over the past 100
years, the only years which compare are 1930 and 1974. Both
these previous years saw big financial shocks which ushered in
a long period of difficult economic conditions which persisted
for many years. And in both cases, when a sustained period of
growth did eventually emerge, it was very different in character
from the period which had gone before. After the turbulence
of the 1930s, the post-Second World War recovery took place
in a much more technologically advanced and socially inclusive
economy than the world of the 1920s and 1930s. There was
also a notable contrast between the characteristics of growth

---

[2] The ideas in this section are set out in more detail in my book: *Rediscovering Growth: After the Crisis* (London: London Publishing Partnership, 2013).

and employment from the 1980s onwards – driven by services industries, finance and information technology – and the expansion of the 1950s and 1960s, which was driven by manufacturing, new consumer goods and post-war reconstruction.

The fact that we have passed a similar watershed to these earlier traumatic years helps to explain why economic conditions feel so challenging and difficult. But we have at least learned from some of the mistakes of the past, and hopefully avoided them in the aftermath of the recent financial crisis. In the 1930s, countries around the world put up barriers to trade which deepened the recession and made the recovery much more difficult. That has not happened in the wake of the Global Financial Crisis – at least not so far. In the 1970s, we moved into a world of high inflation which again complicated and delayed the task of restoring growth. We have hopefully also avoided that mistake this time around.

But in common with the 1930s and the late 1970s, sustained economic recovery has been hard to achieve since the financial crisis and for that reason the current situation is a 'New Normal' for economic growth. The UK economy and many others benefited from some powerful tailwinds before the crisis which are no longer available to help us progress now. From the 1980s onwards, we benefited from a world of easy money, cheap imports and confidence in the policies of central banks and governments. In all three areas, we have seen fundamental changes in our economy which mean that a return to the pre-crisis trend is not on the cards.

The first key change is in the financial system. From the 1980s until 2007, the operation of a highly deregulated and liberalised global financial system provided consumers and businesses with relatively easy access to finance and allowed a large build-up of debt. These financial conditions underpinned a 'global credit boom', centred on the US housing market, which also affected financial conditions in many other countries.[3] This credit boom came to a spectacular end in 2008–9, with the failure of Lehman Brothers and the bank bail-outs which were required in the US, UK and elsewhere to prevent the total collapse of the financial system. Now, banks have become much more cautious and reluctant to lend, with their caution reinforced by new requirements imposed by regulators. While low interest rates and government support have eased these constraints on the financial system for a while, it is clear that we are not going back to the financial practices and behaviour we saw before 2007, and nor should we be seeking to do so.

The second change in the economic climate relates to the cost of imports. From the mid-1980s – when oil prices fell sharply – until the mid-2000s, Western consumers benefited from an environment of cheap imports from the rest of the world. Energy and other commodity prices were subdued. The expansion of the world economy to include new sources of low-cost production from the 1990s – including China and India – initially helped to push down prices of many manufactured products and provided a further boost to Western living standards. As these large emerging market economies have developed and grown, however, the tables have turned. Strong growth in Asia and elsewhere in the emerging world is now exerting more inflationary pressure across the world economy. The world of cheap imports has been eroded by successive waves of energy, food and commodity price inflation since the mid-2000s, creating an income squeeze for Western consumers. Strong growth in China, India and elsewhere is also raising their labour costs as living standards rise. This is good news

---

[3] For a detailed analysis, see Michael Hume and Andrew Sentance, *The Global Credit Boom: Challenges for Macroeconomics and Policy*, External MPC Unit Discussion Paper 27 (London: Bank of England, 2009).

for the populations of these developing economies, but it risks pushing up import prices further and adding further to the squeeze on Western consumers.

A third change since 2007 has been in the ability of governments and central banks to sustain confidence in the private sector. Before the financial crisis, governments and central banks appeared to be able to support growth, contain inflation and maintain orderly financial conditions – by adjusting policy in response to economic shocks. This provided confidence to businesses, households and investors that growth would continue even if there was an occasional brief interruption. And this confidence was borne out by the way our economy appeared to withstand turbulent events in the 1990s and early 2000s – such as the Asian crisis, the bursting of the 'dotcom' bubble in 2000 and the global political instability that followed the 9/11 attacks. The experience of the financial crisis and the difficulty we have had steering our way out of a period of severe economic turbulence shows, however, that we can no longer take this for granted. The prevailing climate is one of nervousness and uncertainty – among businesses, individuals and the financial markets – and it will take some years of sustained recovery before confidence in the continued progress of the economy returns.

In the absence of these three tailwinds – easy money, cheap imports and strong confidence – the UK and other Western economies are going through a prolonged period of adjustment. It is not surprising that economic growth is harder to come by in this changed economic environment. And this low growth 'New Normal' environment is contributing to other problems which had been building up before the crisis, but which were masked by favourable economic conditions. Two particular issues stand out and loom large in our economic debate.

Government spending and public finances

The financial crisis has led to widening public sector deficits and increasing government debts in the UK and other major economies. Contrary to public perception, this is not primarily because the government has provided support to the banking system. Rather it is because the economy has contracted and been slow to recover. As a result tax receipts have been undermined and have fallen well short of the amounts needed to fund public spending. Borrowing has had to make up the shortfall. In the UK, public borrowing rose to over £150 billion in 2009–10 – which meant that the government was borrowing nearly £1 for every £4 it was spending. Since 2009, the UK's deficit on public finances has exceeded £100 billion a year, pushing up the national debt from around £500 billion before the crisis to over £1.4 trillion by late 2014.

Against this background it is not surprising that the government has had to implement measures to restrain public spending and raise taxes. This is starting to bring the deficit down gradually and limit the rise in public debt. While the financial crisis was the key trigger for these problems of rising deficits and debt, however, the control of public finances has also been made more difficult by other underlying issues affecting the UK and other Western economies. Demographic trends and rising public expectations in areas like health and education are putting upward pressure on many areas of social spending over the longer term. An ageing society raises the demand for a number of important areas of public provision – health care, social services provided to the elderly, long-term residential care and pensions. To counter this upward pressure on spending totals, continuing efforts are needed to reform and prioritise spending to keep the overall total at an affordable level.

In addition, the globalisation trends in the world economy are having an impact on some key sources of government revenue.

Companies and high-value individuals now have more choices about where they can locate and earn their income. This has made the taxation of high incomes and corporate profits vulnerable to these location decisions, which themselves can be influenced by the tax system. In the UK in 2013–14, taxes on companies and the top 1 per cent of earners are expected to raise around £86 billion, around 15 per cent of total tax revenue – a significant proportion of the total.[4]

For both these reasons, managing public finances in the UK is not simply a matter of getting the budget deficit down and returning to normal. The large deficits we have seen following the financial crisis have raised important medium-term pressures affecting the structure of public spending and taxation which are likely to remain on the policy agenda for some time.

Income inequality and employment prospects

A second issue being aggravated by the current low growth environment is the inequality of incomes, which is closely linked to lack of employment security and to the low wages available to less-skilled workers. The Organisation for Economic Co-operation and Development (OECD) has observed a rise in inequality in the distribution of incomes in the more advanced economies in the world – including the UK – since the 1980s.[5] According to the OECD and other analysts, the forces of globalisation and new technology have played a major part in this

---

[4] Estimates from HMRC indicate the top 1% of taxpayers paid 29.8% of all income tax in 2013–14, accounting for £46.4 billion of a total £155.6 billion raised. Corporation tax levied on company profits accounted for a further £40.1 billion (data from March 2014 Office for Budget Responsibility, *Economic and Fiscal Outlook* (London: Office for Budget Responsibility, 2014) <budgetresponsibility.org.uk/economic-fiscal-outlook-march-2014/>, accessed 4 September 2014).

[5] Organisation for Economic Co-operation and Development, *Divided We Stand: Why Inequality Keeps Rising* (Paris: OECD, 2011), <http://www.oecd.org/social/soc/dividedwestandwhyinequalitykeepsrising.htm>, accessed 4 September 2014.

change. In the UK and other Western economies, globalisation and technology have advantaged people with high skills and scarce capabilities relative to those with low skills – particularly if the latter are relying on basic manual labour. Even though our economies have tax and benefit systems designed to redistribute income from the rich to the poor, and help the disadvantaged improve their economic prospects, the accelerating pace of economic change is putting these mechanisms under increasing strain.

In the UK, analysis by the Institute for Fiscal Studies (IFS) confirms the growing importance of insecure employment prospects and low-wage growth to the issue of poverty in the UK. Institute for Fiscal Studies economists note that, until the 1970s, the main causes of poverty in the UK were old age and persistent unemployment. More recently, they conclude:

> Poverty has become much more of an in-work phenomenon since the 1970s, as increased earnings inequality in the 1980s and relatively slow growth in earnings since have pushed more low and middle earners into poverty. This shift in poverty from something concentrated among the old and workless to something increasingly felt by employed and self-employed working-age adults is a major socio-economic change.[6]

At the same time, the OECD analysis shows a rising share of income going to high-earners, with the top 1 per cent of earners in the UK doubling their share of income between 1970 and 2005 – from 7 per cent to 14 per cent.[7]

These big changes in the distribution of income and earnings took place before the financial crisis. Since then, it appears

---

[6] Jonathan Cribb, Andrew Hood, Robert Joyce and David Phillips, *Living Standards, Poverty and Inequality in the UK: 2013*, Institute for Fiscal Studies Report R81 (London: Institute for Fiscal Studies, 2013).

[7] See OECD analysis of rising UK income inequality – *Divided We Stand*, <http://www.oecd.org/unitedkingdom/49170234.pdf>, accessed 4 September 2014.

that higher incomes have fallen most sharply – as this is the group most directly affected by the crisis. The indirect squeeze of rising inflation has had a bigger impact on those on lower incomes, however, because they spend a greater share of their income on food and energy which is where the biggest price rises have been experienced.

One group in society which is particularly vulnerable in the economic climate since the financial crisis is those who are leaving school or university and trying to get a foothold in the world of work. Unemployment has risen particularly sharply among the under-25s in the UK, as in many other countries, and now totals just under a million. High youth unemployment is damaging both to individuals and to the long-term health of the economy, as a substantial cohort of the population risks being unable to accumulate the skills and experience needed to contribute to society throughout their careers. Youth unemployment has been a problem for the UK economy, despite the fact that overall employment trends have been much better since 2008 than we have seen in previous UK recessions. Since the financial crisis, unemployment has not risen as high as it did following the 1980s and 1990s recessions – when the jobless rate rose to over 10 per cent, and remained persistently high for a number of years. The UK unemployment rate has also remained lower than many other European economies.[8] Though we continue to see significant regional variations – with the highest unemployment rates in the North West of England and Yorkshire and Humberside[9] – the national unemployment rate

---

[8] In August 2014, only Austria (4.7%), Germany (4.9%), Luxembourg (6.1%) and Malta (5.9%) had national unemployment rates lower than that of the UK (6.2%).

[9] In June–August 2014, the highest regional unemployment rates were in the North East of England (9.9%) and in Yorkshire and Humberside (7.3%), compared to an average rate of 6.2%. The lowest unemployment rates were in the South East (4.4%) and East of England (4.9%), with other parts of the UK in the range 5–7%.

in the UK has remained lower than in most other European economies. Only four European Union countries have a lower unemployment rate than the UK compared with twenty-three where the rate is higher.

The trend towards rising inequality, the deteriorating job and wage prospects for less-skilled workers and the relatively high level of youth unemployment all suggest that education, skills and employment issues need to feature significantly in our thinking about how to chart the way ahead for the UK in the current 'New Normal' economy.

Prospects for the United Kingdom economy

At the time of writing, economic growth is picking up in the UK economy and 2014 and 2015 are forecast to be the best years of economic growth since the financial crisis. Despite the considerable challenges to our economy we have discussed above, it is also important to note that the British economy has some considerable strengths which can help support economic growth and employment into the future.

We have a diverse economy which is particularly strong in a number of service industries, through which we are successful at generating sales in export markets around the world. It might seem unusual to think of exporting services but, when overseas customers spend money which supports employment and activity in the UK, that counts as a services export – just like selling a British-made car or a computer in a foreign market. The UK's strengths in services exports include: travel and tourism; education; creative industries – like film, media, design and music; information technology and software; business and professional services – such as law, accountancy and consulting; as well as financial services. In 2013, services exports contributed over £200 billion of sales to the UK economy, around 12.5 per cent of GDP – a much higher share of our economy than in other major economies.[10] Service industries account for nearly 80 per cent of UK national income and over 80 per cent of total employment.

As an economy, our success in services industries has helped to offset the decline in many traditional manufacturing sectors. The UK still exported over £230 billion of manufactured goods in 2013, though manufacturing now accounts for only around 10 per cent of our total economic activity and 8 per cent of jobs. Manufacturing in the UK is now focused on high-technology and high-value-added sectors, where skills, innovation, design and high quality are the drivers of competitive success. Particular UK manufacturing strengths are aerospace, pharmaceuticals, high-tech engineering and the car industry. Overseas investment has played a key part in rejuvenating some sectors of UK manufacturing industry, including our car industry.

Overseas investment and business is attracted to the UK economy by a number of historical strengths – including our tradition as an international economy, which is open to the rest of the world. We have sought to maintain a business climate in which companies can operate flexibly without too much bureaucracy and interference. This includes flexible employment and labour market practices, which have contributed to the better employment record in the UK following the financial crisis. British culture, history and pragmatism plus the widespread use of the English language are also important advantages for the UK as a business location.

For all these reasons, we should not be daunted by our recent economic difficulties, or the prospect of slower economic growth

---

[10] The comparable figure for the US is around 4% of GDP and for the major continental European economies around 5–8% of GDP. The value of the UK's services exports is second only to that of the US.

than we experienced before the financial crisis. After the two comparable periods of economic difficulty to which I referred at the outset of this chapter – in the 1930s and the 1970s – the UK economy did eventually embark on two long periods of economic growth where living standards rose across society for a prolonged period. The first of these lasted from the late 1940s until the early 1970s. And the second began in the mid-1980s and lasted until 2007, briefly interrupted by the early 1990s recession.

We need to maintain our confidence that, as a resourceful nation with many strengths, a similar transformation can be made in the future. But our economic progress needs to be founded on the right principles, policies and practices. The rest of this chapter discusses these three issues from a Christian perspective.

Three key principles to shape our economy

Having principles which guide our actions is central to the Christian faith and many other faiths as well. Jesus railed against the Pharisees, whom he saw as often hypocritical and not following the principles underlying God's law. The letters of St Paul are full of injunctions to live according to the principles and values of the Christian gospel rather than conforming to the decadent practices of the Roman world. As he writes in Romans 12.2: 'Do not be conformed to this world, but be transformed by the renewing of your minds, so that you may discern what is the will of God – what is good and acceptable and perfect' (NRSV).

St Peter takes up the same theme in his first letter (1 Peter 1.13–14): 'Therefore prepare your minds for action; discipline yourselves; set all your hope on the grace that Jesus Christ will bring you when he is revealed. Like obedient children, do not be conformed to the desires that you formerly had in ignorance.'

So how might we apply Christian values to the challenges of the twenty-first-century British economy, bearing in mind that we live in an imperfect world, albeit one that is still strongly influenced by Christian ideals and values?

There are three principles which are in tune with Christian teaching and which should help us address the current challenges facing the UK and global economies: sustainable growth; shared prosperity; and responsible business. In the discussion below, I discuss their meaning in relation to the current issues surrounding the management of the British economy and in the context of the big global changes affecting our economy in recent years and decades.

Principle 1: sustainable growth

There is a strong strand of Christian teaching which reflects being content with what we have and not being greedy for more. As the writer of Hebrews encourages us (Heb. 13.5): 'Keep your lives free from the love of money, and be content with what you have.'

Should we not therefore be aiming for a zero-growth economy, in an affluent country like the UK – and in other Western economies too? Surely this would release more of the scarce natural resources in the world for use by poorer countries and societies which are catching up with the West? In the post-crisis 'New Normal' world maybe we need to change our perspective and adapt to the absence of economic growth?

However, there are a number of problems with a zero-growth economy. First, we have seen how interdependent the global economy has become, and in the financial crisis we witnessed how a disruption to some key parts of our economy rippled round the world in a fairly indiscriminate way. With many poorer economies dependent on rising demand and invest-ment from richer economies, a zero-growth policy in the West

would most likely stifle the development of poorer economies too.

Second, a zero-growth policy could be very bad for employment. We rely on a degree of economic growth to absorb the
increases in economic output created by a rising population and
technological progress, which tends to raise the productivity
of the labour force over a period of time. By pursuing a zero-
growth strategy, productivity increases reflecting technological
change would displace employees and create a worsening problem of unemployment. While this problem could technically
be solved by encouraging everyone (or some people) to work
less, it is not clear or desirable that this outcome should be
enforced on our economy if it is not in line with the choices
individuals and families wish to make.

Third, a zero-growth economy is likely to be divisive rather
than inclusive. It means that those on lower incomes could
only improve their prospects at the expense of those on higher
incomes and vice versa. A growing economy avoids this problem by creating the potential for everyone to see some rise in
living standards even if there are variations in the experience
of different sections of the population.

So instead of zero growth, we should embrace the concept
of sustainable growth. This means that we do not look for the
maximum possible growth rate in the short-term, but seek a
sustainable rate and pattern of growth which reflects a number
of different considerations. First, we need to have an economic
growth rate which is sustainable through time, and avoids a
rapid boom which then has to be corrected because inflation
has got out of control or we have got too deeply into debt.
Second, we should aim for a growth rate which can be sustained
because it is underpinned by investment – not only in physical
capital and infrastructure but also in less tangible investments
such as human capital (skills and education) and innovation

(new inventions, technology and ideas). Finally, we should aim for a style and rate of growth which is compatible with the resource constraints we face and does not create global environmental instability because of climate change. This latter point means we have to find some mechanism or arrangement for ensuring the sustainability of economic growth and development at the global level. As we have seen in the various rounds of climate change negotiations, this has proved a very difficult task, despite being a highly desirable objective.[11]

Principle 2: shared prosperity

Sharing what we have with others, particularly those in need, is another strong principle rooted in the Old Testament and developed through the teaching of Christ and the Early Church. For example: 'Do not neglect to do good and to share what you have, for such sacrifices are pleasing to God' (Heb. 13.16) and 'They are to do good, to be rich in good works, generous, and ready to share' (1 Tim. 6.18).

The rich are encouraged in particular to share with the poor, though Jesus also praised the widow who gave from her very modest income.

How do we apply this principle to our modern economy and society? It is tempting to think in terms of redistributive taxation, asking the well-off to contribute more so those on lower incomes can benefit through access to welfare payments

---

[11] Scientists have been warning since the 1990s of the adverse consequence of rising greenhouse gas emissions created by human activity – which are already contributing to global warming and are predicted to generate further warming in the future. However, we have yet to reach a decisive and comprehensive international agreement to address this issue. Climate change negotiations are carried out under the United Nations Framework Convention on Climate Change (UNFCCC), agreed in 1994 – for more detail see: <http://newsroom.unfccc.int/>, accessed 10 October 2014.

and/or free public services. That certainly has to be an element in our approach and the UK and other major economies operate systems which redistribute income through taxation and benefit payments. In our modern economy, it is important to ensure that the system is working fairly, efficiently and effectively – and that high taxes are not becoming counterproductive. Modern tax systems are also highly complex and tend to become more so over time – which is one important reason for regularly reviewing and reforming the way our taxation system performs.

This redistributive approach to shared prosperity has to be complemented with another important strand of policy, however, aimed at increasing the opportunities available for individuals to acquire appropriate skills, education and employment opportunities. As we have seen in our discussion earlier, it is those who lack relevant skills who are most vulnerable in the current labour market in the face of the forces of globalisation. And there is a danger of compounding those problems if young people are not able to get a foothold on the job ladder at an early stage of their careers.

Focusing on skills, education and employment opportunities is not an alternative to having a fair tax and benefit system with a strong redistributive element. These two approaches need to sit side by side, and the tax and national insurance system can be used to provide incentives for employers to take on potential workers who may find themselves disadvantaged in the jobs market.

Principle 3: responsible business

Business is the core of our economy. In the UK, nearly 25 million people, over 80 per cent of those in employment, work in a business or other private sector organisation. Business can take many shapes and forms – including large multinational companies, small and medium-sized enterprises (SMEs)[12] and the self-employed (currently around 4.5 million, or 18 per cent of the private sector total).

Businesses are important contributors to our society – as places of work, as organisations we interact with as customers and through the impact that they can have on our communities. If a culture of personal and collective responsibility permeates through the business world, it is also likely that our economy and society will benefit too. The result is likely to be a more harmonious and contented society – and a more successful economy too. As individuals, we do not like to do business with organisations which behave irresponsibly. They will not command our loyalty and respect, and they will ultimately not win our business. We will not be well-motivated and hard-working employees or managers if we do not trust and respect the organisation for which we are working. And while I am focusing this discussion on the business world, the same principles of responsibility also apply within the public sector as well.

Responsibility is an important Christian value. Christians believe we are accountable to God for our actions in our lives. And we are encouraged to demonstrate responsibility towards our neighbours and our wider society. The parable of the Good Samaritan (Luke 10.25–37) highlights an example of responsible behaviour – not walking by on the other side. And the second part of Jesus' summary of the Law encourages us to 'love our neighbour as ourselves' (Mark 12.28–31).

In business life, it is perhaps easier to identify irresponsible actions and behaviour than to set out a comprehensive definition of responsible business. In my view, there are three main dimensions to responsible business conduct: first – honesty,

---

[12] In the European Union, SMEs are defined as businesses with fewer than 250 employees or less than 50 million euros in annual turnover.

transparency, respect for the law and fair-dealing; second – a thorough assessment and consideration of the risks and consequences of business decisions and actions – not just in the short-term but over the longer-term too – so there are not unforeseen consequences; and third – a recognition that the responsibility of business does not stop at the factory gate or the office door. Business has a wider impact on society and can make a wider contribution too – helping to address social issues, engaging with local communities and encouraging voluntary work by employees.

As we have learned more about the financial crisis, we can see that a failure of business responsibility contributed to the problems that led to the crisis. Many banks and financial institutions failed to respect the second of these dimensions of business responsibility – properly assessing risks and consequences – which played a major part in the lending behaviours which ultimately led to the crisis. We have also uncovered problems of honesty, transparency, respect for the law and fair-dealing – such as the LIBOR scandal and some of the allegations which are now emerging about conduct and practice in the foreign exchange markets. Other aspects of business behaviour have been in the spotlight, particularly in the financial world – including the mis-selling of payment protection insurance (PPI) and concerns about the practices of payday lenders. Energy companies – providers of gas and electricity – have attracted criticism for lack of transparency of their charges when the cost of domestic fuel has been rising sharply. Clothing retailers have also faced criticism for the employment standards of their suppliers, following the disastrous fire in Bangladesh in which over 100 people were killed. And the UK's largest retailer Tesco has recently had to admit that its profits were mis-stated. John Cridland, the Director-General of the CBI, has admitted that in the aftermath of the financial crisis 'there's a trust issue in some parts of the large corporate sector' and that bad behaviour in some sectors, notably banks, had contaminated the image of business more generally.[13]

Regulation is one tool we have available to ensure responsible business behaviour – and we see this in operation in a wide range of walks of business life: the minimum wage; employment protection; health and safety; consumer protection; and the regulation of banks and financial institutions. If we rely exclusively on regulation to drive responsible business behaviour, however, we will probably end up with an over-regulated economy and society. We need a society where the values applied in the world of business and at the workplace reflect notions of responsibility, fairness and honest dealing. That relies on the way in which individuals act and behave, and the values which they bring to the task of leading, managing and working in the business world. Christians and members of other faith communities have a key part to play in promoting and encouraging responsible practices within business and other organisations to which they contribute.

From principles to policy and practice

How should we be seeking to apply these three principles to the challenge of charting the way ahead for the UK economy, in a way consistent with Christian values? A detailed agenda lies outside the scope of this chapter but the discussion above has suggested a number of areas which should be the focus of attention in developing policies to chart the way ahead for the UK economy.

First, I have put a lot of emphasis on the development of appropriate skills, education and employment opportunities. This is important not only as underpinning the growth of our

---

[13] *Financial Times* (7 May 2014).

economy but also as helping to address widening inequality and to head off the dangers of persistent high youth unemployment. We will need a mix of policies to do this. One obvious area of emphasis should be developing our system of vocational education outside the traditional university system, including apprenticeships, so young people can develop relevant skills and experience while also earning a living. Another area of focus should be to help those who are trapped in low-pay and low-skilled jobs to acquire new skills which will boost their earning power in the future. We should also be considering a wider range of targeted incentives – possibly operating through the National Insurance system – to encourage employers to take on and train younger workers and those suffering from longer-term unemployment.

Second, we need a comprehensive review of the efficiency, effectiveness and fairness of the UK tax system so that it is in tune with the requirements of a modern, twenty-first-century economy. That means addressing a wide range of issues: the interaction of National Insurance and income tax, particularly for low earners; the structure of the VAT system, which has been relatively unchanged since the tax was introduced over forty years ago and contains many anomalies; the effectiveness of redistribution of income through the tax and benefit system; the taxation of pensions and other forms of saving on which we are reliant for support in old age; and the scope for new or amended sources of revenue – such as property taxes and environmental levies. This cannot be done in a piecemeal fashion. In the UK, we need a much more thorough reform and overhaul of the tax system as a whole, with the broad objective of ensuring it is efficient, fair and simple in the context of our modern economy.[14]

---

[14] See my paper at <http://www.pwc.co.uk/issues/futuretax/publications/a-tax-system-fit-for-the-future.jhtml>.

A third area of focus needs to be re-establishing confidence in the financial system and in business more generally, which underpin the ability of our economy to increase the prospect of achieving sustainable growth. We have seen through the experience of the financial crisis and other recent developments the potential instabilities created by the highly integrated and globalised world economy we now inhabit. Many actions have been taken to correct the vulnerabilities we experienced in 2008–9 – including strengthening the supervision and regulation of banks, and requiring them to build up more capital to safeguard against future shocks. But we will also need to be vigilant against other sources of economic and financial volatility – such as a renewed housing bubble or a sudden upward correction in interest rates. As I have argued, we also need to be realistic about the growth rate that our economy can achieve in the current environment – a steady improvement in the economy is greatly preferable to a short-term boom followed by a bust.

Finally, we need a stronger emphasis on environmental sustainability – and in particular managing the transition to a low carbon economy, which contributes significantly less to the problem of climate change through emissions of carbon dioxide and greenhouse gases. Making this transition without adding additional energy cost burdens to poorer households and key sectors of industry is a major challenge. And to be effective, our policies on climate change need to be aligned with those of other countries, both within Europe and across the wider world.

These policy areas are important, but at the same time we should remember that we can all – whether Christians, members of other faiths or non-believers – influence and shape our economy and society through our individual actions and the way in which we work and interact with others. Our actions, in the organisations in which we work and in the communities in which we live, can make a difference in moving us towards the sustainable, sharing and responsible society we would like to see. We see throughout the Bible, throughout history, and in our own lives examples of how individual actions count and can make a difference for the good – in ways which it is sometimes difficult to anticipate and predict. This happens when individuals go out of their way to help others – following the example of the Good Samaritan. A small act of kindness and generosity can make a huge difference to the life of someone in need. It also happens when churches, other faith groups and communities come together with a common purpose or cause to address local needs, either at home or abroad, or change our national or global society for the better. And individuals can also make a difference by acting responsibly and 'doing the right thing' – whether because of their faith or from a feeling of common humanity – in their everyday working lives.

It is tempting to be intimidated by the forces of economic change which surround us, and the big issues we are facing, not just in the UK but globally. But the UK economy has many strengths which we can build on. We should be optimistic and hopeful that we can find a successful way ahead for the British economy, built on the principles of sustainable growth, shared prosperity and responsible business.

4

Full education in a free society

ANDREW ADONIS*

———•◆•———

A person who has difficulty in buying the labour that he wants suffers inconvenience or reduction of profits. A person who cannot sell his labour is in effect told that he is of no use. The first difficulty causes annoyance or loss. The other is a personal catastrophe. This difference remains even if an adequate income is provided, by insurance or otherwise, during unemployment; idleness even on an income corrupts; the feeling of not being wanted demoralizes. The difference remains even if most people are unemployed only for relatively short periods. As long as there is any long-term unemployment not obviously due to personal deficiency, anybody who loses his job fears that he may be one of the unlucky ones who will not get another job quickly. The short-term unemployed do not know that they are short-term unemployed till their unemployment is over.

(Lord Beveridge, *Full Employment in a Free Society* (1944))

Lord Beveridge's report of 1944 sought *Full Employment in a Free Society*. Once again, at the time of writing, we are enduring mass unemployment. But whenever this scourge returns it has a new complexion. This time round, since the 2008 crash, its most glaring feature is the predominance of unemployment, and

* I am grateful to Adam Tyndall for research assistance. This article was originally published by the Joseph Rowntree Foundation in *Poverty in the UK: Can it be eradicated?*, ed. Jonathan Derbyshire, (London: Prospect Publishing, 2013), pp. 39–42.

underemployment, among the young. In early 2013 – nearly five years after the start of the downturn – the unemployment rate for young people was still above 20 per cent. This equates to nearly a million young people not in education, employment or training. Expand the parameters to include all 16–24-year-olds who are economically inactive (not in work and not looking for work) and the figure reaches 1.65 million.

This compares with an unemployment rate for the population at large that is currently hovering just below 8 per cent. The proportion of young people who are 'idle' – one of Beveridge's 'Five Giant Evils', wider in its meaning than 'unemployment' – is two and a half times higher than among the population as a whole. This is fraught with peril, not only for the individuals concerned but also for society at large.

In contrast, the latest figures from the Office for National Statistics (at the time of writing) show that just over a million people over the age of 65 are in work, the highest since records began. At a time of significant unemployment, the relative position of pensioners is improving while young workers are noticeably worse off than the average worker.

Youth unemployment has many causes and requires bold action across the economy at large. However, a critical factor is education. The OECD reported that 19 per cent of 25–34-year-olds in the UK who left education at 16 are now unemployed, compared to 9 per cent in 2000, while among those with degrees, the unemployment rate stands at only 4.7 per cent. It is not being young that makes you unemployed, but being young and unskilled.

The least educated and trained are always at the greatest risk of unemployment. 'Least educated' does not simply mean those gaining virtually no basic qualifications from school or college by the age of 18 – the 'underclass' of concern to policy-makers before 2008 – but rather the broad swathe of 16–24-year-olds, many of them with some school leaving competences and qualifications but who are part of the 'forgotten 50 per cent' not on a university track. From this broad swathe of young people comes the mass of the unemployed and 'idle' young people – and their plight needs to be addressed with the boldness and urgency of a new Beveridge.

Whereas in 1944 Beveridge called for a policy of 'Full Employment in a Free Society', seventy years on the key imperative is to achieve 'full *education* in a free society'. This is critical not only for national and individual economic well-being but also because education is a key enabler of social integration and individual moral purpose.

The cost of youth 'idleness'

Youth unemployment deprives young people of the opportunity to realise their full potential. It blights communities and stigmatises individuals with a sense of worthlessness and failure. It marks a failure by society to provide the conditions which can enable full human flourishing.

Moreover, its effects are long term. One of the simplest measures of the effect of early unemployment is the impact that it has on the individual's earning potential. That is to say, how much less will someone who is unemployed early in their career earn later in their career?

Using the National Child Development Survey, Paul Gregg and Emma Tominey analysed 'the impact of unemployment during youth upon the wage of individuals up to twenty years later'. Previous studies had found that those who experienced significant youth unemployment could expect wages that were up to 25 per cent lower than average. It had not been proved, however, that it is the unemployment which causes the lower wages. It is not difficult to construct a scenario to explain why there would be a correlation without a causal connection. Those with lower educational attainment – for instance – might be both less likely to find work and have a lower earning potential once in work.

To address this, Gregg and Tominey controlled for a range of factors including 'educational achievement, region of residence and a wealth of family and individual specific characteristics'. But they go further than this and 'employ an instrumental variables technique to ensure that our results are not driven by unobserved individual heterogeneity'.

The result of their analysis couldn't be clearer. Youth unemployment leads to a 'wage scar' of at least from 8 to 10 per cent. Those who experience further periods of unemployment after the age of 23 can expect their earnings twenty years later to be from 12 to 15 per cent lower than those who do not experience youth unemployment.

This is not just a function of the luck and aptitude of individuals. The same results are found when looking at the effects of recession. Lisa Kahn has looked at the consequences of graduating from university in a bad economy and found them to be 'large, negative and persistent'. This is significant enough for Kahn to suggest that, theoretically at least, individuals who graduate in a recession may be better off over their lifetime if they delay entering the labour market until the economy picks up.

It is also worth briefly looking at which young people are most affected and why. Paul Gregg's evidence from the National Child Development Survey indicated a significant 'dependence induced by early unemployment experience for men but only minor persistence for women'. Many studies have also shown that it is the least skilled young people who suffer most. Gregg concludes that 'The evidence of scarring offers a strong justification for early intervention to prevent long-term youth unemployment' and suggests that combining this with an 'attack on low educational achievement' would be most likely to succeed.

This intuitively sensible position is also supported by Simon Burgess et al. They conclude that 'for the unskilled, there is evidence of an enduring adverse effect' with results that mean 'the unemployment experiences of cohorts coming of age in poor labour market conditions are more unequal within the cohort than those of luckier cohorts'.

Another way of measuring the effect of youth unemployment is the extent to which it increases one's chances of being unemployed later in life. In aggregate, it is the tendency for periods of mass unemployment to raise the natural unemployment rate. Put simply, if more people are unemployed now then more will be unemployed in the future.

Olivier Blanchard and Lawrence Summers introduced this idea of 'unemployment hysteresis'[1] in 1986. They argued that the fundamental issue lies in the 'asymmetry in the wage-setting process between insiders who are employed and outsiders who want jobs'. One of the outcomes of the wage negotiation process, they argue, is a wage which ensures the jobs of those who are currently employed. A sudden reduction in employment shifts this 'equilibrium wage rate, giving rise to hysteresis'.

They have, however, been criticised for putting the emphasis in the wrong place. For example, Lawrence Ball believes that 'There is more evidence for stories in which the long-term unemployed become detached from the labor market. These workers are unattractive to employers, or they don't try hard to find jobs.' This line of argument is supported by evidence which shows that 'a long duration of unemployment benefits magnifies hysteresis'.

Whichever of these two explanations one finds most convincing, it is not in doubt that periods of unemployment are extremely damaging to the individual concerned. It might

---

[1] From the Greek *husteresis* (*husteros* – 'coming after' or 'later').

be that changes to the benefits structure or to unionisation legislation could help to minimise hysteresis, but it is doubtful that these policy mechanisms alone will ever produce a hysteresis-free society. And the implementation of either would be unlikely to address the critical imbalance in the distribution of unemployment.

Equipping young people with the skills necessary to thrive in the workplace, combined with preventing extended periods of unemployment while they are young, are therefore the crucial factors in ensuring that idleness is not a recurring theme in an individual's life.

Youth unemployment is not just 'a personal catastrophe'. It is also a significant problem for the national economy.

The UK currently spends over £4.5 billion on out of work and housing benefits for under-25s, a combination of housing benefit, Jobseeker's Allowance, employment and support allowance, income support and incapacity benefit. That's a lot of money that could be put to better use: £4.5 billion could bring back the Education Maintenance Allowance and still have nearly £4 billion to spare. And that's before taking into account the positive effects of an extra million people in work: extra tax revenue, higher GDP growth and so on.

However, £4.5 billion does not begin to price the cost to families, communities, and society at large of mass youth unemployment.

Back to Beveridge in 1944: 'Full productive employment in a free society is possible but it is not possible without taking pains. It cannot be won by waving a financial wand . . . To win full employment and keep it, we must will the end and must understand and will the means.'

Youth unemployment will not be eradicated by waving a fiscal wand. Nor is a revival in demand and employment of itself likely to eradicate idleness among the young. For this to happen, education needs to be extended radically – in schools, in terms of standards and qualifications achieved; in the quality and quantity of apprenticeships for those not on track for university; and in terms of early workplace experiences that offer real training and opportunity.

Schools

The past twenty-five years have seen a significant improvement in school standards. Essential school leaving qualifications – as measured by the achievement of five GCSEs between A* and C, including English and maths – are now achieved by a majority of young people. In the mid-1990s just 30 per cent reached this benchmark; now it is reached by nearly 60 per cent of school-leavers.

However, this is still far short of what is required. Four in ten 16-year-olds are not gaining decent GCSEs; their job prospects are poor and their risk of 'idleness' – unemployment or underemployment – very high. Finding a good job, with a good salary and an opportunity to thrive, is very difficult for them.

The challenge is to transform our '60 per cent school system' into a '90 per cent system'. That is, a system where nine in every ten young people leave school with five good GCSEs including English and maths. And it needs to be achieved as soon as possible.

This '90 per cent system' is achievable, with a will. In 2011, 28 non-selective schools in England reached this 90 per cent benchmark. There were 123 above 80 per cent. There is also good international evidence to show that this is possible. On similar benchmarks, Singapore manages to achieve 82 per cent nationally, while the USA peaked at 80 per cent in the late 1960s and now consistently hovers around 70 per cent. The US is rightly concerned about 'high school drop out': but it is at a lower level than in the UK.

The old conservative social reflex that in education 'more means worse' once dominated public thinking in Britain. Now, thankfully, it is largely dead. The best argument against this outdated thinking is summed up in David Hopkins's book *Every School a Great School*, in which he writes: 'It is salutary to recognise that whether the goal of "every school a great school" is achieved or not, its realisation is more about professional and political will rather than strategic knowledge. It is now twenty-five years since Ron Edmonds asked his felicitous question: "How many effective schools would you have to see to be persuaded of the educability of all children?"'[2]

A 2013 Ofsted report, *Unseen Children: Access and Achievement 20 Years On*, found that only 36 per cent of children who receive free school meals (i.e., children from the poorest families) achieve five good GCSEs, compared to 63 per cent among non-'free school meals' students. Only one in four white boys on free school meals does so. Bridge these class divides and 60 per cent quickly becomes 90 per cent; dropping out becomes further study or training; dipping in and out of unemployment becomes a steady job; and a Britain with too many poor people becomes a low-poverty UK.

A notable success story in this field is the London Challenge, which systematically partnered successful schools and their management teams with their less successful counterparts, driving up standards. In 2007, Inner London schools were second only to the North East as the worst performing schools in England. Only 42 per cent of students achieved five GCSEs at grades A* to C, including English and maths. By 2012, Inner

---

[2] David Hopkins, *Every School a Great School: Realizing the Potential of System Leadership* (Maidenhead: Open University Press, 2007).

London schools were second only to Outer London schools as the best performing in England with over 60 per cent of all students achieving the GCSE benchmark.

The London Challenge programme was established in 2003 and assessed by the schools inspectorate, Ofsted, in 2010. They concluded that, 'Since the introduction of London Challenge, secondary schools in London have performed better and improved at a faster rate than schools in the rest of England.' By 2010, only 2.4 per cent of London's secondary schools received an 'inadequate' rating and 30 per cent were judged to be outstanding. This compares with more than 4 per cent of schools in the rest of England being 'inadequate' and just 17.5 per cent achieving 'outstanding' status.

So how did they do it? Ofsted explain it as using 'independent, experienced education experts, known as London Challenge advisers, to identify need and broker support for underperforming schools'. They also highlight four key factors:

1 clear, consistent leadership from the advisers appointed by the Department for Education;
2 programmes of support managed by experienced and credible advisers;
3 identifying the actual needs of each school, starting with support for the leadership before the main work of improving teaching and learning;
4 robust systems to track pupils' progress and provide effective interventions for those at risk of underachievement.

The London Challenge approach should now be extended nationwide.

For an average secondary school – both in terms of size and attainment – getting from 60 per cent to 90 per cent means an extra six students each year meeting this basic level of GCSE success. Any good teacher would be able to point to which six students in their school could make it across that line with the right interventions. Excellent teachers would be able to tell you what those interventions should be.

This is the next crucial point with regard to improving school standards: we must expand the supply of outstanding teachers. Teach First, which in 2013 recruited 1,300 top graduates to teach in schools serving deprived communities, is an example of what can be done, where there is the will. This from an organisation which was only established in 2002.

Every school also needs a strong governing body and leadership team providing a powerful vision and ethos. This too can be achieved even in the toughest neighbourhoods, as demonstrated by the success of the programme to establish academies – independent state schools managed by high-capacity sponsors dedicated to educational transformation – since its launch in 2000.

Dynamic partnership between the State, families and social institutions – including religious institutions – can help show the way here. Combine brilliant teachers with brilliant leadership and family, community and social involvement and 60 per cent could quickly become 90 per cent, dramatically – and systematically – reducing Beveridge's curse of 'idleness'.[3]

Apprenticeships

Alongside a revolution in school standards, there needs to be a revolution in the quality and quantity of youth apprenticeships.

---

[3] Such partnerships can also provide a way through training into work for those who, for whatever reason, have fallen outside the school system. Handcrafted is a Christian project in Durham that provides tailored training to help people disadvantaged by crime, unemployment, alcohol or substance abuse to find a job, and also serves the local community by providing affordable repairs – <www.handcraftedproject.com>, accessed 5 September 2014.

Apprenticeship numbers are deceptive. Most of those called 'apprentices' are well into their 20s, and are in reality mainstream employees. The government claims big increases in apprenticeship numbers, but most of these are aged 25 or over and 70 per cent of current apprentices turn out to have been working for their apprenticeship provider beforehand. Many of them have simply been given the title 'apprentice' by re-badging adult training schemes.

Focus on school-leavers and what they go on to do and the status quo is dire. Of 2011's 780,000 19-year-olds, about 300,000 went on to full-time higher education. Fewer than 130,000 – including under-19s too – started an apprenticeship. There is a black hole of unemployment, or unskilled and part-time work with barely any education and training, into which from 250,000 to 300,000 young people are consigned each year.

Now, thanks to the Richard Review (published in November 2012 by businessman Doug Richard), we have the beginnings of a plan to make it happen. Richard recommends one apprenticeship qualification per occupation, devised by employers, as opposed to the staggering 11,775 that are currently meeting public funding criteria.

Richard recommends a minimum standard of numeracy and literacy to be an integral part of every apprenticeship assessment. He recommends a competence test at the end of the scheme – more akin to a driving test than the current modular system which leaves many apprenticeships incomplete. In Germany, apprentices undergo a final examination in the vocational school and an oral examination and practical test in the workplace. The same should happen in Britain.

We need far more apprenticeships, specifically designed for young people, on the Richard model. Many firms are leading the way – Rolls-Royce, Jaguar Land Rover and Network Rail all provide models of best practice. A Whitehall apprenticeship scheme has recently been launched. It needs to become a gold standard in the public sector, like the civil service 'fast stream' is for graduates.

UCAS, the university admissions service, says it would be willing to become an integrated higher education and apprenticeships admissions service if the government and employers approached it to do so. This is an excellent idea. It would help give a rocket boost to youth apprenticeships and enable school-leavers to apply both for university and apprenticeship places in tandem. This could be valuable in raising the profile of apprenticeships and effectively advertising vacancies nationwide.

Only one-third of large employers and one in ten SMEs offer apprenticeships. Much of the public sector also offers few apprenticeships. A revolution is needed in the supply of youth apprenticeships, both quality and quantity, with employers in the public and private sectors doing more on their own account, and with government and employers working in more inventive partnership.

There are two other key issues. First, higher-level apprentices. Barely a quarter of the 126,000 apprentices under the age of 19 are studying at the equivalent of A level or higher. Although apprentices are expected to be 'working towards' an acceptable standard of functional maths, English and information technology, it is unclear how often that is achieved. We need far more higher-level apprenticeships, especially in engineering, where there is an acute shortage of graduates.

Second, apprenticeships need to last a decent length of time. Over recent years, almost half of all apprenticeships have lasted a year or less – many a matter of weeks. No university would award a degree on this basis. Apprenticeships should not be dumbed down either.

Trade unions also have a part to play, promoting and supporting apprentices in the workplace. Some of the most exciting work being done by trade unions is in the area of training and apprenticeships, such as the brilliant UnionLearn project being run by the TUC. All partners in the workplace have a key role to play in training a workforce fit for the future.

Jobs

Learning does not stop when young people leave formal education. As outlined earlier, initial experiences in the labour market can be equally formative. We must see this as an integral part of a young person's educational and professional development because it is crucial to their life chances, earning potential and likelihood of avoiding poverty.

But in-work poverty is a real risk even for those young people who avoid unemployment. The National Minimum Wage (NMW) has been a success but it has only risen by 42p since 2011. The fact that the NMW is not sufficient to avoid poverty – especially for those in London – is demonstrated by the rise of support for the Living Wage (LW). This is the idea that everyone should be paid enough to live decently and provide adequately for their family. It is an ethical argument against in-work poverty and it is a calculation that takes into account local variation in the cost of living.

For young people, there is even more cause for concern. Those under 21 have a lower NMW rate than those over 21. Over three-quarters of 16–20-year-olds are paid below the LW compared to just 14 per cent of 41–50-year-olds. Nearly half of all people paid below the LW are aged 30 or under. This is not surprising given salary progression over the course of one's career but it means that in-work poverty is a reality for many young people.

There is a strong case to be made for raising the NMW. Once again, it is both moral and financial. If the NMW were to be increased to the LW rate, the taxpayer would save over £2 billion. That's approximately £3.6 billion in savings from the private sector – roughly a third of which comes from income tax, a third from National Insurance Contributions and a third from a reduced benefits bill – coupled with an increase in public sector pay of £1.3 billion.

When the NMW was introduced, the naysayers predicted mass unemployment as a result. No such effect occurred. Recent research from the Resolution Foundation has also found that large parts of the UK economy could afford to pay a higher minimum wage. Raising the NMW must be done sensibly, over time and in conjunction with the Low Pay Commission. But it must be done if we are to end in-work poverty.

We must take a holistic view of education, employment and training for young people and not allow so many of them to slip through the net. There should be virtually no Young People Not in Education, Employment or Training (NEETs) under the age of 25 and there should be no in-work poverty. As Angel Gurria, OECD Secretary-General, said on the publication of their report: 'High youth unemployment is not inevitable, even during an economic crisis; it is the product of the interaction between economic context and particular policies.' The State needs to act to improve these 'particular policies' and build a low-poverty UK.

Conclusion

Getting our educational system right is crucial to our future economic and social well-being. Schools, colleges and universities are critical in fostering social cohesion and sound common values, and in providing individuals with the means to flourish. For the religiously inclined, this is a moral imperative; for the policy-maker, it is a social and economic necessity.

The keys to success are simple to identify, harder to deliver:

- an equal care for all, across the whole spectrum of social class and ability;
- an end to artificial barriers to achievement, whether these are social or economic or simply a result of academic fashion;
- a holistic approach to planning and execution;
- adequate investment;
- full family, social (including business) and community engagement;
- a clear ethical framework;
- encouragement and support for brilliant teachers, brilliantly led.

Difficult to deliver, but by no means impossible – as the recent improvements in standards and the individual examples I have mentioned show. With continued attention to these points, we can achieve full education which both strengthens our free society and empowers its citizens.

5

The changing face of poverty

JULIA UNWIN

————•◦•————

Introduction

The debate about how to tackle poverty is neither new nor over.

The suffering of people and places in poverty is well documented, and costs, risks and waste are well known. There has been poverty in the UK since records began.

There is no shortage of lamentation about the evils of poverty, and a shared recognition that poverty limits human potential and shames us all.

York is a particularly important place from which to consider poverty because it was here that Joseph and Seebohm Rowntree so assiduously reported poverty, and shocked a nation into recognising that something needed to be done. Our current approach to the relief of poverty is rooted in their rigorous research, the crusading ability of Archbishop Temple, and the administrative skills of William Beveridge.

A number of principles have underpinned this approach and have been a fundamental part of the social contract – the settlement between the people and the State, describing what people can expect of each other, of market and community institutions and of the State itself.

The first principle is that work is the best possible way out of poverty, with a shared understanding that hard work should therefore provide sufficient income to enable the individual, and household, to survive. The second principle is that families should support each other, owing a duty of care to other members.

From the early years of the Poor Law, these two principles of individual and family autonomy were supported by a third: the acceptance of the need for the wider community to offer support at times of individual vulnerability or market change.

A complex network of support has existed for centuries, motivated variously by a fear of civil unrest, by religious principle (the recognition of God in every individual), and by the government's need to limit its financial commitments.

The public policy environment of the UK has for a very long time had an investment in relieving poverty, through both prevention and protecting against its worst impacts.

This investment, with its restrictions designed both to mould behaviour and ration demand, has always been contested.

The dominant roles have moved between the State – at parish, local and national level – the voluntary sector, churches, mutual friendly societies and the market. For centuries, the patchwork of support, some national, some local, has struggled to find a way of preventing poverty and has provided for its (usually very limited) relief.

The social contract

The UK social contract is an implicit one. It changes over time, and is described differently in different situations. What is more, its very existence is questioned. Yet the bones of the social contract on poverty and inequality can clearly be seen in custom and practice, in expectation and in law.

There are expectations on the individual – that they will try to be self-sufficient and to do their best to secure the income that they need. Additionally there is an expectation that family members will, as far as they are able, support each other and that the first duty is to support the immediate family.

There are expectations on the market too. There is an expectation that the welfare of the worker will be protected, that there will not be exposure to undue risk, and that unlawful discrimination will not be tolerated. There is regulation of holiday time and working hours, and rights to paid time off in particular circumstances. The housing market is also subject to expectations and to regulation. Homes that are fit for habitation, priced at a level that can be afforded, are fundamental to the nature of the contract.

And there are expectations on the State. These give the State, at local and national level, not only the powers to intervene but also the obligation to support and provide a safety net that protects against destitution.

This implicit and rarely articulated social contract is constantly changing, but changes in the behaviour of one partner – the individual, the State or the market – will always have implications for others. Crucially the level of pay provided by employers will have a direct impact on the demands made on the State. So too will the levels of rent charged and landlords' expectations about the level of return on capital. This in turn requires a level of subsidy for people on lower wages who are to be housed.

The nature of this social contract is at the heart of our concerns for society.

Three dimensions of poverty

Poverty is always with us, but it is by no means inevitable, nor is it constant. It operates in different dimensions and in different ways. The New Testament (Mark 14.7) may tell us that poverty will always be with us, but this has never been an excuse for acceptance. Rather it serves as a reminder that, for Christians, addressing the position of people in poverty is a constant demand.

Poverty is associated with money – both income and costs. It is also associated with the operation of markets, because labour markets, housing markets and the operation of systems essential for survival bite hard on people living in poverty. The third dimension is the dimension of place – the recognition that poverty is both local and national, is not evenly distributed, and will be experienced differently in different places.

These three dimensions provide a framework for considering poverty, for understanding a generous and proper response, and provide some indications of what might now be done.

Money

Household income is the greatest determinant of poverty, and by any measure, adopted anywhere in the world, an assessment of income, and therefore available cash, is vitally important to any household. The absence of money in a household erodes autonomy and self-expression. It creates stress and anxiety, and rapidly saps confidence, motivation and capability. This much is well documented.

In recent years, great public attention has rightly been focused on the system of income support for poorer people and more recently on attempts to reform how this is provided. The historic anxiety has been that if State subsidy is too generous it will remove the willingness to work and this is now profoundly affecting the income of poorer people and places. Cash transfers from the State in the shape of tax credits and benefits are obviously hugely important, and the way they are calibrated and delivered is part of any good society's contribution to alleviating poverty. Over the past fifteen years (at the time of writing), considerable strides have been taken to improve the income conditions of families with children and older people. These have demonstrated that State interventions – continuously and consistently applied – can make a difference.

The income available from work, always prescribed as the best and safest possible route out of poverty, now provides no such assurance for many people. A low-wage economy, likely to become even more so with rapid automation, means that hard work does not provide a reliable route out of poverty. Even once secured, work is inconsistent and does not offer progression. The fact that so many people in middle age are subsisting below the Living Wage (LW) is one indicator of the penury in which many working people live. This failure of work to provide sufficient income for households signals a significant rupture in the social contract.

But the pockets of poor people are affected in other ways. The very high costs faced by households in poverty inevitably have a big impact on their available income. It is a truism to say that the 'poor pay more'. Food in poorer households will cost more if the cooking facilities are inadequate, and if the nearest shops are those selling the more expensive convenience food. Household bills are higher, as arrangements for spreading the cost are unavailable to poorer households. In any event, the costs that are most subject to rapid inflation are precisely those that take a larger proportion of income from poorer households.

The very high costs of housing mean that an elaborate system of subsidy has been created, and that people who are working full-time increasingly need Housing Benefit in order to pay rent. Childcare – that absolute requirement for parents who need to work – is another cost that means there is little disposable income left.

The risk of debt, and the likelihood of it, has stalked the lives of poor households throughout recorded time. In our current credit-fuelled economy, debt is an ever-more consistent feature in the lives of poorer people. Changing work patterns, sudden expenses and crises in health mean that people with limited assets, having exhausted the capability of family and friends, can rapidly become heavily indebted. As with the other costs devouring the limited funds available, debt in poorer households is an even more costly expense.

Money has always defined poverty. The lack of it, the search for it, and the need for it is a constant. Poverty in the UK in the twenty-first century is characterised by an absolute lack of money, and a struggle to cope. It is different because the demands on that limited money are different, and the cash available in the rest of society is so significant. Giving alms (money or goods) to poor people is older than Christianity itself, and charity will always have its role. The unconditional gift of money, with expectation of no return, is a requirement of all the world's religions, and Scripture tells us that such action benefits the giver as much as the recipient. But ending poverty, both in individuals and in society, requires a concerted, long-term and sustained response that needs to offer equity and certainty in ways that charitable donation can never supply.

In the UK this approach has had many manifestations, but the involvement of the State, both locally and increasingly nationally, has been an accepted feature for centuries. State intervention theoretically allows for the sharing of risk, for equitable and fair distribution, and for practically applying a shared public responsibility for vulnerable people.

The founding principles of our current welfare state, rooted in notions of reciprocity and mutual insurance, were also formed at a time of much greater acceptance of State intervention. The control of price, and critically rent, alongside a centrally directed economy, provided the means to create jobs where they were needed, and to align income and costs.

That alignment has been broken. State responsibility for the subsistence needs of its poorer citizens has always been contested, and has rarely been popular, but as the context changes, and the powers and choices of the State change, the debate has become particularly difficult. For people who are in poverty and receiving benefits, the experience has been much more difficult: attacked and criticised, described as idle or fraudsters, it has become easy to demonise those who receive benefits and credits from the State as somehow culpable for the current market condition.

All the main political parties currently approach the provision of 'welfare' based on a critical assumption – that, unless the receipt of help is made as unpleasant as possible, poor people will always opt not to work. This latter-day conception of the Victorian mantra of 'less eligibility' assumes that poor people hold a set of motives and aspirations that are entirely different from everyone else's. This has no basis in evidence. Indeed most of the evidence and experience is that people who are poor are desperate to change their circumstances and try extraordinarily hard to do so.

This assumption means that political debates about 'welfare' are essentially arguments about the nature and severity of conditions to be applied to the delivery of benefits. The current sanctions regime is the latest manifestation of an approach that tries to mould behaviour through the provision of benefits. At heart it is based on the view that the motivations of poor people are entirely other than those that drive the rest of us.

Undoubtedly there are people who attempt to defraud the system. This is true in every possible walk of life. There will be those who prefer an impoverished life on benefits to one spent working, and there is no doubt that this can fuel hostility to people who rely upon benefits. Simple statistical rebuttal is clearly no answer to those who believe that there are vast numbers 'milking the system', and the constant repetition of stories about the dishonest few is undoubtedly driving public discourse. But this concern is rooted in anecdote, not reality. The ancient distinction between those who are 'deserving' and those who are 'undeserving' threads through all public debates, ignoring the reality. The income of many people in poverty is governed by a combination of economic circumstance, physical and mental capability, family structure and pure bad luck, which profoundly affects their ability to be independent.

The availability and dignity of work is a cornerstone of much of Scripture, but so too is a belief in the inalienable and eternal value of the individual and recognition of their assets, whether material or otherwise.

In contrast, the dominant deficit model assumes that individuals, left to their own devices, would prefer a life of idle penury to one in which they are engaged and contributing. It risks associating material gain with real value, and confusing the contribution people make in unpaid, unrewarded and frequently unrecognised work. By focusing on a very material definition of productivity, this approach to work can also obscure the very great social value of care and community.

Markets

The extent to which education, enterprise and employment provide a reliable and straight route out of poverty has also changed. The hollowed-out labour market is well documented. Today, the nature of work available – more particularly the prospects offered through employment, enterprise and education – have a very different flavour.

The historic link between unemployment and poverty, or pauperism, has been broken. It is now, as study after study has demonstrated, more than possible to be employed and still live a life of considerable poverty. Work currently available is low paid and frequently unreliable and inconsistent. It offers little in the way of progression. The notion that hard work will enable people to leave poverty and build a life of self-reliance is no longer true for many. Instead the prospects of work provide intermittent activity, limited reward and no security.

Work is becoming ever-more casual, as highlighted by the much-discussed 'zero hours contracts', and there are many forms of self-employment. The fluid boundaries between work and unemployment mean that many people persistently experience grinding poverty, whether working or not. Perhaps even more tellingly, very low pay is now experienced in every decade of life. Recent research from the Joseph Rowntree Foundation (JRF)[1] recorded that two thirds of those earning below the LW were in the prime of their working life, disproving the notion that low pay is somehow a 'starter' wage, with inevitable promotion and progression to follow.

The rapidly changing circumstances of individuals and families, whether working or not, result in a fluctuating and usually very limited income. With one in eight members of the working-age population applying for Jobseeker's Allowance in any two-year period, it is hard to continue with the view that poverty somehow marks out another, distinct and different population. Perhaps the single most striking, and certainly the most publicised, aspect of the new face of poverty is the break in the link between poverty and unemployment. While the Catholic Catechism has always listed 'defrauding the labourer of his wage' as one of the four sins crying out to heaven for vengeance, the debate about the proper reward for work is more routinely discussed in terms of worker productivity, automation, economic demand and global pressures. Wages that do not provide adequate income may reflect poor productivity or the low value accorded to the work. But the outcome is, essentially,

---

[1] See <http://www.jrf.org.uk/media-centre/report-reveals-new-face-uk-poverty>, accessed 5 September 2014.

a rupturing of the social contract, on which so many assumptions about the structuring of society are based.

The same is essentially true about the conditions of work. The hallmark of Christian writing about work is that it contributes intrinsically to shared, abundant prosperity, but when work is so flexible that it provides no security at all, and so sporadic that it is genuinely unreliable, it is hard to see it in this way. Work that traps people in poverty is, in these terms, as culpable as systems of social support that equally trap people and make transition so very hard.

However, money is about expenditure as well as income. The costs faced by poorer households are great, and increasingly so. A market approach to setting prices makes some essentials unaffordable, and leads to the creation of lower-quality, frequently expensive alternatives, because it does not acknowledge that these goods are central to a functioning society.

The unrestricted market will not help people to become better off. But the ways in which markets operate undoubtedly affect both the experience of poverty and the extent to which people are able to provide for themselves. The rising cost of essentials – and the continuing struggle to pay for them in a world where consumption is so highly valued – is a characteristic of modern poverty.

Of course this has always been true, but there are aspects of the modern market that mean poor people experience higher costs and better-off people benefit more, including:

- the impact of online communications and marketing;
- the very significant reductions in cost that can be achieved through electronic payment;
- the ability to shop around and search digitally for better value;
- payment plans, which favour better-off people, and cost poorer people more.

Housing is all too often a cause of poverty, with an extra 3 million people deemed to be in poverty once they have paid their housing costs. This is caused in large part by the major emphasis on housing as the most common means of accumulating wealth, and the shortage of housing in many parts of the country where work is most readily available. The very high rent paid by people who cannot buy, as much as the insecurity and sometimes poor quality of rented housing, is a direct result of the operation of the housing market. The historic victory of the UK housing system, which had broken the link between poverty and poor housing, is at risk of reversal as poverty again becomes associated with conditions of squalor.

The other market biting upon the income of poorer households is the market for finance itself. The assumed higher risk in lending to poor people results in high charges that penalise those with limited means, who are forced to borrow to meet the costs of emergencies and crises. Studies of those in long-term debt describe a desperate cycle. Changes in working patterns, reaching the limits of a family's capacity to support, sudden illness and delays in benefit and tax payments, all contribute to a spiral of debt. This is then exacerbated by responses to otherwise normal domestic crises. For poorer families, the combination of a broken washing machine, a fast-growing child and a delay in processing a tax credit can result in deep and persistent debt. Escaping from such debt is virtually impossible, and contributes to a hugely diminished disposable income.

Place

The third dimension of modern poverty that challenges perceptions of poverty, and crucially shapes responses, is the dimension of place.

Places, through family and neighbourhood networks, through churches, trades unions and community organisations, have always provided the first bulwark – the first defence and protection – against poverty. Strong communities, even the very poorest in material terms, can and do provide solidarity, comfort and practical aid. Employment-generating schemes, credit unions, networks to support people who are lonely, food banks and lodgings schemes are just a few examples of how places support those who are poor. The circulation of relatively small sums of money among family and friends to help tide people over is, and always has been, a feature of poverty, and is usually firmly rooted in place.

This vital place-based response to poverty is undermined and threatened in the very places that need it most. Poverty is not distributed evenly across the country. The causes and experience of poverty differ across the country and so do responses.

In part, this relates to the unevenness of the economy, and the way the restructuring of the post-industrial UK economy changed the prospects of some parts of the country. The great period of de-industrialisation is a defining, and perhaps familiar, aspect of the modern geography of poverty, because of the dramatic changes it heralded for the north of England, and the reversal of its fortunes. The former industrialised cities and towns of the UK, with the sudden removal of the source of (usually male) employment, suffered a shock from which most have yet to recover fully.

In towns and cities with relatively few opportunities, those who can will leave. The magnet of opportunity is nothing new. People have always 'gone to London to make their fortune'. What remains in the cities they leave behind has always been a cause for concern. But in our much more mobile and fast-moving economy, the strong sense that some places feel 'left behind', resulting in an ageing, impoverished and largely underskilled population, is presenting real challenges to the authorities with responsibility.

The concept of the declining city, variously known as the weak market city or the failing city, attracts different policy prescriptions in different countries. In the USA, for example, there is a much greater readiness to abandon towns when the demand for work shifts and the rust-belt cities are testament to this approach. In stark contrast, the cities of the former East Germany have been regenerated with considerable expense, and a clear political commitment to develop new centres of wealth.[2] Without intervention, however, accepting the inevitability of decline presents not just a political challenge, but a moral challenge about how to support the people who live in those areas to lead full, engaged and productive lives.

Other areas, with greater economic prospects and ambition, will try to ride the waves of economic growth and many will do so with huge success. Others too will seek to harness the return to economic growth to improve their local prospects, and businesses and local authorities will work in tandem to improve the economy of those towns and cities. In doing so they face choices about communities that are poor, underskilled and poorly resourced. They can see them simply as inconvenient obstacles to local growth and development, but this risks a return to growth that simply ignores the poorest neighbourhoods and households, thereby pushing them further away from any prospect of economic viability. Economic growth that merely displaces poverty, or further isolates poor households, brings its own risks. For much of the latter half of the twentieth century, regenerating parts of our great cities has jostled uneasily with supporting those in greatest need. The recent history of some London boroughs illustrates powerfully how the concentration of great wealth, while improving

---

[2] A. Power, Jörg Plöger and Astrid Winkler, *Phoenix Cities: The Fall and Rise of Great Industrial Cities* (York: Joseph Rowntree Foundation, 2010).

amenities and increasing the tax base of local government, may only be achieved by the displacement of poorer households.

Or they can work with the grain of the communities that are there, understanding their assets and strengths, and make their organising purpose the alleviation, prevention and reduction of poverty. For example, Acumen Development Trust[3] works to achieve social and economic regeneration through learning, enterprise and employment. Its principal area of activity is in East Durham, but it now works across the North East of England. Acumen was founded in May 2003 to provide support for social enterprise and to bring together community engagement and outreach provision in business coaching, skills for life and employment advice.

Features of the changing face of poverty

The experience of poverty is, in so many ways, unchanging. The risks faced by poor people and the tragic waste of skills and ability are a constant through the centuries. So too is the disdain with which people in poverty are viewed. Poverty is feared, and those who experience it lead lives of fear, and also of shame.

Much social change is led and fuelled by those affected, those with a voice and the ability to make others listen. But modern poverty in the UK lacks such a voice. It is only in the rare cases where bodies, and especially faith organisations like the Church of Scotland, take the initiative to set up a Poverty Truth Commission[4] that people who are themselves poor get a platform to describe their experience of poverty.

---

[3] See <http://locality.org.uk/our-members/acumen-development-trust-ltd/>, accessed 5 September 2014.
[4] See <http://www.povertytruthcommission.org/>, accessed 5 September 2014.

They describe, vividly and powerfully, the impact of experiencing poverty and how the dimensions of money, markets and place can always be found in it. So too, however, can new features, and ones that are frequently overlooked.

The spectre of destitution now stalks people who are poor as the threat of withholding benefits is used in an attempt to mould behaviour. While all systems of public support have conditions attached to them, it is new for the UK to have institutionalised the ability to withdraw all obvious means of financial support for failure to comply with regulations. The sight of people with no money at all has been the spur for food banks and emergency shelters, and is increasingly described by those who support people in poverty.

Experience from elsewhere suggests that such a fierce application of sanctions can do one of two things: in European countries that have trialled this approach, the evidence is that people do comply so that they do not lose vital income, but they will do so by taking inappropriate jobs that they cannot possibly maintain. In the USA, in contrast, the evidence suggests that a more common response is to avoid the process of benefits altogether. While this has the effect of reducing the 'claimant count', it also places some people entirely outside the system,[5] leaving them vulnerable – and they ultimately call on the resources of the State anyway, as they end up in hospital or in prison. The development of an alternative, undocumented economy, living somehow below the radar in conditions of real penury, poses risks to the solidarity of society.

These threats then pit poor people against very poor people, with a sort of rhetoric that seeks to blame people for

---

[5] See JRF work on sanctions: <http://www.jrf.org.uk/media-centre/response-dwp-welfare-sanctions-statistics>, <http://www.jrf.org.uk/blog/2013/08/sanctions-welfare-poverty> and <http://www.jrf.org.uk/publications/monitoring-poverty-and-social-exclusion-2013>, all accessed 5 September 2014.

their poverty, and ascribe malign motivation to those who are suffering most. Even a cursory glance at the reporting of poverty illustrates how working people in poverty are distinguished from those who are not working, even though, as we have seen, these are the same people. Hostility to travellers and migrants is used to suggest and foster deep and damaging divisions between those whose circumstances are desperately straitened.

These features of modern UK poverty erode the prospects for solidarity, poisoning its wellsprings by elevating difference and ignoring the common good.

Responses to these dimensions of poverty

Each dimension will receive its own particular attention, be subject to different constraints and be interpreted differently. But all responses will be underpinned by a view of the inevitability, or otherwise, of poverty.

The Nobel Prize-winning economist Amartya Sen, in his JRF lecture[6] on 22 January 2014, argued that while ignorance allows poverty to continue, accepting that it is inevitable and impossible to relieve is just as significant. This raises challenging questions, perhaps especially for Christians. While it is possible to construct a view that poverty is the inevitable collateral damage of a fast-moving global economy, to do so in a way that condemns many to a life of material deprivation and highly limited opportunity entails a willingness to reject individuals. If you believe that poverty is inevitable, you are also accepting the abandonment of individuals, the waste of human potential and the reduction of capability.

---

[6] Podcast available at <http://www.lse.ac.uk/newsAndMedia/videoAndAudio/channels/publicLecturesAndEvents/player.aspx?id=2205>, accessed 5 September 2014.

> Overcoming poverty is not a task of charity: it is an act of
> justice. Like slavery and apartheid, poverty is not natural. It is
> man-made and it can be eradicated and overcome by the actions
> of human beings. (Nelson Mandela)[7]

Social justice cannot be pursued by one actor alone. The State, operating entirely alone, can never end poverty. Neither can the untrammelled market. Equally, and just as self-evidently, we cannot expect individuals or families always to improve their circumstances by their own effort alone.

It is both desirable and essential to engage the State in the relief and prevention of poverty. The State, both at local authority and national level, is where we can most obviously share responsibility, pool risk and work for the common good. The UK State has a major role to play in the quest to end poverty, with its role in redistribution through the system of tax and benefits, market intervention through its regulatory bodies and support to community-based organisations. This is vital and ought to be non-negotiable, along with the State's role in organising and marshalling resources, intervening where necessary and offering leadership.

State engagement is necessary, but it is not sufficient in responding to the changing face of poverty. The role of markets (as well as those who seek to regulate them) is also vital. Housing, energy, finance and childcare need to be provided at a price that poor people can afford. Without this, the costs of being poor will simply consume whatever income can be secured.

Employers within the market also need to recognise their role in perpetuating and entrenching poverty. Employment practices that offer no security, no progression and an insufficient income make the fight against poverty a futile one. Employers

---

[7] From his speech to a rally at Trafalgar Square, London, on 3 February 2005, at the invitation of Make Poverty History.

with a stake in their communities know that paying a wage that more properly reflects their employees' income needs will result in more engaged and more empowered workers. Clearly no business can pay a wage it cannot afford, but many businesses now working towards the LW have concluded that the benefits of an increased wage bill justify the additional costs. Apprenticeships, progression and conditions of work that enable a dignified and sustainable approach are all possible for companies that take the welfare of their staff seriously. This in turn allows for workers who can make a longer-term commitment, with a real stake in the success of the business.

Low wages that do not provide for subsistence contribute strongly to poverty. So too does a pattern of work that offers no security or reliability.

The third and final group in the war against poverty is those community groups, churches, trades unions and others that have historically offered aid and comfort, while also working tirelessly to prevent poverty. Working locally, understanding the nature of their community, too often these organisations and their efforts are dismissed as purely palliative, which misses the point. It ignores the importance of resilient communities, enabling everyone to thrive – communities in which assets can be shared and support offered; the advice and assistance offered to maximise income; and the friendship offered to those who are isolated. Crucially, running like a bright thread through every discussion about poverty, it discounts the willingness to see and treasure the humanity and potential of each individual, whatever their income.

Conclusion

And the King shall answer and say unto them, Verily I say unto you, Inasmuch as ye have done it unto one of the least of these my brethren, ye have done it unto me.   (Matt. 25.40, KJV)

109

Society will always be judged by its treatment of the poorest and those most in need. To pretend that this is simple or that there are ready answers is to deny the complexity of individuals' lives, as well as the competing demands on the State. A commitment to value each individual, maximise their capability and contribution, and so secure a greater, more sustainable prosperity, however, will always require a focus on the poorest people.

The principle of solidarity has a long and distinguished pedigree. It recognises that the debts and obligations we owe to each other are not symptoms of outdated paternalism. Nor do they assume the creation of a long-derided dependency. Rather they understand that mutual insurance against risks – whether personal or the headwinds of a global and volatile economy – is a priority for all, and that a settled and strong social contract protects the most vulnerable, while insuring all of us against the social evil of despair and division.

To treat people in poverty as somehow different from everyone else, and to demonise and stereotype those who receive benefits as 'scroungers' or 'shirkers', is to turn a blind eye to the evidence and to turn away from the social contract. The truth is that there is no convenient distinction between those who are 'deserving' and those who are 'undeserving'. Policies, debates and attitudes built on this ancient yet false distinction are based on prejudice rather than reality and attach a stigma to all people in poverty.

We can only end poverty with a fair, sustained and co-ordinated response, based on evidence and a real understanding of what twenty-first-century poverty is, how it works and its impact on people and places.

We may believe that 'the poor will always be with us', but why should we accept it?

6

Reflections on work

OLIVER O'DONOVAN

———◦•◦•———

We talk a great deal about the circumstances of work, about unemployment, working conditions and remuneration, but it sometimes seems that we avoid talking about work itself. This, perhaps, is because the subject takes us too deep for comfort into questions about our human nature, questions that belong to religion and ethics before they belong to economics. Yet policy, too, needs to take into account what makes our work satisfying or frustrating. If, as the wise man said, 'There is nothing better than that a man should rejoice in his work' (Ecclus. 3.22 (ESV)), we need to ask how that enjoyment is achieved.

Three essential aspects of 'good' work

First, in the ancient narrative of creation the human race appears on the scene with a vocation to work, engaging with the material world and exploiting its potential. It is said that the Lord God 'took the man and put him in the Garden of Eden to till it and keep it' (Gen. 2.15). Work makes a difference to the world – a purposeful difference, not merely the difference that any event makes to those that follow it, as when a herd of elephants trample vegetation and deny other species their habitat. In work we not only *affect* things but also *effect* things.

We may often call our best work 'creative', though the analogy with God's creative work is only a loose one. If God in creation grants being and sense to a world that would be nothing without them, human creativity is an exercise of sympathetic intelligence, exploring and revealing the good things already latent in the order of nature. The first example of Adam's work which the ancient narrator gives us is not digging or sowing, but naming the forms of non-human animal life, a work of recognition and classification that unlocks the order within the variety of the animal kingdom (Gen. 2.19). To work well is to go with the grain of our worldly material, whether that is inert stuff, living beings, or abstract relations of things. It requires both intelligence and love.

Second, work is also a communication with other human beings. It satisfies our social instincts, shaping the complex patterns of human society. Cooperation is a basic condition of civic friendship, whether we think of the casual good humour that may colour an exchange between retailer and purchaser, or of a long-term collaboration between partners who contract to work together on a common project. One of the ways in which we distinguish 'work' from 'leisure' (which may involve many of the same activities) is that when we are at work our cooperation can be relied on. The amateur and the professional chef may both deserve their cordons bleus, but the professional must turn up at the restaurant come rain come shine, since management and staff depend on it.

The labours of work – the constraint of the diary, the difficulty of taking time off when the sun is out, the backache from being too long on our feet, the need to go on late into the night, the wearing meetings in search of a common approach to a project – these are the necessities that society imposes. We may often resent the sweat of the brow they exact from us, and sometimes they may become positively oppressive. But it is not oppressive in itself that we are bound to others in our work, and it is no hardship that our work is sometimes hard. It is simply a sign of its social importance. Through our labour we give ourselves, and make ourselves indispensible to others. That is the social dignity that work confers on us, the responsibility it permits us to bear. It makes us a 'something' for other people.

Third, without rest, however, labour does become oppressive. Work depends on rest, and rest on work. Uninterrupted and undifferentiated exertion is not work, but merely labour. When we lose sight of the alternation of work and rest, because the labours are too heavy or because we have no satisfying work to do, everything is experienced as labour. Work is what we rest *from*, rest is what we work *towards*. This truth is easy to misunderstand; it is not simply that we need relief from the expenditure of effort. A good deal of effort is poured into non-working activities too: activities chosen to suit our fancy, which we call 'leisure', and also the often tiresome tasks involved in sustaining life – shopping, preparing food, running a home, attending to children and sickness, receiving and answering routine communications and so on. True rest from work involves reflection. It is as we rest from it that we can see our work as an accomplishment, not merely a task. We can take satisfaction in its completion. And because we can anticipate a moment when we *shall* take satisfaction in its completion, we can look forward to the work that lies before us, and think of it as something of which to take ownership.

The importance of rest is embodied for Jews and Christians in the institution of a weekly day of worship. The narrative of creation invites us to see our work and rest in the light of God's work, culminating in the rest of the seventh day, when God saw what he had done and found it 'very good'. In entering God's rest through the Sabbath celebration we learn to share his evaluation and to apply it to our own work. Articulated into weekly units of exertion rounded off by a day of rest and worship, work leads us into fellowship with our creator. This weekly rhythm tells us that work is not its own justification, but a medium of something more important. It brings God's purposes, which make our human work purposeful, before our minds, so that work and worship together become constitutive of ourselves, shaping our vocation.

We have touched on the theological term 'justification', which is the question of how a human life may be meaningful and acceptable before God. We are probably familiar with the doctrinal formula that we are not justified by our works – a paradox, since, on the face of it, nothing could possibly justify us *other than* our works, for justification *is* the blessing of God on what we are and do. Yet the effectiveness of what we are and do is not simply a function of this or that being done. It is possible, even inevitable, that work well done may amount to precisely nothing. God, we are told, can *invest* what we do with a value it cannot achieve in itself, making it the form of his blessing on our lives. Through work we may be granted to be a 'someone', receiving a personal identity from God.

These three aspects of work, material, social and spiritual, are bound up together. Communications with others in our handling of the material world provide a form for the service of God, which is the goal of our existence. George Herbert's famous poem speaks of how all activity is capable of being directed to God – 'what I do in anything, to do it as for thee' – and how this makes the world appear new to us, as though we had polished up a dish or a piece of furniture:

> Nothing can be so mean
> Which with this tincture, 'For thy sake',
> Will not grow bright and clean.

With that image, work itself in its most unglamorous form enters the picture with its burdens and responsibilities:

    A servant with this clause
    Makes drudgery divine;
  Who sweeps a room as for thy laws,
    Makes that and th' action fine.

The household servant is not only God's servant but also someone else's, for the room is cleaned for other people to occupy. But the whole cluster of relations – the room, the labour, the people who will benefit – forms a testimony to the ordered graciousness of God's world, and makes us aware of his presence.[1]

That work is the form of human vocation holds good for all humans, not excluding those who by virtue of handicap, illness or age are unable to undertake material work. No one can be so aware of the importance of work to human existence as someone who is suddenly disabled for work for which he or she was perfectly fitted. John Milton's sonnet on his blindness gives voice to the deep frustration of everyone in such a position: 'Doth God exact day-labour, light denied?' The answer to that question is so striking that it has entered our language as a proverb: 'They also serve who only stand and wait.'[2] Motionless, with eyes fixed on the master and ears trained to his command, the waiting servant contributes to his service simply an attentiveness to his will. But this, too, is necessary. The restless posting to and fro of other servants demands it as a complement.

The wrongs of work

Work is a sphere in which we can do wrong and must learn to put wrong right. Precisely because work is our human vocation,

---

[1] Herbert, 'The Elixir', *The Works of George Herbert*, ed. F. E. Hutchinson (Oxford: Clarendon Press, 1941), pp. 184–5.

[2] Milton, 'Sonnet XIX', *Poetical Works*, ed. Douglas Bush (Oxford: Oxford University Press, 1966), p. 190.

it can be corrupted by failure (our own, or others') to observe the conditions of true humanity. The wrongs of work are as pervasive as the wrongs of speech. Just as lying becomes possible wherever there is truth to tell, where there is service to be given, disservice and damage can be done. The wrongs of work have wide effects, and for this reason are often systemic: I fail to work well because you do not work well, and you do not, because I do not.

Restraints designed to protect against wrong may be built as disciplines into traditional working-practices; or they may be externally imposed, as legal or quasi-legal constraints. Either way, they strike us as restrictive rather than constructive. They are not like techniques, which help us do the work better, but simply guard us against the harm that we may do, consciously or unwittingly, in the course of work. No work can be entirely without such constraints; there will always be room to wish that we had more freedom in work than we actually have. Nor will the constraints always be the same, but will vary with the wrongs to be guarded against at a given time. There is a standing danger, then, that external constraints may be ill-adapted to the requirements of the work, too restrictive or too permissive, or both in different ways.

The wrongs of work are the concern of all of us, and require us to begin with the work we ourselves do. They cannot simply be left for management or government to worry about. In work, as in other matters, it is the 'law written on the heart' rather than on the 'tablets of stone' that is the way to freedom (cf. 2 Cor. 3.3). Those working traditions that have incorporated appropriate restraints into ordinary working-practices are in a happy position, comparatively, and are more likely to escape clumsy external regulation. Yet the law is not always written on the heart, and regulatory constraints, like statutory laws, can be needed.

At first glance we might divide the wrongs of work into two opposite categories: those created by *lack* of activity and those created by *surfeit* of activity. We may call them 'idleness' (as used by Beveridge)[3] and 'drudgery' (from Herbert's poem). Drudgery does not mean that work is forced or un-consenting. The very best forms of work can become drudgery when we misjudge what we can accomplish, value financial rewards more highly than the work itself, accept destructive compromises in our standards of work and so on. Idleness, for its part, does not mean 'unemployment'. Unemployment is simply the lack of a contractual agreement to work for someone else. Idleness is the lack of effective activity. Many an unemployed person is anything but idle, and some activities that count as employment are comparatively idle.

This distinction, however, takes us only so far. By concentrating on the quantitative question of how much effective activity there is, or how little, it tends to highlight symptoms of problems rather than causes. If we follow the interpretation of work we have already outlined, we reach a sharper view of three ways in which work may fail us and degenerate into idleness or drudgery. Taking the points in reverse order, work may (1) fail to provide us with a vocation; it may (2) fail to put us in a satisfactory social relation to others; and it may (3) fail to set us in a creative relation to the material world.

First, an age which has trouble believing in God will also have trouble believing in work. The absence of God entails a loss of confidence in practical wisdom. We can no longer see that work is 'for' anything that might support the meaning of our personal existence. Work may be touched by an inner alienation. It is a matter of our life, and the question of what

---

[3] William Henry Beveridge, *Full Employment in a Free Society* (London: Allen & Unwin, 1944).

it amounts to 'ultimately', in the light of judgements higher than those of our employers or peers, is a question that strikes down right to our own self-evaluations.

There are aspects of alienation that can only be resolved by the individual whose experience it is, and cannot be structurally provided for. A certain restlessness with work is, perhaps, a normal aspect of working experience, a reflection of work's transcendent dimension as a calling to be ourselves. Yet good working structures can help combat the vocational vacuum. The access work offers us to our calling depends to a great extent on the wisdom it affords us, and good work provides us with opportunities for learning and development. Provision for this can very often be made within the structures of organised work, simply by ringing the changes on working activity and offering widening experience, quite apart from career development opportunities that help us prepare for higher levels of responsibility.

But here the stability of employment is of decisive importance. If a certain element of coming and going is a natural, and even helpful, feature of any workplace, enabling people to spend time in one kind of work before moving to a different one, fear of unemployment or underemployment can be a destructively alienating force. We can hardly expect people to give the best of themselves in work if the context is never secure. The economic gains of a preference for short-term and part-time employment contracts cannot be more than short-term gains, if they are won at the cost of the demotivation and alienation of the workforce.

Second, work may sometimes afford us no real experience of cooperation. Coordination is not a substitute for it. Adam Ferguson in the eighteenth century was already disturbed at how those who labour both in industry and administration can be 'made like the parts of an engine to concur to a purpose, without any concert of their own', lacking a sense of their place in the whole, and concomitantly a sense of commitment to one another.[4] If some kinds of work have always had rather limited connexion with their clients – manufacturers who never meet consumers, for example – in an age such as ours, where globalisation and electronic communications mean that many people never meet those they work with and for, the problem becomes much more acute. We may describe the problem as the 'displacement' of work – using 'place' as the most general term for a centre of communications. It can undermine quite ordinary political and social connexions when we are uncertain who we are communicating with and where in the world they are.

Displacement feeds a general nervousness about the all-pervasiveness of the market model in assigning work. The 'market' we so often refer to is, of course, only an abstraction; it has left real markets far behind. The market was a device to overcome the distance between producers and purchasers, which it did by constructing places where they could meet. Old market crosses peppered across our urban landscapes remind us that they were focal sites for surrounding regions, places where goods could be assembled, compared and bargained over, and finally bought and sold. The market of modern economic practice is largely placeless, and therefore lacks cooperative engagement. The anonymous electronic placing (and withdrawal) of large investments has become the symbol of what market exchange becomes when the market cross has disappeared: an ensemble of instantaneous transactions which never amount to a rational social whole. And so forms of work which require stable social relationships, consistent expectations and acquired practices are undermined.

---

[4] Adam Ferguson, *An Essay on the History of Civil Society 1767*, ed. Duncan Forbes (Edinburgh: Edinburgh University Press, 1966), p. 182.

One of the things the Fair Trade movement reminded us of in relation to the food retail business was the indispensable collaborative relation between retail and production. A lesson was learned in this area, as large retailers struggled to shake off their image of always driving a hard bargain, and began to highlight their producers in their publicity. It was an interesting indication of how a business often marked by dislocation (remember, in that respect, the difficulty of tracing the horse meat to its source!) felt a need to relocate itself in its working context. It is important, not only for strategic reasons but also for working morale, that sectors of an industry reflect on their impact on other sectors and on their wider social contexts, forming a conception of the human significance of what they do from day to day.

The third thing that can go wrong with work is its abstraction from the meaning of life. Labour becomes separated from achievement, 'work' from accomplished 'works'. A gap opens up between the worker and the material world, the result of abstracting the labour from its goal and meaning. An age in which a great deal of intellectual work is done – much of it, despite its pretensions, quite inconsequential – suffers acutely from this problem. No one who deals primarily in words can be free of the thought that they can all be blown away with the wind, and, I imagine, no one who deals primarily in figures, either. But the abstraction need not be intellectual, as in these illustrations. The industrial 'helots' so well described by Marx were abstracted from the world in which they lived, too. They had a human self-consciousness, with thoughts, loves and hopes for realisation in the world, but their working life was wholly dissociated from these, and, since it gave them no time for them and yielded too meagre resources for them, they lacked a self-determining interest in what they were doing.

What work needs in order to make contact with reality is a participation in the thinking process that shapes it. We are alienated from our work when we cannot sufficiently understand what it is for, and how it is to be done. And here we must explore the importance of working practices. A practice is an ensemble of activities, skilled operations and principles governing them, which can be learned. It is not simply an operation we may learn to perform, or an activity of many operations in which we may engage, but a capacity to deploy the activity and its operations to perform a work according to its governing aims and principles. In acquiring the practice we acquire also the exercise of discretion and reason in applying it. It involves the exercise of judgement and the building up of experience. Good work is distinguished from routine labour precisely by the practices that it develops, and that is why our working-practices are a guarantee of our freedom in work – not the freedom to do as we like, but the freedom to act on our best judgement of what the work demands.

Because practices have to be learned, they demand communities of training and induction in which they can be taught and handed on. All good forms of work generate forms of learning, wisdom and community. One of the most troubling legacies of the industrial past is the complacency with which it accommodated the distinction of an 'unskilled' from a 'skilled' labour force. There are many varieties of skills; there can be no place for institutionalised unskills. Communities of work grow up not only among those types of work that are typically collaborative but also among those that are pursued individually and even competitively. They are constituted by a common understanding of what the point of the practice is, and what it means to be good at it; they enable social interactions among practitioners which sustain the practice and help it reflect changing circumstances.

There is a sad tale often told of the impact of evolving technology upon human work. It goes back to the first wave of the Industrial Revolution: long-developed skills made useless, whole trades disappearing overnight, work reduced to technical operations of such limited scope as to make the worker effectively mindless and so on. In the recent era of computerisation some of this story has been lived through again, and some of the pains suffered by industrial workers in a previous era have been felt by white-collar workers in their turn. Change must be managed, if work is to remain possible in changing circumstances. But change is not managed well without a reflective evolution of working practices on the part of those who have acquired and sustain them. Change is a matter of appropriating new opportunities thoughtfully, and must proceed in a way that fits the work, not imposed according to some one-size-fits-all conception from without. It must therefore be guided by those who understand and value the working-practices that have evolved up to that point.

Employment and management

This brings us inevitably to employment. Employment is the practice of determining each participant's work and remuneration within a collective enterprise by a bilateral agreement, formal or informal, between the individual worker, on the one hand, and the business as a collective whole, on the other. The sphere of good and useful work is much broader than employment. We know, or ought to know, the great value society reaps from work done within the home, by voluntary associations and by what bureaucracy names (with a curious contradiction in terms) the 'self-employed'. There are agreements made between two equal parties to work together and share the profits in given ways, where neither of them is employed by the other. Yet the employment contract has in our times been the primary social mechanism of assigning work and relating it to the distribution of resources for living. Unemployment, correspondingly, is the primary signal to a modern society that all is not well with its work.

Employment statistics govern a great deal of our common thinking about policies for work. Like all statistics, they need care. They reveal what they have to reveal, like the ancient sphinx, in riddles, and we must make sure that the questions we put to them are the questions that they are intended to answer. They can tell us, within reason, how well the demand for work is met by enterprises that employ workers, how many people are seeking opportunities at any time and how long they have sought without success, whether there are sections of society (women, men, the young, the old) who find opportunities specially elusive and so on. Things well worth knowing, which can signal outstanding difficulties and stimulate policies to address them. High unemployment among young people is especially worrying, since failure at this point fails a whole generation, and its ill effects can be felt for decades.[5]

But as employment is not the only work there is, and unemployment not the only unmet need there is, our policies need to look beyond quantitative measures of unemployment to qualitative problems of underemployment, mismatches between work and workers, failures in education and training for work, unsatisfying or degrading work, exploitation and so on. The greatest problems confronting us may sometimes lie not with the work that is not available, but the work that is, which may weave together elements of idleness and drudgery in troubling ways.

The employment contract tends by its structure to establish a difference in power – sometimes to the advantage of employees,

---

[5] On this matter see the observations of Andrew Adonis in his essay for this volume.

if their skills are valued and scarce, but more normally to the advantage of employers who, as corporations embodying the continuity of the work and owning the materials of it, are in a stronger position than a replaceable individual. So long as the threat of unemployment is felt to be a real one, the power of the employer to give or withhold work will be formidable, and may sometimes be used oppressively.

But this disequilibrium is only one aspect of a wider disparity of power, that of management in relation to the workforce, which has often seemed to resurrect on a larger scale the old master–servant relation characteristic of the small household-business of the pre-industrial age. 'The masters' was the term still used of management in manufacturing a century or so ago. It suggested that initiative always belonged to the one side; nothing was expected of the servant but compliance; nothing was expected of the master but an insistence on the demand. Whether the compliance and insistence was good humoured or surly, hardly seemed to matter. In reality that was never the whole truth of working-relations in the past, even in manufacturing, but the model had its own imaginative logic and tended to fulfil its own worst predictions in times of stress.

To escape from the dominance of this imagined relation we need to conceive working-relations as *cooperation*. In an earlier age, faced with a society whose industry was largely in the hands of household-businesses reinforced by servants who were legally slaves, the Apostolic Church laid its emphasis on how this relation might be re-envisaged as a cooperative equilibrium of brothers and sisters engaged upon a mutually supportive service: 'The master has more need of patience in ruling the household than the servant in being ruled,' as Augustine wrote.[6] To establish a cooperative equilibrium, where the specific skills

---

[6] Augustine, *City of God* 19.16.

and authority of each sector are appreciated as a contribution to the work of others, is the primary moral concern we must bring to our working-relations.

There are, however, special difficulties in realising this conception in the modern manager–workforce relation, which arise from the tendency of the modern enterprise to grow in scale beyond the reach of interpersonal relationships. As a business enterprise takes root and grows, it absorbs more entropic energy in securing its position in its social context. Strategic planning, publicity, accounting, appointment and management of personnel, all demand specialised attention with specialised skills, and a business does not have to be very large before it recruits dedicated administrative staff to supply it. So a sector grows up within the business which has different working-practices, different educational requirements and different immediate objects of work from the primary workforce, and, as administrative skills tend to be transferable, administrative personnel may well have more in common with their peers in other enterprises than with those they work with and for.

The fact that we often refer to 'workers' *as distinct from* 'administrators' shows how deeply this division of roles can be felt. It is not, of course, that the administrators do not work, but the immediate object of their work is not the primary object that is the reason for the business (manufacture, retail, teaching, performance, whatever it may be), but a secondary one, the smooth administration of its internal and external functioning. This raises the demand for partnership and cooperation to a new level. When administration inclines to proceed in ways that seem to undermine working practices, for example by imposing unrealistic timetables or workloads, or skilled practitioners are, for their part, unrealistic about contextual constraints (of budget, personnel, etc.) within which the business must operate, it takes sympathetic imagination on either side to grasp the practical problems and aspirations of the other in the service of the common business.

In principle, administrative specialisms simply follow the logic of the principle of division of labour, allowing those who perform the core work of the enterprise to get on with it undistracted. But inevitably the exercise of certain powers that belong to the enterprise as a whole – the power to engage in contracts, for example, including employment contracts – devolves to the administrative sector, creating an imbalance of power in decision-making. It is with this imbalance in view that we speak of 'management', meaning that centre of administrative activity which commands the key processes of decision.

The imbalance is sharply increased when a third participant is taken into account alongside the partnership of worker and manager: the owner, or the provider of capital. An alliance between capital and management can appear a very natural one. In an age where private enterprises must grow if they are to hold their own against competitors, more capitalisation is constantly called for, and it is the responsibility of management to secure it. The administrative objectives of management, which may anyway be in some tension with the interest of the workers in upholding their working-practices, now depend upon satisfying the investment objectives of their backers, to get a return on their capital.

Publicly funded work, meanwhile, has its own version of the problem: the need constantly to compete for government favour and to conform to political objectives of kinds that may be quite unhelpful to the work. There is not one 'bottom line' in modern work, but two parallel lines, economic profit and political profit. But, of course, they are not *really* the bottom lines. A business needs to be profitable, but only to such a degree as can secure the foundations of the work and sustain it effectively. Public-sector work needs to satisfy government aspirations, but such aspirations as have to do with getting work well done which will of its nature serve the common good. The real bottom line is the primary objective, the effective performance of the work in hand and an opening to further work which will follow on from it.

Pope John Paul II, in his important Encyclical on work, *Laborem Exercens* of 1981, asserted the principle of 'the priority of labour over capital', and also that 'a good labour system overcomes the opposition between capital and labour'.[7] The priority, in other words, is not that the interests of the workers should always trump all other interests, but that the primary concern of the enterprise, which is to engage in a certain kind of human work effectively, has to *remain* primary in the thinking of all the participants, whether they engage as workers, administrators or investors. This requires a breadth of thinking which is difficult to legislate for and difficult to inculcate where it is missing. But it is not impracticable, and we can see its effects, when it occurs, in well-run enterprises that pay their bills and reward their investors (sufficiently, not excessively), but primarily provide for their own future by recruiting, training and supporting a skilled and intelligent workforce, renewing their plant, exploring new markets and new techniques, and so on.

The key is a focused concentration on sustaining and evolving skilled working-practices as the primary *intellectual* resource which any business inherits. These are a repository of wisdom about the work and its performance, not fixed and unmoveable, but capable of growth. Where there are many strands of practice, primary and secondary to the business's concerns, as there will be in any complex enterprise, they can be developed in ways that begin to accommodate to one another, incorporating the goals and values that each tradition embodies. The ability to

---

[7] John Paul II, *Laborem Exercens* 12, 13.

harmonise the objectives of the different working sectors in a business will be the mark of successful management. And together with equilibrium on that front good management will seek to establish some comparable equilibrium in the sharing of the risk, whatever it may be, that the business runs. A specially 'imperilled' sector of the workforce, liable to be laid off before anybody else is laid off, will be a sector that cannot acquire and contribute skill, a helot class which is useful not for its work but only for its labour.[8]

We should notice at this point a change of nomenclature which has become common in recent years. The buzz word 'leadership' has increasingly replaced 'management' not only in popular discussion but also in government thinking, and it seems to imply an aspiration to a broader and less sectional view of the good of work. Yet this language causes some anxiety, not least for the suggestion of a certain restlessness, favouring change and innovation over stability and mature growth.

Properly, 'leadership' is a service to a common task rendered by someone *performing* the task. You can coach swimmers from the bank, but you can only lead them from the water. Leadership is given at the level of the primary practices whenever one worker helps others acquire and maintain the practices of the work, as for example an experienced craftsman guiding an apprentice. To be a 'leader' is to be someone other workers look to for help in doing what the whole community of work does. It is distinct, then, from the kind of adjunct help that a primary practitioner may receive from an administrator.

To apply this notion to industrial enterprise is to engage in a tricky transfer of thought. 'Leadership' ought to imply a role in which the various functions that are discharged in a complex

---

[8] Julia Unwin's observations in this book about the break in the link between poverty and unemployment (pp. 99–101) are of relevance to this.

business are held in an equilibrium of value, and in which transferable skills of administration do not constantly overwhelm the core-practices of the work itself. Leadership cannot be a specialism on its own. It can only fulfil itself by appreciating specialisms and enabling them to cooperate in a common enterprise. If that appreciation is not apparent, the suspicion will be aroused that this language merely rebrands the abuses of managerialism under a new name.

There is one characteristic fear which recurs constantly in different manifestations. It was characteristic of the Industrial Revolution, and has equally been a feature of the communications revolution. It is the loss of skilled practices, whether constrained out of existence by economic or other external pressures, or corroded from within by a generalised managerial conceptuality that does not value them. With their loss we fear a greying of the world, a shrinkage of its meaning. And at the heart of what we fear there is an element of collusion: the reason our skills will disappear rather than develop is that we cannot make the effort to learn them and to teach them. Managerial categories, since they are transferable and need no patient work of explanation and discovery, are more convenient to communicate in as a general lingua franca. And so we enter a trajectory on which we begin to think of all work as being alike, and lose sight of what makes it most interesting – its diversity.

In fighting these fears there is something for government, something for leadership and something for every worker to attend to. The scope for government is more limited than it is often taken to be, but important: to safeguard the economic infrastructure to the extent that living by their work remains a normal possibility for men and women, and to guard by sanction or regulation against the worst abuses of working relationships, however they may arise. In addition to which government supports some kinds of work directly in the pursuit of its own tasks, and may do this either well or badly. The effects of government over-involvement in the details of work, however, is almost always likely to make work more difficult and unrewarding.

Leadership, for its part, will maintain the humanity of work if and only if it can imprint upon the consciousness of a business the value and integrity of the special skills and practices that make it possible. But neither the government's contribution nor that of leadership can do what is needed if those of us who simply work, in whatever role or whatever context, cannot imagine finding the mystery of our own vocation and fulfilment in our work, for a working population with no existential interest in its own work can take no interest in other people's, either.

Which is why, perhaps, a theologian should not neglect to say that the fruitfulness and sustainability of our work, the healthy evolution of working-practices and the cooperative endeavours they give rise to should be a matter for prayer. We have a model in the Collect for Trinity XVII in the Book of Common Prayer, where we are invited to pray that God's grace may 'prevent and follow us', that we may 'continually be given to all good works'.[9]

Every word in that prayer is worth pondering. The 'we' means not just 'each of us separately', but society as a whole, the only context in which work can be undertaken and effected. That we, as a society, may be continually 'given *to*' our work – not merely given it – it is necessary that our works be 'good', well conceived, well fitted to their circumstance, broadly and wisely designed, and that we be fit to attend to 'all' good works, and not only those fashionable ones which carry éclat or put

---

[9] Cranmer's beautiful translation of the equivalent collect from the Gregorian Sacramentary adds the word 'all'. 'Given to' is his expressive rendering of *intentos*, 'attentive to'.

us at the cutting edge of progress. And that can be so only if they can call not only on such strength of labour as they require to execute but on such wisdom as is needed to conceive them well, for which we must ask the 'grace' of God, not only 'accompanying', as the scholastic phrase had it, but 'preceding' and 'following'. God's grace is required not merely for the *execution*, but for the *imagination* of good works, as well as for their *successful outcome*. Is it not at the heart of the principle of the equality of workers declared so strikingly in the parable of the vineyard (Matt. 20.1–16), that not only the reward for work but also the opportunity to work in the first place are the gifts of a generous master? If we are wise, then, we pray for our work, and especially that, since good works are a cultural gift of vast importance, too easily lost by forgetfulness and negligence, we may be 'continually' given to them.

7

Health and well-being in Britain

KERSTEN ENGLAND

There is much to celebrate. Life expectancy rates continue to rise, diseases such as cancer and HIV/AIDS are in many cases no longer terminal and survival rates for people born with or who develop long-term and chronic conditions are impressive. People born in the UK today can expect to live well into their eighties. We are on many levels the healthiest we have ever been.

But there are huge disparities across the nations of the UK today. Life expectancy varies dramatically and the faultline is largely socio-economic. Our children have among the lowest levels of health and well-being in Western Europe. The demand for health and social care services is escalating beyond the resource base available through the public purse for its provision.

Our approach to health and well-being is neither equitable nor sustainable.

This chapter explores a Christian vision for health and well-being, and the shifts in both policy and practice which would assist in its realisation within families, communities and institutions within the wider health and social care system.

At the heart of this vision is the proposition that the common good is secured through high levels of personal responsibility, mutuality and reciprocity, and a commitment to those most in need. Aspects of our societal and institutional approach to health and well-being fall short on these principles – often unintentionally – and stand in the way of the fullest expression of the common good.

The health of the UK at the start of the twenty-first century

In the past hundred years the population of the UK has grown by 50 per cent. The ten years between the census of 2001 and that of 2011 saw the largest population growth in any decade since the 1801 census.[1]

The median age of the population increased from 25 in 1911 to 39 in 2011. In 1901, life expectancy for men was 45 years and for women it was 49 years. By 1999 it was 75 years for men and 80 years for women. In 1911 there were but 13,000 people aged 90 and over. In 2011 there were 430,000.

These statistics reflect the dramatic improvements in the living conditions (and subsequently health) of the population through the twentieth century. But, as has been argued by Sir Michael Marmot,[2] the key determinants of health are social, rather than genetically inherited or related to the provision of health services. 'Enlightened' industrialists and civic leaders of the late-nineteenth and twentieth centuries – such as Joseph Rowntree, Titus Salt, Robert Owen and Margaret McMillan – understood this and were hugely influential in promoting policies and campaigns to improve the health of workers and their families. Some of the greatest leaps forward in the underlying health of the nation have been secured through actions such as slum clearance, delivery of effective sewerage and sanitation, the Clean Air Act and the introduction of universal education.

---

[1] <www.ons.gov.uk/ons/rel/census/2011-census-analysis>, accessed 6 September 2014.
[2] *Fair Society, Healthy Lives. The Marmot Review. Strategic Review of Health Inequalities in England Post 2010* <www.uclac.uk/marmotreview>, accessed 6 September 2014.

The development of health services, world-leading medical research, the National Insurance Act of 1911 – which enabled access to primary diagnostic services for those in work and contributing – and the creation of the National Health Service (NHS) in 1948 have also undoubtedly played their part in the improvement of the nations' health. The provision of health care which is 'free' at the point of use and perceived to be 'un-rationed', the elimination of many communicable diseases, effective treatment of previously life-threatening conditions and specialist care for those with chronic and debilitating conditions are perhaps the most widely recognised achievements of our NHS.

Despite this picture of a relatively affluent and healthy UK, there is an urgent need to reflect on how we secure the health of all in our four nations if we are to create the common good in the twenty-first century.

Reflection about this must touch upon the balances to be struck between personal responsibility and self-help; mutualism and reciprocity in families, communities and organisations; the potential impact of greater investment in preventative and community-based services; the pursuit of greater socio-economic equality; and the affordability and efficacy of our current models of health and social care.

Challenges

Seven major challenges face us.

First, the expectation of a long, healthy life is not enjoyed by everyone and all communities in the UK.

A 2005 article in the *British Medical Journal* remarked: 'Life expectancy at birth varies with deprivation quintile and is highest in the most affluent groups. The differences are mainly attributable to differences in mortality rates under 75 years of age. Regional life expectancies display a clear north–south gradient . . . analysis shows that deprivation explains most of the geographical variation in life expectancy.'[3]

In 2013 figures released by the Office for National Statistics[4] showed that people born in Manchester can expect, on average, to live 5 years less if they are men and 3.7 years less if they are women than the average English person. Men born in Kensington and Chelsea – the area with the highest life expectancy in England – can expect to live 10 years longer than men from Manchester. Even then this masks very significant differentials between communities within places. Men from the poorest communities in York, for example, can expect to live about 7 years less than their counterparts in the most affluent areas of the city.[5]

The correlation between income level, poverty and ill health remains – depriving individuals of years of healthy life, diminishing the productivity of communities and increasing the cost to the State.

Second, our children have among the worst levels of well-being in Europe and the developed world.

The UK is sixteenth in Unicef's most recent report card on child well-being[6] in the world's 21 richest countries. In this assessment, indicators of well-being include educational

---

[3] M. Shaw, G. Davey Smith and D. Dorling, 'Health Inequalities and New Labour; How the Promises Compare with Real Progress', *British Medical Journal* (28 April 2005), pp. 1016–21.

[4] *Interim Life Tables, England and Wales, 2010–2012* (24 October 2013), <www.ons.gov.uk>, accessed 6 September 2014.

[5] It might be thought that, in today's more mobile society, location is a poor indicator of life expectancy, as an individual's experience of health service provision will vary as they move around. But in fact, with few exceptions, deprivation by geographical area changes very little over time. Environmental and social factors which may impact on life expectancy also vary by area, as does the availability and quality of healthcare provision itself.

[6] <www.unicef-irc.org/reportcard-11/>, accessed 6 September 2014.

attainment, mental health, substance misuse, involvement in the criminal justice system and economic inclusion as well as incidence of disease and premature death. Unicef UK has undertaken its own analysis of why children in this country experience such strikingly low well-being while some children from countries with less economic security have a greater sense of well-being. One explanation, they believe, lies in the damaging effects of inequality.

This echoes the assessment of Kate Pickett and Richard Wilkinson in their work *The Spirit Level*[7] which argues that there is a direct correlation between levels of income inequality and well-being. Using data from twenty-three affluent countries and fifty US states they find that health issues are anything from three to ten times more prevalent in more unequal societies.

Third, a dramatic and costly upwards demand curve for health care is due to lifestyle-related disease.

A Department of Health circular published in March 2013 stated: 'Most people in England are overweight or obese. This includes 61.9 per cent of adults and 28 per cent of children aged between 2 and 15. People who are overweight have a higher risk of getting type 2 diabetes, heart disease and certain cancers. Excess weight can also make it more difficult for people to find and keep work and it can affect self-esteem and mental health. Health problems associated with being overweight or obese cost NHS England more than £5 billion every year.'[8]

Obesity is just one of the diseases directly related to lifestyle which, with alcoholism and smoking, is putting acute pressure onto health services. The use of the word 'lifestyle' should not be taken to dismiss the part that income, culture, societal

---

[7] Richard Wilkinson and Kate Pickett, *The Spirit Level: Why Equality Is Better for Everyone* (London: Penguin Books, 2010).

[8] <www.gov.uk/government/policies/reducing-obesity-and-improving-diet>, accessed 6 September 2014.

pressure, self-esteem and the availability of choice play in our adopted lifestyles, or to blame those whose well-being is affected. What is clear is that the cost to our well-being, the State and the tax payer is very high.

Fourth, there is a major demographic change – more people living longer – with increased demand for complex and specialist care for longer periods of time.

A committee of the House of Lords reported in 2013 that the UK is 'woefully unprepared' for the social and economic challenges presented by an ageing society.[9] The report went on to say: 'With the number of people living with long term medical conditions set to rise sharply a "radically different model" of care would be needed to support people in their own homes and to prevent pressure on the NHS.'

The particular challenges of dementia, physical frailty and isolation often see older people expensively hospitalised with variable outcomes, not least of which is frequently lower levels of choice, independence and well-being. Despite a system which prioritises longevity and the treatment of serious disease, there is relatively little attention to well-being in later life and indeed to end-of-life care.

Fifth, there is a relative lack of investment in and spending on preventative, community-based and mental health provision.

In 2013–14 the budget of NHS England was £95.6 billion.[10] Of this, £1.8 billion was allocated to Public Health England to discharge NHS England's public health responsibilities. The amount available for funding Health Improvement projects by local authorities was £2.52 billion. In a health system set up to

---

[9] House of Lords Committee on Public Service and Demographic Change, *Ready for Ageing?* (25 March 2013), <www.parliament.uk>, accessed 6 September 2014.

[10] NHS England, *High Quality Care for All, Now and for Future Generations: Transforming Urgent and Emergency Care Services in England*, <www.england.nhs.uk/allocations-2013-2014/>, accessed 6 September 2014.

treat ill health rather than to promote well-being, and at a time of tough financial settlements, it can be challenging to make the case for increased investment in these areas, for redesign of the system and for the cultural change which would be required for it to be effective.

The transfer back to local government of many of its original public health responsibilities provides a significant opportunity to tackle the wider determinants of health through the involvement of wider local authority functions in the promotion of health. There are striking case-studies from parts of Scandinavia and indeed from the USA and the UK, where genuine co-design and delivery of services in and with communities is having a positive impact on well-being indicators. I will return to these later. But we have yet to see a significant policy or attitudinal shift in the UK about how we might best prevent disease and ill health within our communities. The debate about how to promote well-being is marginal.

Sixth, there is a relative lack of integration in health and social care provision, and no neat distinction to be drawn between the two. Currently, however, our systems for providing for people in need divide significantly along such lines. The complexities of integration between a national health system which is designed to be free at the point of use and a local social care system whose cost is assessed against an ability to pay are challenging. It is very difficult to produce 'joined-up' services which are designed with the perspective of the individual at their heart.

In addition, central funding for local government, which has responsibility for social care, has reduced dramatically. This can produce significant tension in debates between providers, for example around hospital discharges and eligibility for long-term and continuing health care. As a commentator bluntly remarked, 'our district general hospitals will be like warehouses of older people – lined up on wards'[11] because of a lack of good preventative services, community-based support and poor co-operation between health and social care services (including disputes over funding and responsibility).

Seventh, the health system, although relatively protected from cuts as part of the deficit reduction programme of national government, has seen demand and costs rise ahead of available funds.

In 2013–14 the NHS England budget of £95.6 billion equated to a 2.6 per cent growth compared to 2012–13 baselines and, as the NHS England website remarked, 'a real terms increase of 0.6 per cent at a time of limited resources'.

However, an Institute for Fiscal Studies (IFS) report commented: 'Public funding for health is set to be tight until at least the end of the decade. If NHS productivity does not increase sufficiently fast to bridge the gap between funding and demand pressures, then access to and quality of care is likely to deteriorate.' The report went on to say: 'Serious thought must be given to options for the NHS. These include reconsidering the range of services available free of charge to the whole population or the level of taxation needed to finance those services in the future.'[12]

A Christian approach to health in the twenty-first century

In the context of these fundamental challenges, what might a Christian perspective contribute to debates about the health of our nations?

---

[11] From a speech by Andy Burnham, Shadow Health Secretary, to the King's Fund, 24 January 2013.
[12] Rowena Crawford and Carl Emmerson, *NHS and Social Care Funding: The Outlook to 2021/22* (Institute for Fiscal Studies July 2012), p. 5: Nuffield Trust evidence for better health care.

In Christian thinking the health and well-being of individuals and communities and the building of the common good are inextricably linked. Building the common good is about creating the conditions for individual human flourishing – which is not possible without attending to our spiritual, emotional and physical health.

From the book of Exodus, through the Gospels, to the book of Revelation the Bible is an account of individuals, families, communities and nations seeking to live well and to live well together. Parts of the early books of the Old Testament such as Leviticus read like an early attempt at a set of standards for environmental health! The exhaustive sets of rules and prohibitions reflect those societies' understanding of the threats to their health and survival. In the New Testament, while there is a continued focus on the rules for living a good and godly life, more nuanced stories start to explore broader moral questions such as the intrinsic value and right to health of each human being – as Jesus healed even those considered unclean, including a leper, a woman who was haemorrhaging and a Samaritan.

Religious orders of men and women undertook some of the earliest research, cultivation and preparation of remedies and medicines; ministered to the afflicted, the sick and the dying; supported women in childbirth; and provided hospitals and elements of poor relief. From that time on and through the early modern world, the Church and religious institutions undertook many of the functions of what came increasingly to be expected of the State and a progressive taxation system. Many of the pioneers of British social reform, such as Tuke, Rowntree, Temple and Beveridge, were inspired by Christian teaching and passionate about the provision of health and care for all.

Through all Christian thinking on the issue of health and well-being certain core tenets persist:

- that our well-being and human flourishing are concerned with the spiritual, emotional and physical dimensions of our lives;[13]
- that our well-being is inevitably and inextricably connected with that of others (as in St Paul's image of the parts of the human body each of which relies on the others for its well-being);
- that we have been given the gift of life and with that comes a responsibility to look after our own well-being;
- that everyone is loved and entitled to care – no one is beyond God's love;
- that there is a journey of life of which dying and death is an inevitable and important part;
- that inattention to the above can damage our well-being.

These tenets can form part of an agenda for reflection on how we secure our health and well-being in the twenty-first century. Far from providing easy answers to what must be done, they draw attention to some of the frailties of our current approach to well-being and to the challenging nature of some of the changes which may be required if health and well-being is to be experienced in all of our communities.

These challenges are for us as individuals, for our families and communities as well as for the institutions and civic leaders who design and fund our health and social care systems.

We live in a world that is increasingly marked by individualism, consumerism and transaction rather than a world of the common good marked by responsibility, mutualism, co-operation and redistribution. Even health which is predominantly delivered in the UK 'free at the point of care' is increasingly seen as a commodity, from which we as 'customers' expect to have certain

---

[13] 'A joyful heart is good medicine, but a broken spirit dries up the bones' (Prov. 17.22, NASB).

outcomes and in the process of which we are relatively passive recipients rather than active participants. We have raised our physicians to the status of 'gods' and invested them with expectations they cannot fulfil. With significant exceptions health is seen as a private transaction between an individual and a service rather than the activity of people in relationship together, as families and communities with responsibility both for their own health and the well-being of their neighbours.

As individual liberty, freedom of choice and responsibility are strenuously upheld, those who wish to foster debate about the equity of access to choice and the consequences of life-limiting choices are often pilloried as representing 'the nanny state' and infantilising individuals. Vested institutional and professional interests – often driven by sincere principled commitment to health care – can lead to polarised and therefore fruitless debates.

This is unsustainable with increasing demand, decreasing resources and the lack of attention to some of the most corrosive and damaging impacts on our health and well-being. In the rediscovery of what makes for the common good we can begin to articulate an agenda for change in the pursuit of our individual and communal health and well-being.

Key questions

There are some key questions.

- What are our expectations, and what are the limitations of the State which we fund and of the leaders whom we elect, in relation to health provision?
- What are our personal, familial and community rights, responsibilities and contributions? How much tax do we want to pay?
- What is the role of the market, individual choice, the role of patients/service users in design and delivery of services?

• What is the right balance between preventative, community and specialist services and action to tackle the wider determinants of health?

In the concluding section of this chapter I advocate an agenda for change which begins to address these questions and to seek a way forward.

An agenda for our health and well-being

Five main propositions frame this agenda:

1 Tackling poverty and inequality is fundamental.
2 We need to ensure equitable access to health and social care provision for people of all socio-economic backgrounds.
3 A transformation is required in the delivery of health and social care services, rebalancing health and social care spend and activity from the treatment of disease to the prevention of ill health and creation of well-being – with individuals at the heart of design and decision-making.
4 The creation of vibrant and active communities with high levels of mutualism and association will increase well-being.
5 There is an individual duty/responsibility of self-care.

Tackling poverty and inequality

As the Marmot report states: 'Reducing health inequalities is a matter of fairness and social justice. In England the many people who are currently dying prematurely each year as a result of health inequalities would have enjoyed, in total, between 1.3 and 2.5 million extra years of life.'[14]

The strongest correlation between life expectancy and healthy years of life is income. In addition, overall levels of health

---

[14] Fair Society, Healthy Lives. The Marmot Review. Strategic Review of Health Inequalities in England, p. 15.

and well-being are significantly affected by wide disparities of income and social status. The best chance of a long and healthy life is to be born into a working household with sufficient income and to be employed in similarly good work, throughout one's life.

This perspective sits at the heart of the six policy objectives proposed by the Marmot Review for the reduction of health inequalities, namely:

- give every child the best start in life;
- enable all children, young people and adults to maximise their capabilities and have control over their lives;
- create fair employment and good work for all;
- ensure a healthy living standard for all;
- create and develop healthy and sustainable places and communities;
- strengthen the role and impact of ill health prevention.

Other chapters of this book deal more directly and in more detail with issues of economic growth, child poverty, societal unfairness and work. But the importance of these issues to the health agenda is clear.

Indeed one very positive aspect of the transfer of public health responsibility to local government is that many local authorities now have poverty strategies which bring together work on jobs, cost of living and financial inclusion with work on health inequalities.

An example of the impact of this is that an increasing number of local authorities are adopting the Living Wage (LW) as the minimum wage payable to their employees and are seeking to extend this approach to contracted work and casual staff. Coalitions of private, voluntary and community organisations and the public sector committed to paying the LW are being established at local level. The experience of the introduction of the LW is that it lifts self-esteem, workforce morale and organisational productivity as well as enabling people to live decently.[15]

Ensuring equitable access to health and social care provision for people of all socio-economic backgrounds

The NHS was built on the basis of service provision which is free at the point of access – social care is constructed to enable everyone to access a level of care and to pay a financial contribution for that in proportion to their ability to pay. Both systems were designed to ensure that income was not a barrier to receipt of benefit.

Recent studies reveal, however, that this is no guarantee of equitable provision. Although the funding formula for Clinical Commissioning Groups (CCGs) is designed to reflect the underlying assessed needs of its population, this is no guarantee of the distribution of benefit. For example, in a 2011–12 study of the funding of health in York and North Yorkshire there were more General Practitioners (GPs) per head of population in affluent areas and the flow of people through GPs and subsequently referred for secondary care was similarly skewed.[16]

A significant challenge in a free and demand-led system is to ensure that benefit is equitable and not disproportionately experienced by those who are most confident about seeking health care. It is an important challenge for the relatively newly established CCGs – made up of GPs – to identify those who don't present themselves through their practices and clinics but who have health needs. Working with the joint strategic needs

---

[15] An independent study of the business benefits of implementing a living wage policy in London: GLA Economics Executive Summary prepared by London Economics, February 2009.
[16] Independent Review of Health Services in North Yorkshire and York: report of independent commission, 2 August 2011, p. 11.

assessment for their communities and local Health and Wellbeing Boards and through the focus of the Health and Wellbeing strategy, there is an opportunity to prioritise delivery of shared interventions to build access to and take up of preventative health programmes in deprived communities.

Transformation in the delivery of health and social care services

The structures for delivery of health and social care are different across the UK and its devolved administrations. In each nation, however, there have been major reforms with the objective of bringing greater integration in the delivery of health and social care and an increased focus on prevention to tackle the upward curve of demand as a result of demographic change.

As the Welsh Assembly Government said in its 2009 publication *NHS in Wales: Why We Are Changing the Structure*: 'We need to provide more care closer to people's homes and more self-care programmes to help people live more independent lives, provide more joined up services between health and social care, and increasingly focus on public health, creating a wellness service, rather than a sickness service. It means looking at whole systems not just hospitals.'[17]

More recently both the major reorganisation of the NHS in England outlined in the White Paper *Liberating the NHS*[18] and the Care and Support Bill have the stated intent of increasing local practitioner and user-led commissioning of integrated health and social care services, as well as the long-term affordability of service provision. In England, Health and Wellbeing Boards – statutory bodies led by local authorities – have responsibility

---

[17] *NHS in Wales: Why We Are Changing the Structure* (2009), <www.wales.nhs.uk/documents/nhs>, accessed 6 September 2014.

[18] Department of Health, *Liberating the NHS: An Information Revolution: A Consultation on Proposals* (London: Department of Health, 2010).

for preparing 'joint strategic needs assessments' and 'health and wellbeing plans' which enable local commissioning of services which reflect need and promote well-being.

A specific requirement is to produce 'Better Care plans'. These plans articulate how the funds and activities of health and social care services will be brought more closely together – so that there is greater focus, for example on preventing hospital admission and equally on support for people metaphorically to 'get back on their feet' after a period of time in hospital.

Although structures and plans may have clear intent, delivery is much harder, especially in a time of turbulent change, with anxiety about scarcity of resources, understandable individual and institutional interests, and a desire to hold on to the safe and the known. It may be better for the health and well-being of a community to shift resources from hospital beds to community and preventative activity, but without constant dialogue and agreement between individuals, communities and providers of services such proposals will become mired in emotive controversy. Defence of the status quo will be understood as defence of the NHS.

There are, however, many good examples, here and internationally, that are worth noting. At the heart of each is deep attention to building common understanding, trust and the involvement of all in pursuing both individual and the common good.

Jonkoping is a province in Sweden. Its health and social care system was once one of the most expensive in Sweden and produced weaker results than other provinces.[19] Over twenty years Jonkoping has transformed its health and social care system and now provides quality health care at relatively low cost. It meets the Institute for Healthcare Improvement's 'Triple

---

[19] <www.lj.se/qulturum>, accessed 6 September 2014.

Aim' of better health care for the individual, better health for the population and lower cost per capita.

According to Goran Henriks, the Jonkoping Director of Development, what was most significant in the achievement of these improvements was a comprehensive shift of culture to:

- concentrate on what patients value, not what professionals value;
- involve all suppliers and caregivers in prioritising those patient values;
- understand that each step in a process is dependent for its success on the steps that precede and follow it.[20]

This approach was extended across the health and social care system – enabled initially through the creation of a 'qulturum'. The qulturum is a place in which service users, carers, community associations, health and social care staff, academics and researchers work together to create new approaches to well-being and care, with individuals at the heart of design. In the qulturum there is explicit emphasis on the equality of all participants, e.g. titles and ranks are removed. Over the past ten years almost every person working in health and social care in Jonkoping has been involved, embedding common values, language and approaches across the whole system.

In Monmouthshire, in Wales, the explicit intention of health and social care provision is to help people to 'live their own lives'. Health and social care teams have been brought together and work from community hubs across the county. Work with individuals and families is structured around what people want for their lives and not about 'what is wrong'. People are seen as capable rather than needy – bringing abilities and their wider

---

[20] <www.kingfund.org.uk/. . . /goran-henriks-lessons-from-sweden-esther-project>, accessed 6 September 2014.

networks of care to the discussion about developing individualised solutions. The contact between individuals and service providers is described as a 'conversation'.

There is clear intent in Monmouthshire to work at three levels:

1 community: building resilient individuals, families and communities;
2 service: building flexible, empowering and responsive services;
3 individual: helping people and families to find solutions that build on their strengths, aspirations and networks.[21]

Similar approaches – frequently now described as the co-design and co-delivery of services – from around the UK are described in a series of publications by the Innovation Unit and Nesta[22] in their *People Powered Health* series. In describing Lambeth's collaborative commissioning Dr Adrian McLachan says:

Before, commissioning tended to be hierarchical and profession-led. Now we have co-produced decisions – there's no one person who is the boss. We work by consensus. And this works because a lot of time went into laying a foundation of trust and understanding. Now the commissioning collaborative is working with communities and individuals to 'understand their needs, their assets and their aspirations in order to fund and guarantee effective, meaningful and efficient support'.

In all these examples, the abiding disciplines of research, building evidence of need, prioritisation of spend, clear definition of required outcomes, and commissioning and evaluation of provision continue. What is fundamentally different is who is involved in all of these processes, how they are involved

---

[21] Monmouthshire County Council, *Your County Your Way* (2012), <monmouthshire. cc.wordpress.com/tag/your-county-your-way/>, accessed 6 September 2014.
[22] Nesta, *People Powered Health*, <www.nesta.org.uk/project/people-powered-health>, accessed 6 September 2014.

and the influence that they have in the decision-making. In the establishment of integrated health and social care designed with individuals, families and carers, passivity and disempowerment can be replaced by an active and creative partnership which leaves people a level of dignity and choice and higher levels of well-being. Within all of this is an assumption of the much greater role which communities and networks of support can play in the delivery of health and well-being.

Vibrant communities, healthy communities

People's well-being is first experienced in family and community settings. Vibrant communities – which may not be particularly affluent communities – build and sustain individual, family and community well-being. Places and spaces in which communities can come together in activities underpinned by mutualism and reciprocity build trust, confidence and connection between people and underpin well-being. Relatively speaking, in such communities, people experience less isolation, watch out for one another in times of illness or hardship, lend a hand, do a good turn and share in one another's joys and sorrows.

In many parts of the UK, in both urban and rural settings, we appear to have lost much that can be good about community life, with fewer of us knowing or trusting or getting involved in community activities.

Our lives have become more focused upon securing income with which we can provide for our families through purchasing decisions than in collective activity to create the quality of life which we seek. The common experience is that time is short, jobs less secure, income levels are lower – all of which impact on well-being and lower the likelihood of people giving of their time to community activities. People socialise most easily around established shared interests – sport, religion, culture, professional associations, family ties – rather than geographic locations where they may happen to live. Increasingly, communities can be virtual and facilitated through social media and other internet-enabled communication platforms. These connections and the mutual support that flows through them can have a significant positive impact on well-being. Virtual communities and communities of interest undoubtedly have an important contribution to make.

But I want to return to the core infrastructure and activities within a geographic community that can support its health and well-being. In fact, it is to the notion of the parish – the dwelling beside of peoples – as the original and still key building block of community life that I turn first. Regardless of the issue of belief, Christian churches and other religions' buildings are important assets in the infrastructure of community life. In many communities across the UK the church and its hall are the setting for pre-school play schemes, luncheon clubs, yoga, keep fit and dance classes, youth clubs, fundraising activities, etc. Churches are places where people who do not generally attend church celebrate the festivals of the year. All of these activities have positive impact on the health and well-being of that community and for visitors who make use of the facilities, breaking down isolation, building relationships and providing support for mental and physical health. But the contribution of a church and its congregation to the well-being of a community can be much greater if it sets out to promote the common good. There are many examples of churches across the UK who see this as central to their purpose and witness.

The Bromley by Bow Centre, now much celebrated for its inspiring work, provides a focal point for one of the most income-deprived communities in the East End of London. The four main ways in which the Centre works are:

- to support people to overcome chronic illness and unhealthy lifestyles;
- to enable people to learn new skills;
- to support people to become less grant dependent and to find work;
- to provide the tools to create an enterprising community.

The Revd Andrew Mawson describes speaking at a World Health Organization conference and how, after four days of speeches 'by politicians, policy makers and aspiring academics talking about poverty, health and the demands of a planet with ever-diminishing resources and an apparent environmental nightmare', he was asked to speak. He observes:

> I had spent four days looking at large graphs and hearing about policies for change and endless statistics from around the world. No one had actually mentioned anyone with a name and an address. The messy details of people's real lives were startlingly absent from the platform. I then told our Bromley by Bow story . . . and received a standing ovation. I don't think this had anything to do with my abilities as a public speaker. I think it has everything to do with touching a raw nerve and daring to suggest that the way we think about government and its relationship to people . . . is profoundly out of kilter with the realities of life experienced by millions of people.[23]

There are similar examples of churches up and down the UK – such as The Thornbury Centre in east Bradford, built around St Margaret's Anglican church and now hosting the local library, start-up businesses, skills training, Home Start and conferencing facilities; and the Acomb Gateway Centre in York with its kitchens, café, food bank, youth provision, lifelong learning and health self-help support groups. An organisation called One

---

[23] Andrew Mawson, *The Social Entrepreneur: Making Communities Work* (London: Atlantic, 2008), p. 12.

Church, 100 Uses – a community interest company – works with congregations to help them connect with their community.[24]

Of course vibrant and healthy communities are certainly not the preserve of church or religious communities. But there are consistent threads which run through some of the most powerful examples of community-generated change, namely, the centrality, agency and capabilities of individuals, an entrepreneurial approach to development of actions and solutions, a willingness to take on and challenge self-serving bureaucracy, and the importance of building relationships and trust between people, communities and organisations.

The example of a small ex-textile town – Todmorden – at the end of the Calder Valley on the border between Lancashire and Yorkshire brings these dimensions to life. 'Incredible Edible Todmorden' – described as a breakthrough idea for the twenty-first century by the then-Sustainable Development Commission – has transformed the community infrastructure and well-being of Todmorden through the use of food as a means of bringing people together.[25]

With a passion for local food growing, a group of local residents, social entrepreneurs and small business people came together. Planters of herbs and salad vegetables appeared at the railway station in the town, patches of uncultivated, unused ground started to sport vegetables, the local café started to offer loyalty cards in which after every-so-many drinks a fruit tree would be planted locally. 'Food trails' started across the town and people were encouraged to pick and eat the vegetables that were ready for cropping.

The focus in Todmorden was food because food is a universal currency – we all need to eat. The outcome has been an

[24] <www.onechurch100uses.org/>, accessed 6 September 2014.
[25] <www.incredible-edible-todmorden.co.uk/>, accessed 6 September 2014.

overwhelmingly positive impact on the health and well-being of the town and its residents. As with the Bromley by Bow Centre, Incredible Edible Todmorden looks to a very practical culture of change based on 'learning by doing', embracing human creativity and diversity and applying business ideas to social questions.

There are important lessons and some unsettling challenges here for institutions, bureaucracies, statutory partnerships and their 'orderly' practices of need identification, prioritisation, funding and commissioning of services. How willing are they not only to change processes fundamentally – so that the individuals and communities for whom benefit is intended are involved with power and influence in design and delivery decisions – but also to respond to and be led by community-initiated work on health and well-being which may or may not work neatly with the timescales of health and well-being strategies and Better Care Fund submissions?

Individual rights and responsibilities for health and well-being

The intrinsic value and sanctity of each human life is central to any definition of what constitutes the common good. Our society is, or ought to be, underpinned by a consensus that everyone should, by right, have access to the opportunities which enable individuals to achieve their full potential in life and that no one who is unwell should go untreated.

Within our health and social care system this belief has helped establish a broad right of access to health services free at the point of care irrespective of contributions through the national insurance and taxation system. This notion of entitlement has run deep in our culture since the formation of the welfare state.

The discourse about human rights has, however, been con-taminated by that of customer rights – the rights of those who buy goods and services – which can be exercised without reference, care or commitment for others. Taxation comes to be seen as payment against services to be received as a customer rather than an investment by citizens – in proportion to their ability to contribute – in the creation of the common good.

It is time for a renewed debate about the rights of individuals and how those are exercised. It is a debate that must include discussion of responsibilities and citizenship, because the debate is fundamentally about our connections with each other, our 'social contract' and about the type of society we want in the UK.

Each human being is the custodian of the body and soul with which they live their life. We take decisions every day about how we live in our bodies. These choices directly impact upon our and others' health and well-being. A significant element of the escalating cost of ill health is related to lifestyle 'choices'. Levels of consumption and waste both damage the environment and limit the health of others. Our short-term convenience, standard of living and demand for treatment of preventable diseases have implications for the health and well-being of others. We cannot shirk the moral and ethical questions which this raises.

Responsibility for health should be a collaborative effort between the individual and the society in which they live. That responsibility is recognised in – but not limited to – the taxes we contribute. It does not transfer to others our own responsibility for the health and well-being of ourselves, our families and our neighbours. The common good is not ultimately created in the payment of monies for the provision of services by the State and the market. It is created through individual acts of human kindness, care and compassion for others who are known and unknown to us – which require us to recognise the responsibility we have towards our own health as well as towards the health of others.

Conclusion

On the whole, people in the nations of the UK are living significantly longer, healthier and more prosperous lives than any previous generation.

But good health is not universally enjoyed. In today's Britain some of the deepest socio-economic divides in the Western world give rise to much poorer health and life expectancy for the children and adults of income-deprived communities.

Increasingly we have expectations of our health and social care services as customers. We expect that provision will be available when we need it and that it will be able to cure our ailments and prolong our lives. Many of the ailments which now require treatment are not the result of communicable diseases. They are the product of lifestyles chosen by us more-or-less freely and consciously. But simultaneously we are becoming less and less comfortable about the costs which we might have to bear to sustain a health system in which demands and cost pressures are rising. We have also become less involved in the active care and support of others, whether family, friends or neighbours.

Despite broad acceptance that the prevention of disease and promotion of well-being can deliver great public good, enabling personal resilience and self-care, allocation of spend in the health service remains heavily skewed towards acute and secondary care. Physical health is prioritised over mental health and well-being, and the relationship between the two is infrequently addressed in care planning. The aim of 'prolonging life' is one of the five pillars of purpose for the National Health Service but the development of quality services and the quality of life available to those who are terminally ill is patchy. Our model of health remains largely focused on treatment of disease rather than the creation of health and well-being.

These are big and complex challenges and they require policy responses and change at many levels. As this is about how a whole system functions, there are crucial interdependencies between the actions which are required.

Key dimensions of Christian teaching about well-being emphasise the connection between physical, emotional and spiritual well-being; our interdependence with others for well-being; our responsibility for self-care and the care of others; the universality of God's care and compassion; and the journey of life towards death. Collectively these create a framework for thinking about the policy shifts and practical action that would deliver greater well-being.

Here are four distinct but interconnected calls for action:

1 *A re-energised debate*, which starts in our hearts and homes and broadens into the life and debates of our churches and our public, private, voluntary and community organisations locally and nationally. It is crucially a conversation for us as citizens with those whom we choose to represent us about the nature of the social contract in the twenty-first-century UK. What kind of society do we and our families want to live in? In the pursuit of the common good what are our obligations to one another? What are we personally responsible for? What are our rights? How much are we prepared to contribute? What is a fair share? Are there limits to our kindness, care and compassion for others? Who should benefit from prosperity and, when times are hard, what collective obligations do we have to those whose health and well-being are poor, for whatever reason?

2 *Concerted work to strengthen community life and well-being in neighbourhoods across our nations.* This work can, as we have seen, take root and inspire significant change in different ways in different communities. It may be the energy

of a worshipping community, or a school enmeshed in its neighbourhood with a deep knowledge not just of its children but of their families, neighbours and friends. It may be the creativity and drive of a local social entrepreneur who sees possibility in forging connections between previously disparate activities. But in all cases where this work has led to the flourishing of community life it has been built on: an assumption that every community has potential and untapped capabilities rather than assumptions of incapability; the energies and passion of diverse individuals in that community; deep ongoing conversations about needs and dreams; and creative, innovative and unexpected solutions. The public sector can play its part but it is a responsive not controlling part – as often about removing unnecessary obstacles as providing services, guidance or funding.

3 *Sustained work to redesign the delivery of health and social care services*, working with robust population data and understanding of clinical efficacy but crucially with the lives, involvement and influence of individuals at its heart:
  - to produce integrated services and care pathways co-designed with communities, service users and carers, which recognise that people do not experience their needs in neat categories of 'health' and 'social care';
  - to rebalance the attention, activity and resources of the health and social care system to the creation of well-being focused on self-care, circles of care and preventative and community actions;
  - to transform the provision of mental health and end-of-life care;
  - to ensure provision and resources are distributed appropriately against the differing needs of communities.

4 *National action to tackle the unequal distribution of health and well-being:*
  - against a backdrop of a slow return to economic growth, decisions on income and taxation which address, through mechanisms such as the minimum and living wage, increased income inequalities and lowered standards of living for the poorest in society – recognising the impact of poverty and income inequity on the health and well-being of individuals and communities;
  - constant attention to the distribution and demand pattern of health and social care services to ensure equity of access and provision;
  - a national resetting of the debate about entitlement to prosperity and well-being – beyond polarised debates about 'shirkers and workers', the worthy and unworthy, us and them, and the stigma and embarrassment that attaches itself to the lives of some of the most vulnerable in our society. This is at root about the fostering of a whole-nation discussion about our 'social contract', from which policies, systems, plans and actions for our improved well-being must ultimately emanate.

We can refocus our policy-making and our efforts by putting our collective well-being, not profit, as our prime motivator and setting goals for the public good, not just growth, in recognition that well-being and health are far more important indicators of wealth than money or material gain.

8

Ageing: blessing or burden?

JAMES WOODWARD

━━━━━●◆●━━━━━

Introduction

This chapter begins with a personal story about the relationship of self to age.[1] From this moment of connectivity with an older person I argue that imagination and compassion are the core spiritual virtues that should underpin our thinking about older people, our responses to ageing and the possibilities of the transformative contribution of the elderly to society. The second section examines the significance of demographic statistics before identifying some questions and issues raised by an ageing society. The third section looks at the challenges posed to older people in living a healthy, engaged and dignified old age. The fourth section discusses the much contested issue of how best to organize society to deal with the economics of health

---

[1] The title of the chapter 'Ageing: blessing or burden?' was first used by Bishop David Jenkins who taught me the importance of the social dimension of theological reflection and encouraged me to dig deeper into this area of study. For further information about my work in this area see <www.jameswoodward.info>, accessed 14 September 2014.

There are a growing number of older people narrating their stories of old age: Diana Athill, *Somewhere towards the End* (London: Granta Books, 2008); Philip Toynbee, *End of a Journey: An Autobiographical Journey 1979–81* (London: Bloomsbury, 1988); and Barbara G. Myerhoff, *Stories as Equipment for Living: Last Talks and Tales of Barbara Myerhoff*, ed. Marc Kaminsky, Mark Weiss and Deena Metzger (Ann Arbor: University of Michigan Press, 2007).

and social care in later life. In the fifth and sixth sections we shall look at the possibilities of reimagining old age, acknowledging both the blessing and burden of ageing and seeking to see how the Christian tradition might support our nurture of the common good through a valuing of age.

Who's that in my mirror? Imagination and compassion as the basis of our relationship to age

In our world today even if you are going nowhere, you go there quickly! I am late for a meeting in Birmingham and I can't find my mobile phone to let my colleagues know that I am behind. I negotiate a busy junction and then meet a pedestrian crossing. There are three cars in front. My eyes catch the sight of an old man waiting to cross. He hesitates and then moves back while none of the cars ahead let him pass. I decide to let him cross, even when my anxiety levels about the meeting continue to rise. I stop. He hesitates. Then slowly and laboriously he takes several steps from the kerb. He is frail and the journey across the road seems to take for ever.

The man, it seemed, was so alone and so vulnerable. I saw his weakness and his pain. He had probably crossed that road for many years but suddenly that path had become treacherous and strange. How many minutes did I wait as he slowly placed one foot in front of another? How much longer would he be able to do this? Was he at the end of his life? Where was the man going? Who was he becoming? Was anyone helping him along his way?

As I drove off, something very profound and disturbing struck me. He was me! The thought preoccupied me for the rest of my journey. The day would come when I, threatened by a jungle of cars, would hesitate, and wonder how the familiar had become so foreign, how and why my

161

body had become so heavy and difficult, and how my reactions had become so tranquillized. The old man had become a stark foreshadowing of what I would become. His vulnerability would become mine with all its dependence and imperfections. His appearance challenged the mask of my illusions. His ageing reflected my own ageing.

I both sympathized with that old man and feared him. His presence spoke about my passage through time, my own physical changes, and my own inevitable death. I did not want to receive this message but it was written very clearly on the page of my busy day. It made me sad and gave me hope. He exhibited patience that reminded me that we all have to slow down. This discardable, throwaway person is the product of our culture, a bundle of experience, wisdom, knowledge, life, concerns and wisdom. Who is he? I do not see him in my car wing mirror – he disappears strangely into the landscape.

This man's story is important, just as your story is important. They belong together. These are the tales of unique human existence, fabric that took years to weave. Whoever we are, we are all worth something.

Some underpinning theological values

There are some key theological themes that run through this chapter. The first is that we all have value in the sight of God and that part of our responsibility to affirm the dignity of humanity is to recognise that all stages of our living and dying are of equal worth.[2]

---

[2] Many writers argue that in order to tackle some of the particular challenges of old age we must attend to the tasks of personal development through which we all pass. See Daniel J. Levinson, *The Seasons of a Man's Life* (New York: Ballantine Books, 1978). This book has influenced much reflection in the area of intergenerational learning.

The second is related to this. Put rather crudely: what is old age and what are older people for? This is related to how we are to understand the nature of personhood and our engagement with many of the unmanageable and ambiguous aspects of our existence. As T. S. Eliot once remarked, 'there are two kinds of problems in life'. One kind requires the question, 'What are we going to do about it?' The other calls for different questions: 'What does it mean? How does one relate to it?'[3]

The first kind of problem is like a puzzle to be solved with appropriate technical resources and pragmatic responses. This approach poses a deeper range of challenges, which no particular strategy, policy or technique will overcome. We constantly run into the danger of a reductionist model of the person and ageing that understands ageing primarily as a scientific problem amenable to technical solution. We cannot live for ever and most of us shall need to negotiate this stage of living. Our consumerist and materialist eye cannot contain or even allow for the paradoxes of later life: ageing is a source of wisdom and suffering, spiritual growth and physical decline, honour and vulnerability.

Finally, there is the value of sharing the wisdom that comes with age. In the Jewish tradition, much has been said about what makes for a blessed old age. Among the features of such blessedness are a lack of infirmity, the presence of children, economic success and being afforded respect. It follows, therefore, that if persons are blessed in old age they are the veritable embodiment of holiness. The Jewish tradition assumes that if one has lived a long time, one has learned a great deal and is consequently deemed wise. The ideal state, of course, is a combination of wisdom and old age. A Yiddish proverb says it

[3] Cited in Thomas Cole and Sally Gadow (eds), *What Does It Mean to Grow Old? Reflections from the Humanities* (Durham, NC: Duke University Press, 1986), p. 247.

best: 'Old age to the unlearned is winter. To the learned it is harvest time.'[4] This value embodied in an older person points to why a society that values older people is a richer place in which all may flourish.

An ageing society: what are the facts?

Both globally and in the United Kingdom, we are experiencing a revolution in the opportunities that are offered by a steady increase in life expectancy. The statistics offer a picture that is translated into all kinds of practical realities.[5]

In 2014 there were 10 million people in the UK over 65 years old. By the year 2030, this figure is projected to rise to 15 million. By 2050, the number will have nearly doubled to around 20 million.

Let us look at those projections from a different perspective. Today almost 1 in 10 people are over 60 years old. By 2050, 1 in 5 people will be over 60. By then, they will outnumber children aged 0–14.

These facts affect us all directly. A man born in the UK in 1981 had life expectancy at birth of 84 years. For a boy born today, the figure is 89 years, and by 2030 it is projected to be 91. The trend for women is similar. A girl born in 1981 was expected to live for 89 years and one born today might expect to live to 92. Projections suggest a girl born in 2030 might live to 95. We are all living longer and we should expect, in our

---

[4] Amy Elizabeth Dean, *Growing Older, Growing Better: Daily Meditations for Celebrating Aging* (Carlsbad, Calif.: Hay House, 1997).

[5] The statistics that follow are summarised from the UK Office for National Statistics <www.statistics.gov.uk/hub/population/ageing/older-people/index.html>, accessed 17 February 2014. This section also draws upon the work of Age UK, <www.ageuk.org.uk/professional-resources-home/knowledge-hub-evidence-statistics>, accessed 2 February 2014; and The King's Fund <www.kingsfund.org.uk/time-to-think-differently/trends/demography/ageing-population>, accessed 15 December 2013.

families and communities, to have increased numbers of older people. There can be few of us who do not know friends or neighbours who are literally 'living with age'. Each of us will need to anticipate and prepare for living longer.

At this point it is important to bear in mind that the projection of accurate demographic figures is problematic. It is not possible to project accurate figures because of variables in fertility and mortality rates. In some parts of the world gaining accurate information can be difficult and some projections have been based on false assumptions. These variables all have implications for policy-makers planning services for older people.[6]

Within this total statistical picture, however, the number of very old people grows even faster. This brings particular challenges to the debate about our provision for meeting the needs of older people. Much of today's public spending on benefits is focused on elderly people. Sixty-five per cent of Department for Work and Pensions benefit expenditure goes to those over working age, equivalent to £100 billion in 2010–11 or one-seventh of public expenditure. Continuing to provide state benefits and pensions at today's average would mean additional spending of £10 billion a year for every additional one million people over working age.

Growing numbers of elderly people also have an impact on the NHS, where average spending on retired households is nearly double that for non-retired households: in 2007–8 the average value of NHS services for retired households was £5,200 compared with £2,800 for non-retired. These averages conceal variation across older age groups, with the cost of service provision for the most elderly likely to be much greater than for younger retired people. The Department of

---

[6] See Kevin Morgan and Christopher Smith (eds), *Gerontology: Responding to an Ageing Society* (London: Jessica Kingsley Publishers, 1992), chs 8 and 9.

Health estimates that the average cost of providing hospital and community health services for a person aged 85 years or more is around three times greater than for a person aged from 65 to 74 years.

We can be sure that in the coming decades, rapidly ageing populations will increasingly strain health, welfare and social-insurance systems, putting potentially unsustainable pressure on public budgets.[7]

Some issues raised by an ageing society

Reframing our relationship to time and work

Living longer offers us the chance to reframe our relationship to time and to the various stages of our living. We need to rethink what we believe about the nature of work and the relationship between paid and unpaid activity. Concepts of retirement have changed, with older people over the age of 65 feeling that they still have a useful part to play in society. There are issues relating to family and the responsibility that the different generations have for one another, especially when older age presents health and social care challenges.[8]

The consequences of an ageing population present society with major issues of public policy, issues that face both the voter and those seeking a mandate to govern. These issues are in part related to finance and are wide ranging. For example who should be responsible for pensions and other income support? How do we provide the best health care for older people within the limitations set on health care spending, particularly given the increase in those living with dementia-related

---

[7] See Anthony Warnes, Lorna Warren and Michael Nolan (eds), *Care Services for Later Life* (London: Jessica Kingsley Publishers, 2000).

[8] Kirk Mann, *Approaching Retirement: Social Divisions, Welfare and Exclusion* (Bristol: Policy Press, 2001).

conditions? Can the State be expected to meet the needs and associated costs of social care? How and where should older people live and how innovative are we in the provision of suitable housing?[9]

The physical and spiritual dimensions of growing older also present some real anxieties and fears. In an individualistic, consumerist and materialistic world, is it possible to affirm that we are blessed by the presence of older people? Indeed as we face the prospects of ageing what are we to make of the negative images and stereotypes of old age? How far do these representations shape our sense of what age means or are we shaped by the denial of ageing in twenty-first-century Britain?

Transforming attitudes towards old age

I have long argued that what is needed is a fundamental change in how we as a society think and feel about old age. It should be possible to nurture the valuing of age as a blessing, from within a theology of human dignity and flourishing. This is a core theme in our shared commitment to the nurture of the common good in our communities.[10]

In order to realise this vision, however, there will need to be some social, financial, political and theological change in order for old age to fulfil its potential in us and, through us, in society.

---

[9] Sheila Peace and Caroline Holland (eds), *Inclusive Housing in an Ageing Society* (Bristol: Policy Press, 2001).

[10] For more information about the development of my thinking in this area see <www.jameswoodward.info>. See also my *Valuing Age: Pastoral Ministry with Older People* (London: SPCK, 2008). This work needs to be done across the professions. It was modelled in the Leveson Centre for the Study of Ageing, Spirituality and Social Policy where professionals tackled subjects of theory and practice. See also the work of Methodist Homes for the Aged (MHA), the Outlook Trust and the Diocese of Oxford SCOP project.

What are the challenges that older people face?

Older age can bring a range of challenges to independence.[11] These might include physical frailty, pain and dependency. A small proportion of older people have to accept the need for help from relatives and neighbours. Some may need to have paid carers to help with basic tasks of living, while a small number may need to accept a transition into residential care. Age can bring with it some cognitive impairment and even dementia. These and other factors combine to make this age group vulnerable to both abuse and neglect.

My pastoral experience has indicated that it is often loneliness that besets many older people.[12] This may be caused by the way in which an individual's social networks shrink. Family members, including children, may well live at a distance. Isolation may be the result of the death of a partner or indeed of children.

The context and culture within which ageing takes place are significant shaping influences for older people. Grandchildren are important for grandparents but often grand-parenting takes place at a distance or in the context of family breakdown. Older people can sometimes find it difficult to cope with the gaps and differences in values and ways of living (e.g. the reliance on modern technology and social networking as part of keeping in touch). Older people have expressed their concerns especially about the economic fortunes of their families as all live with the reality of differences in property and income.

---

[11] See Stan van Hooft, *Caring about Health* (Farnham: Ashgate, 2006); Susan Carmody and Sue Forster (eds), *Nursing Older People: A Guide to Practice in Care Homes* (Oxford: Radcliffe, 2006); Barry McPherson, *Aging as a Social Process* (Oxford: Oxford University Press, 2004).

[12] See Jan Reed, David Stanley and Charlotte Clarke, *Health, Well-Being and Older People* (Bristol: Policy Press, 2004); Robert Slater, *The Psychology of Growing Old: Looking Forward* (Buckingham: Open University Press, 1995).

Ageing is also an inner journey as there are emotional, psychological and spiritual tasks to be faced. Older people need to come to terms with their lives as they reflect on its shape and fortunes. There may be a need to face bad and often traumatic memories. There is infinite value in this process. The inner work done in later life can be the means by which the treasure of wisdom can be passed down to younger generations.[13] There is a need for the elderly to consolidate their identity, which will include a healthy acknowledgement of mistakes and the aspiration to leave a legacy of something worthwhile after death.

Older adults, like people of all ages, will have to find their own way of dealing with death. Some may deny it, resisting at all costs any open conversation about understandable fears of living and dying alone. Some will even avoid any preparation for death that takes the shape of planning and paying for a funeral. There can be few, however, who do not wonder what shape their death might take and what chances there may be of dying with dignity. It remains our shared responsibility to embrace the realities of death through encouraging a more open approach to conversation, reflection and preparation for dying and death. This may also mean a clearer sense of what the choices and decisions may be around the end of life.[14]

Finally, we should not understate how prevalent negative attitudes towards older adults affect older people. These attitudes include indifference (many older people feel invisible and

---

[13] Vern Bengston makes a significant contribution to our understanding of how wisdom is or is not transmitted within families across generations. See his book *Families and Faith: How Religion Is Passed Down across Generations* (Oxford: Oxford University Press, 2013).

[14] There is a considerable body of literature in this area. For an example of an open, honest and reflective account of an older person narrating the shape of the end of her life see May Sarton, *End Game* (New York: W. W. Norton, 1992).

unvalued), pity, resentment and fear, which could even lead to a stigmatising and stereotyping of mature adults as out of date, and even greedy and selfish.[15]

Financial and political issues

The statistics that concern 'population ageing' give rise to a number of stories about increased longevity and often have a number of things in common – it is bad, it is new, and it will overwhelm us all. The major fear is the burden of cost and caring that having more older people will create.

We should note that 'population ageing' has been taking place for almost two centuries in the UK. We should also note the diversity of the ways in which people age and the interconnectedness of culture, economic status, housing, employment and the provision of health care.

Some, though not all, would add that a person's spiritual and religious world also impacts significantly on how they age. It will be important to ask those who generate public policy to include within their vision a holistic view of human personhood and the intrinsic value of all stages of living and dying as we seek to make the best provision for the common good.[16]

In this context far too much of the 'care debate' has concentrated on the important but rather narrow agenda of whether we shall be able to 'afford' ageing. This is a significant debate and still largely unresolved, which may well be to the forefront of political debate in the 2015 General Election.

We would do well to attend to the way this debate is conducted. In order to make choices, we need information. Too

---

many of the conversations that take place about older people are simply inaccessible to the general public. The more politicised the discourse, the less we are able to negotiate the contested areas of policy. These debates (necessary as they are for democracy) often fail to place these issues into a broader and wiser historical and cultural horizon. To pick up the image of that man in the wing mirror of my car, we fail to make the connection between older people, the fabric of our lives and the prospects for our own ageing.

The Dilnot Report as a way forward for funding care

There have been a number of attempts to offer solutions to reform of the Funding of the Care of Older People. Recent discussion has focused on and around the proposals outlined in the Dilnot Report.

The report's main findings were that:

1 public policy must face the fact that public expenditure in England on older people's social care is not keeping up with rising demand;
2 care costs for any one individual are uncertain and can, in some circumstances, be very high indeed;
3 the current system of funding individual care in England, which requires people with more than a very modest level of capital assets to use those assets to cover the cost of their care, leaves many in fear and uncertainty as they approach one of the most vulnerable periods of their life;
4 a system is required for funding care which enables the risk to any one individual to be pooled, through taxation or insurance or, preferably, a mix of them both. The report proposes a system under which the individual will be responsible, on a means-tested basis, for the costs of his or her care up to a suggested level of £35,000, after which the State would

pick up the cost. The current asset threshold for those in residential care would also be extended, from £23,250 to £100,000.

Such a system, the report argues, will provide sufficient certainty to enable people to plan ahead, and allow the financial services industry to develop insurance and other products to help them with their planning. It will also help the poorest in our society the most.

The research underpinning the report estimated the cost to the public purse of its proposals at less than £2 billion. While we continue to be in a time of some economic constraint, finding the funding for old age care will clearly not be easy. There will certainly be debate about the priorities for government spending. But there is also a conversation to be had about the values that should undergird decisions made about the levels of tax necessary for the kind of society we wish to see where all may flourish. In this debate we should remember that the £2 billion that Dilnot suggests would fund care is to be compared with a total annual government expenditure of just under £700 billion.

The persuasiveness of the argument about resource constraints should be viewed against the implications of not making this investment. One implication is that the cost of caring for older people already falling on the NHS and other parts of the national budget is likely to go on increasing. In other words, resistance or delay to the introduction of a fairer system of funding means that problems and pressures on the system will continue, not be avoided, and incur further unexpected cost.

The government has incorporated the idea of a 'cap on care costs' proposed in the Dilnot Report into the Care Act which became law in May 2014. It has set the cap at a higher level (£72,000) although future governments would have the option to lower it should the fiscal climate improve, or indeed raise it (it is intended that the arrangements embodied in the Act will come into force in April 2016). The government also propose to raise the upper threshold for means-testing to £118,000.

These steps have been welcomed as important, albeit not sufficient. As time passes, concerns are growing about the extent to which the changes will be experienced as an improvement, or whether the new system will be found to be as confusing and complex as the current one. Deliberations continue about fairer and more sustainable ways to fund health and social care – for example, in the context of the report of the independent Commission on the Future of Health and Social Care in England set up by the King's Fund which was published in September 2014.[17]

The Dilnot Commission also recommended other reforms, including a major information and advice campaign to help people plan ahead; better information and needs assessment for carers; and better integration of health and social care. The aim of this approach to justice and human flourishing is to achieve the right balance between individual responsibility and publicly funded provision. Getting that balance right is a core dimension within a Christian vision for Britain.

A new social contract is needed which – on the basis of an honest assessment of the respective roles of the State, voluntary associations and individual citizens – assures the weak and vulnerable of proper protection and gives all of us confidence that we are committed to building the conditions necessary to assist human flourishing.

The blessings and burdens of age

The discussion about the funding of care needs also to be put into the context of some of the organising narratives and

[17] Final Report of the Independent Commission on the Future of Health and Social Care in England, the King's Fund, September 2014.

possible misconceptions that shape the ways we look at age. Might we be able to hold together some of the burdens of older age with the opportunities and blessings of mature years? Longer life and increased numbers of older people result in many positive things for the community and our common life. In this part of the chapter I look at the defining of age; myths of dependency and health in old age; the relationship of poverty to old age; the pensions debate and the notion of retirement; and the perceived threat of dementia.[18]

Redefining old age

We must be careful about the ways in which we frame how 'old' age is defined. There are many who are thankful for the possibility of living longer and view getting old as a good thing. We may actually relish the prospect of living longer. Age redefined might affirm that we are *actually getting younger* if you count the years we actually have left to live! A wider view of these statistics can see that over time we can expect people of successive generations to be healthier and fitter and have longer to live at any age than their predecessors. This is a situation that could bring an abundance of opportunities and blessings.

An age in years that we might think of as 'old' now may not seem so in fifty years' time. We shall need to redefine age in the light of this and look again at what we mean by old.

The exploration of a positive defining of age will have to contend with the reality that a great deal of our culture is frenetically oriented towards youth. This may be understandable: people want to put down markers for the future as they see it and to capture the attention of a younger generation. Nevertheless it should be possible to hold together our perspectives of the

---

[18] Mike Featherstone and Andrew Wernick (eds), *Images of Aging: Cultural Representations of Later Life* (London: Routledge, 1995).

generations in a way that does not ignore the reality of responsible, active people in older life, who are still participants in
society, not passengers. Younger people forget that they are
ageing themselves, and should play their part in planning for
how we think about and prepare for older age. Younger people
will be in need of positive and hopeful models for their own
later years. We tolerate a very eccentric view of the good life,
or the ideal life, as one that can be lived only for a few years,
say, between 18 and 40. So the work of defining age becomes
critical if we want to break out of either wanting older citizens
to go on as part of the productive machine as long as possible
or of giving in to an ageism that accords them a marginal and
humiliating status, in which older people become tolerated but
not valued.[19]

Are all older people dependent?

A key part of reframing our relationship to older age is to
remind ourselves that most old people are not 'dependent'.
For the first time, *a million people* aged 65 or over are still in
paid work. Indeed if we define dependency as 'not in paid work'
then there are more dependants of 'working age' in the UK
than there are people over state pension age who don't work.
The number of people working past state retirement age has
almost tripled over the past fifteen years. A TUC survey showed
that 258,000 women and 338,000 men are still working at the
age of 65 and over, against 93,000 and 112,000 in 1998.[20]

A great many older people report their health as good. At
the time of the 2011 census there were about 300,000 people
aged over 64 in care homes (including public and private, with

---

[19] Bill Bytheway, *Age and Time in Unmasking Age* (Bristol: Policy Press, 2011), ch. 3.
[20] From <www.theguardian.com/society/2013/aug/24/over-65s-work>, accessed 23
March 2014.

or without nursing) – just over half a per cent of the population of England and Wales. Many of them are not dependent financially but are affluent and support younger family members.

Old age, poverty and pensions

We should not confuse old with poor. Those who are poor are rarely poor because they are old: they are poor now because they were poor when they were younger, unable either to accumulate assets or pension rights to draw on in later life.

Discussion of the economics of ageing is very often dominated by the concern that we cannot afford pensions. A little over a century ago, annual working hours in the UK were *double* what they are now (at around 3,000 hours per year). Working lives were also longer: boys and girls might leave school at 12 or 13, whereas now employment rates don't peak till the mid-20s as students leave higher education, and many retire from work before reaching the state pension age. The issue here is not that we cannot afford pensions but that the nature of work has changed and we need a different set of arrangements for pensions to reflect this.

Individuals retire at different ages and the present generation of people over 60 have the advantage of well-resourced pensions. Only those who have not accumulated the assets necessary to choose retirement will be forced to work on. The affluent will continue to be able to afford to retire early. Worst of all, it is those most likely to end up working up to the state pension age who will be least likely to survive to enjoy a long retirement. The poor, those in manual jobs, or living in areas of social deprivation, have life expectancies *from five to ten years below* their more privileged peers.[21]

---

[21] For further information in the area see <www.ons.gov.uk/ons/taxonomy/index.html?nscl=Life+Expectancies>, accessed 23 March 2014.

None of this means that older people shouldn't be encouraged to work longer – if that is what they choose to do. To suggest, however, that an economy as productive as that of the UK 'cannot afford' to let its least affluent members leave work until they are 68 or 70 is quite mistaken. This is not about a policy driven by economic or demographic pressure but reflects the political debate about the place of the State and particularly the resourcing of the welfare state in a cash-limited economy.

The fear of dementia

One of the reasons that we have an ambiguous relationship with age and ageing is the fear of what shape old age might take in us. As the number of older people increases, there are few of us who do not know the effects dementia and related diseases have on individuals and their families. Definitions of dementia vary across time and place (at what point does the general weakening of cognitive function that accompanies 'normal' ageing cross the threshold to dementia?) but there is a close connection to age and 'early onset' dementia is very rare.

As life expectancy increases we could expect many older people to live with, and die with, dementia. It is anticipated that the number of people in the UK with dementia will double in the next forty years (800,000 people with dementia in 2012; 1,000,000 people with dementia in 2021; 1,700,000 people with dementia in 2051).[22]

If the dementia from which someone is suffering is mild and compatible with independent living, it has few implications. If it is severe, it has the potential rapidly to increase demand for social and health care.

What we really do not know is how the relationship between age and dementia prevalence is changing. The dream scenario

---

[22] See <www.alzheimers.org.uk/infographic>, accessed 23 March 2014.

is that longer lives also mean later dementia: the nightmare one is that longer lives come with a fixed relationship between age and dementia, so that a rapidly increasing proportion of the extra years in longer lives are spent with the condition. We do know of factors that appear *to delay the age of dementia onset*, including more mental, physical, or social activity, something vibrant communities can provide. There have been a number of government initiatives to address the increased number of people living with dementia.[23] Our response to this threat to well-being will be critical in how we collaborate for a good and blessed old age.

The contribution of older people to intergenerational care

Despite the problems associated with ageing, there are many positive attitudes of respect, interest and compassion for older people based on our experience of them as heroic, sacrificial and wise. In communities across the country older people play an important part in sustaining the common good through (for example) volunteering, unpaid childcare and support of neighbours, and they often play a critical part in the care of older partners. Older people in faith communities are often carriers of memory, story and identity.[24]

Grandparents are the most important source of childcare after parents themselves, more important than either public or private childcare. Older people make an enormous contribution in so many ways to the common good of our families, communities and churches. It is not easy to calculate with

---

[23] The dementia friendly communities champion group (of the Department of Health) has been working with the Alzheimer's Society and the Dementia Action Alliance on a programme of work. See <http://dementiachallenge.dh.gov.uk/category/areas-for-action/communities/>, accessed 14 September 2014.

[24] For a fascinating collection of stories about spirituality in later life see Keith Albans and Malcolm Johnson (eds), *God, Me and Being Very Old* (London: SCM Press, 2013).

accuracy the net contribution of older people to the common good of societies. Figures from the United Nations (UN) show that more than 70 per cent of men and nearly 40 per cent of women over 60 continue to work.[25] Age Concern UK published the following figures for unpaid care in the UK (2010): 3 million unpaid carers (replacement value of £15 billion); grandparent care – one-quarter of families use grandparent care each week (replacement value of £4 billion); volunteering – 5 million older volunteers (replacement value of £5 billion). This equates to a total value of £24 billion (equivalent to 3 per cent of the economy).

There is one area that is particularly important – that of the intergenerational relationship. As family structures become looser and more scattered geographically, it is vital that there be regular opportunities for interaction between younger and older people.[26] As we explore what might make for a good community we shall need to address the ways in which the good of older people can practically be part of the well-being of all people. Our vision must embrace the need to strengthen the bonds that bind all generations in our community together, especially at a time when these are under particular strain.

Valuing age: how might theology shape our debates?

Much of the research that has taken place in North America over the past twenty or thirty years has indicated that people

---

[25] See *The Forgotten Workforce*, <www.helpage.org/download/4c3cf79de7a82/>, accessed 29 March 2014.

[26] In some congregations, there are older people with time to establish mutually nourishing relationships with younger children who need some support in reading. Older people play an important part in the sharing of memories through formal and informal oral history projects.

beyond mid-age become more spiritual, and therefore more open to some of the religious questions that theology asks.[27] Among the many reasons for this increased 'religiosity' are two core realities.

The first is that beyond mid-age people are closer to their deaths than their births. This increased sense of awareness of mortality is linked with another feature of the second half of life. This is a preparedness to face up to one's limitations, deficiencies and disappointments that both hurt and threaten us. As individuals face their failures and mistakes, questions open up about what makes for human flourishing and well-being. Old age is the time when a person may look back over their significant relationships, the security that comes from homes made, children nurtured and careers developed. This increased and developed sense of the spiritual is forged out of life's failures as well as its successes. This research is validated through my own experience of pastoral work with older people, which reflects the significant reality of spiritual growth in the final years of living.[28]

The second core reality, found at the heart of all pastoral work, is the belief that every human being of whatever age is unique and equally precious in the sight of God. We belong together and our vision of the common good is dependent upon understanding what each of us has the capacity to contribute to the rich tapestry of humanity. This will differ at different stages of our living and will not depend solely on our economic status, our independence and youthfulness, or our capacity to be consumers. We shall need to explore a variety of

---

[27] See Eugene Bianchi, *Aging as a Spiritual Journey* (New York: Crossroad, 1990); and Melvin A. Kimble, Susan H. McFadden, James W. Ellor and James J. Seeber (eds), *Aging, Spirituality and Religion: A Handbook* (Minneapolis: Fortress Press, 1995).

[28] Susan A. Eisenhandler, *Keeping the Faith in Late Life* (New York: Springer Publishing, 2003).

ways in which everyone at each age might be able to make a contribution from the wisdom of their particular experience and sustain a sense of self-worth and purpose in society.

A failing of today's society is to set the old over and against the young, in a state of mutual incomprehension. In fact, the old need the young and the young the old. An integration of the generations is critical to a mutually supportive society.[29]

Three tasks which face all who are growing old provide distinctive gifts that we can offer to all the generations:

1 the task of completing our work – not just of finishing it but of deriving from it the wisdom of experience to be passed on to our successors;
2 the task of reflecting on our life – of reflecting on its underlying coherence as a service of God and its failures to realise the opportunities of service which we were given;
3 the task of hope – of witnessing not only to the value of a life well lived but also to the gift of faith in a God who will sustain us even in and through the moment of death itself.[30]

Together these tasks provide the distinctive contribution the elderly can make to all the generations, and the means of bridging the gaps between them. They offer the prospect of fulfilment both to those who are old and to those who one day will be.

I want to make a plea for us to support the development of very different ways of speaking about what we struggle with as we grow older. How ought we to grow old? Or what does it mean

---

[29] See Michael D. McNally, *Honoring Elders* (New York: Columbia University Press, 2009); and Amanda Genier, *Transitions and the Life Course: Challenging the Constructions of 'Growing Old'* (Bristol: Policy Press, 2012).

[30] See Peter Coleman, *Belief and Ageing; Spiritual Pathways in Later Life* (Bristol: Policy Press, 2011); Elizabeth MacKinlay, *The Spiritual Dimension of Ageing* (London: Jessica Kingsley Publishers, 2001). Robert Archley writes about these issues from an American perspective in *Spirituality and Ageing* (Baltimore: Johns Hopkins University Press, 2009).

to grow old? How do we nurture virtue in older age? How can we enable older people to make their valuable contribution?

Ageing has been brought under the dominion of scientific management, which is primarily interested in the physical aspects of ageing in order to explain and control the ageing process. How do we find a way of giving voice to the things that really matter? And if we can find a voice, who will listen to us?

Christians can offer alternative understandings of the moral significance of growing old. The cross is not a symbol of the fragility of a virtuous life. It is not just a story but the ground of a reality that subsumes the stories that all our lives would tell. The cross of Jesus is the grace of God; it is the ground of our hope; and it is the promise of our deliverance. Part of what we learn from the death of Christ is the central reality of sin and the necessity for us to learn to forgive others. In the cross the scars and pain and vulnerabilities of all the ages are absorbed into the love of God. In this embrace there is healing, forgiveness and transformation.

Old age is forever stereotyped. For some it simply does not matter and any attempt to attach particular significance to it is misplaced. We all age in different ways. We have older people that we admire and some whom we might be determined not to imitate.

While visiting some of the innovative work being undertaken by the Church in Sydney (especially in the area of housing for people living with dementia) I asked an experienced nurse why she thought that Church and society found it so problematic to engage with age. 'I am sure I know why that is,' she confidently replied, 'we are afraid of growing older: we need to befriend the elderly stranger in ourselves.'

We might take ourselves back to the car journey that I described at the beginning of this chapter. Can we imagine what old age might be like for us? Could this reimagining possibly be the basis of the shaping of public policy? And what spiritual resources would we need to help us do this?

Conclusions

In this chapter we have taken an overview of some of the issues that shape our present public debate about age and ageing in twenty-first-century Britain. It remains to be seen how far these questions might frame or shape the way people make democratic choices, but we must keep the human reality of older people to the forefront of our debates. In the choices that we make about how to provide for those most vulnerable in our communities, we shall want to work across professional boundaries to provide the best care and support of older people. This will include a commitment to person-centred care that seeks to maintain health, independence and active life in older age. The rising numbers of older people living with dementia will make particular demands on mental health services. An older population will put demands upon how communities and families organise for housing and both formal and informal care. These are economic issues about resources but also questions about how far the State can meet our expectations.

There will certainly need to be a change in attitude to inheritance, retirement and patterns of work. We shall need to ask ourselves about our responsibility for the vulnerable and poor older people in our society. These are issues of care and how we empower individuals, professionals and institutions to deliver better services for the sake of our communities.

At the beginning of this chapter I shared a lesson in the importance of recognising ageing in ourselves through others. This is about generating a compassion shaped by imagination that can help us to appreciate the true meaning and significance of ageing. Age can be a wise and challenging teacher. Older people can show how little time we give, in all our bureaucracy and busyness, to consider what substance and depth mean in being human. It is no accident that older people become more spiritual, and that they can help us to perceive that age is essentially a spiritual task.

This making of the soul takes shape when our human life is expressed in and through our stories. We need to value older people by listening to them. Their narratives need pondering, retelling, organising and appropriating. How might the Churches work together in moving age, older people and our responsibility to them further up the political agenda? How can those with the power to engage with ageism deal with the impoverishment of living that some older people embrace? It is perhaps the mature aged, rather than the young, who can become for us the prophets of our time, witnessing to a present pregnant with wisdom for living and pointing to a future filled with hope.

9

Improving the health of our representative democracy

RUTH FOX

————•◆•————

Introduction: disillusioned, disengaged but not uninterested

An opinion poll by Ipsos MORI in 2014 found that nearly three out of every five voters now expects more from government than they do from God.[1] The comparison is of course facetious, but it encapsulates one of the central problems at the heart of representative democracy today. There is a huge gap between public expectations and the capacity of our elected representatives to meet them; between the public's democratic ideal and the reality of day-to-day politics.

For all its imperfections, representative democracy remains the best form of political decision-making at our disposal. Few among us would relish the alternatives and, over the past half century, our political system has delivered relative peace and stability, economic prosperity and living standards unimaginable to our forebears. And yet, a damaging 'anti-politics' mood is gnawing away at the democratic roots of our society which, if left unchecked, threatens to cast doubt on the legitimacy of representative politics regardless of which party may be in power in the future.

---

[1] Ipsos MORI/King's College London, *Political Leadership Poll*, 14 January 2014.

The most public manifestation of public disillusion is evidenced in declining levels of voter turnout at general elections and the hollowing out of political parties. But this is just the tip of the iceberg. Members of Parliament and political parties are increasingly treated with public contempt. The discontent is directed at all the mainstream political class and goes well beyond particular dislike of any one party or politician. Although generally proud of our democracy, the public loathe politics and although they recognise Parliament's essential role at the heart of that democracy they are deeply dissatisfied with it and with the representatives they elect to it.

There has never been a golden age in politics and historically politicians have rarely been held in high regard. William Hogarth's satirical depictions in the eighteenth century were just as cruelly damning as the Spitting Image puppets of the late twentieth. And such was public contempt for the political class in nineteenth-century Britain that, as fire took hold of the Palace of Westminster on 16 October 1834, contemporary accounts record much cheering and jeering from the crowd that gathered to watch the conflagration. The public outcry at the parliamentary expenses scandal of 2009 – echoed in the Maria Miller and Patrick Mercer affairs of 2014[2] – represents merely the latest chapter in public disaffection with the political system rather than the emergence of a new narrative.

But the challenge facing politicians today is perhaps greater in depth and scale than anything previously witnessed. For on almost every indicator of democratic health the trends

---

[2] Maria Miller MP, Secretary of State for Culture, Media and Sport, resigned from the government in April 2014 following an investigation into her expenses by the Parliamentary Commissioner for Standards. That same month, Patrick Mercer MP resigned from the House of Commons, prompting a by-election in his Newark constituency, when he learned that the Committee for Standards was to recommend his suspension from the House for six months for engaging in paid advocacy and failing to register his interests properly.

have been downwards since the early 1970s and have worsened since 2000.

In the late 1950s and early 1960s the public were generally content with and proud of the political system and its competence in delivering for citizens, as well as in their own ability to influence the decision-making of that system both nationally and locally. Today, however, the reverse is largely true.

For over a decade the Hansard Society has tracked public attitudes to politics in our *Audit of Political Engagement*, the only annual health check on our democracy.[3] Where opinion polls in the early 1970s showed that nearly half the public thought our system of governing generally worked well, today our *Audit* shows that just a third of the public agree.[4] In terms of the role individuals believe they can personally exercise in the system, consistently around only a third of the public say that if people like themselves get involved in politics they can really change the way the country is run. This low sense of their own personal political efficacy is buttressed by the perception that they have very little influence on decision-making: only around a quarter feel they have some influence over local decision-making and around just 15 per cent say the same about their influence at the national level.[5] In stark contrast, in 1963, 60 per cent of the public believed that they would be taken seriously if they raised an issue with the government.[6]

Nonetheless, the public's interest in politics and desire to be involved continues to outpace their sense of efficacy and influence. The terms 'apathy' or 'apathetic' are frequently used

---

[3] <www.hansardsociety.org.uk/research/public-attitudes/audit-of-political-engagement/#reports-and-data>, accessed 15 September 2014.

[4] Hansard Society, *Audit of Political Engagement 11* (2014), pp. 49–51 (see <www.hansardsociety.org.uk/wp-content/uploads/2014/04/Audit-of-Political-Engagement-11-2014.pdf>).

[5] Hansard Society, *Audit of Political Engagement 11* (2014), pp. 51–8.

[6] G. Almond and S. Verba, *The Civic Culture Revisited* (Boston: Little, Brown, 1980).

in popular commentary on public attitudes. But the public is neither uninterested nor indifferent to politics. The Scottish independence referendum demonstrated that to powerful effect: 97 per cent of the public registered to vote, 84.6 per cent actually did so, 16- and 17-year-olds voted for the first time, and the campaign was notable for the vibrant level of civic engagement. Here the issue was so important, the stakes so high, that people felt their participation could make a real difference. But when it comes to Westminster party politics, the picture is very different.

Over the past decade the level of interest in politics has remained around the 50 per cent mark.[7] And today, broadly four in ten people say that they would like to be involved locally or nationally in decision-making and eight in ten say that they would be prepared to undertake some form of political activity if they felt strongly about an issue.[8] But in practice they are disengaging from the formal political processes focused on Westminster rather than seeking to play an active part in them.

These problems of political engagement can be found in most industrialised democracies but the UK situation is particularly acute because the decline is happening across so many indicators and the rate of deterioration continues to sharpen.

The causes and consequences of 'anti-politics'

Declining electoral participation

Our democratic system is designed for mass participation on the part of the electorate and political parties. But the past three general elections have produced the lowest turnouts on record

---

[7] Hansard Society, *Audit of Political Engagement 1–11* (2003–14).

[8] Hansard Society, *Audit of Political Engagement 11* (2014), p. 28.

since 1918. Participation levels of 59 per cent, 61 per cent and 65 per cent in the 2001, 2005 and 2010 elections respectively are significantly below the 75 per cent plus turnout levels recorded on a regular basis until the early 1990s. The problem is mirrored in other elections for posts outside Westminster. In November 2012, for example, elections were held for the first time for 41 new police and crime commissioners across England and Wales. The government argued that electing the new commissioners would empower the public, increase local accountability and give people a direct say in how their streets are policed. And yet, just 15 per cent of the public voted in the elections and in one ward in Newport in Gwent no elector visited the polling station.

And there is growing inequality of participation: younger and less affluent voters are increasingly unlikely to vote. Just 44 per cent of 18–24-year-olds voted at the 2010 general election compared to 76 per cent of those aged 65 and above. Until the late 1980s voter participation levels were broadly the same across all social classes; but by the 2010 general election the most affluent voters participated in much higher numbers than the least affluent. The result is that older, better off voters are accorded a disproportionate degree of attention and influence in the political process.

Electoral participation is not the only indicator of a democracy's health, nor perhaps even the best one. But in our parliamentary system it is the foundation that underpins the principles of representation and accountability. We elect politicians locally and nationally for a set period and then have the opportunity to make a judgement at the end of the term about whether to return them or to 'kick the rascals out'. So the decline in voting at elections raises challenging issues for the future in terms of the credibility and viability of conventional politics as we know it.

The decline of political parties and civic associations

These concerns are compounded when we look at the state of party politics. In our democracy political parties perform several functions: to articulate and aggregate interests, to foster political participation, to recruit political candidates and organise effective government. In the 1950s nearly 4 million people (approximately 1 in 10) in this country belonged to a political party. Today, it's estimated that just 1 per cent of the adult population – fewer than half a million people – are members.[9] Parties remain the key entry point to representative politics but, being atypical of the populations they serve, they are increasingly perceived to be out of touch and are no longer the vital deliberative link between representative government and civil society that they once were. And the declining social base of political parties means that political leaders are increasingly drawn from a small pool of professional political activists so disliked by a public that abhors what they perceive to be their lack of 'life experience'.

A strong civil society is essential to the quality of our democracy but the decline of political parties has also been mirrored by a decline in allegiance to trade unions, churches, and voluntary groups that previously provided the trusted networks of mutual assistance and reciprocity that helped mobilise political interest and participation and developed and honed their in-depth knowledge of local communities. Such associations brought people together to work co-operatively, an essential feature of democratic engagement. But associational activity and a sense of belonging has been overtaken by individualistic, time-limited forms of participation.

---

[9] F. McGuinness, *Membership of UK Political Parties*, House of Commons Library Standard Note, SN/SG/5125 (2012).

A culture of consumerism

The decline of social capital coupled with the emergence of an individualistic, consumerist culture does not provide the nurturing environment required for representative politics, at the heart of which is the achievement of compromise through the peaceful mediation of different, often competing, interests. There is rarely a unified public view on any issue. Politicians therefore have to chart a complex, difficult course between clashing interests, competing resource demands and the variable needs of different segments of the population. The policy decisions that result from this process of negotiation and conciliation are often a necessary compromise between the ideal and the possible. And the forging of such compromise can often be messy and difficult. It is not well suited to a consumerist culture where instant consumption can sate any personal desire and people are encouraged to believe they can always have what they want.

The culture of consumerism also feeds a marketisation of politics that damages politics and politicians. Rather than contending visions between politicians of integrity, each committed to their own perception of the national interest, politics has increasingly been reduced to a marketing game. In this game, each side offers up promises to the public but rarely engages in open and forthright debate about the negotiations and compromises that are required to achieve those promises.

The public sense that today's politicians lack the courage to engage properly with them about the serious issues facing the country. And when the bargain of candour between government and the governed is abandoned it destroys public faith in the political process. The combination of culture and communication – the unwillingness to answer a straightforward question, the evasiveness and adversarial finger-pointing – feeds the sense that people are being deceived, manipulated and kept in the dark.

When members of other professions engage in argument and competition, they generally conduct their disagreements in a private way, hidden from public view. In contrast, politicians engaged in partisan battle routinely go on television and radio and openly criticise each other in the strongest terms, all of which has a corrosive impact on public attitudes in the long term. Imagine visiting the doctor for diagnosis of a worrying medical condition to find on leaving the waiting room that another doctor is waiting to greet you, only promptly to accuse the first one of incompetence, dishonesty and mistreatment. But such behaviour is the daily cut and thrust of politics. The onus must be on political leaders to find a way to engage with the public in more effective, authentic ways that highlight differences between them but in a less rancorous manner. A new art of political conversation and dialogue is needed to replace the unedifying shouting match.

The increasing complexity of government

Public frustration is also rooted in a pessimistic belief that no matter who is in office, or what they do, in the end nothing really changes. The institutional framework of our democracy has become more complex as a result of managerial reforms in public policy, the marginalisation of local government, devolution and the growing role of the European Union. As the range of functions performed by government has expanded into new, complex, often highly technical areas of policy-making, the very same forces of globalisation which have augmented this expansion of the policy sphere also serve to highlight the limits to the power of elected representatives. And as the areas of decision-making for which politicians are deemed responsible have expanded, parliamentarians have conversely, in the light of declining public confidence and trust, increasingly delegated responsibility and oversight to independent experts and arms-length bodies, consequently changing the contours of political accountability. Yet at the same time they have further complicated the picture by creating new layers of elected representation whose role, powers and relationship to other levels of government remain a mystery to most people.

Citizens thus find it almost impossible to track and understand the processes that led to a particular decision and are left feeling confused and disorientated by the political system. Unsurprisingly, declining levels of public satisfaction with and influence on politics are linked to a pervasive perception that decisions are now made by distant, unaccountable institutions: by unelected judges, the European Union, or multi-national corporations, to name just a few.

Perceptions of influence

Coupled with this there is a rising perception that citizens' interests are subverted by unaccountable concentrations of influence, power and money in our politics. The way we pay for politics and permit the exercise of influence in the political system is central to our democracy because it both reflects and shapes our social values. Democracy cannot work fairly if the resourcing of our political system leads to the over-representation of some interests and the unfair under-representation of others.

Our system is rarely, if ever, corrupted by a direct offering and acceptance of a bribe, but the web of reciprocity that envelops politicians, often disproportionate to the scale of influence, money or in-kind support offered, causes lasting reputational damage. The first wound inflicted on Tony Blair's reputation came just six months after winning a landslide election victory in 1997 when he was accused of granting Formula 1 motor racing an exemption from the new tobacco advertising ban shortly after a meeting with the head of Formula 1, Bernie Ecclestone, who was also a major donor to the Labour Party. More recently the coalition government has similarly suffered, most notably when evidence emerged of the amount of contact between the Culture Secretary Jeremy Hunt and his advisers and the lobbyist for Rupert Murdoch's News Corp at a time when the Minister was considering the company's proposed £8 billion takeover of BSkyB and News Corp was embroiled in the phone hacking scandal.

When evidence of alleged impropriety emerges, it is harder for citizens to believe that decisions are rooted in the public interest, and made on the basis of principle or a rigorous evidence base. Even small, systemic distortions to the policy agenda and decision-making process undermine public faith and confidence in our system of governing. This, in turn, contributes to a reduced public interest in politics and undermines the motivation of citizens to engage in the political process.

The media and its effect on political behaviour

The approach of the 24/7 media also has a corrosive impact on public attitudes to politics and their willingness to engage in it. Our *Audit of Political Engagement* shows that the media generally – including television – do little to benefit our democracy in terms of nourishing political engagement and from the perspective of political citizenship it is better to read no newspaper at all than to read a tabloid.[10]

In the guise of appearing impartial the press has become more adversarial and aggressive, fusing reporting and comment. Much of the political coverage is negative in tone, often bordering on the cynical. Controversial measures attract headlines but much

---

[10] Hansard Society, *Audit of Political Engagement 9, Part 2: The Media and Politics* (2012), pp. 38–41.

political work, in terms of the real impact on people's everyday lives, is often technical, detailed and non-controversial. There is, as a consequence, a tension between the visibility of parliamentary work and its importance and the extent to which it is reported.

Politics is treated as a game with an array of commentators on hand to issue snap judgements and award points. Performance rather than the substance of debate largely takes precedence and the politics of personal destruction is often to the fore. The idea of politics as a theatre of controversy, where the only interest lies in conflict and who emerges from it, effectively precludes serious consideration and coverage of any politicians who are more consensual in their approach.

Both the traditional and new social media culture are also important contributory factors in the short-termism that dominates political action and feeds the public's sense that, regardless of whichever party is in power, nothing ever really changes. Democracy often works best when it works slowly and deliberatively but this is at odds with a media culture that favours an instant rather than a reflective response, and preferences simplicity over nuanced complexity.

Politicians can at best plan five years ahead courtesy of the Fixed Term Parliament Act, but for many of the big strategic problems facing the country this is still too short a timescale and the attention-span and patience of the public and media undermine the prospect of a more considered approach. Big, long-term challenges facing the country such as economic renewal, housing provision, climate change, pension reform, energy security and delivery of transport infrastructure such as high speed rail cannot readily be explained in 30-second soundbites on the evening news or 140 characters on Twitter. These forums simply do not provide the space for political conversation about the important choices facing the country.

Perceptions of politicians and Parliament

It is one of the great paradoxes of modern politics that MPs live and work in closer connection with their constituents than any generation before them and yet the public is less satisfied with them than ever. Less than a quarter of the population report being satisfied with the way that MPs generally are doing their job and only a third say the same about their own local MP.[11] The political class is now drawn from a narrower base than ever before, thus perpetuating a sense of 'us' and 'them': regardless of how MPs start out, most people believe that MPs are not like 'ordinary people' and are remote from the everyday lives of the people they represent. They are perceived to be in politics only to make money or advance themselves socially at the expense of others, rather than to represent their constituents or the country's interest. When their trustworthiness is ranked alongside other occupations, politicians occupy the relegation zone alongside tabloid journalists, estate agents and bankers.[12] Only one in five of us say we would be 'proud' if a child or relative became a politician; in contrast, 75 per cent of us would be 'proud' if one of our relatives became a doctor and 64 per cent a school head teacher.[13]

The perception of Parliament as out of touch – a place for the wealthy, public school elite – is particularly pronounced at present because so many senior politicians, especially in the current Cabinet (in 2014), so readily fit this stereotype. But the unrepresentative nature of politics – a democratic deficit that feeds public disillusion – will only be resolved if *all* the

[11] Hansard Society, *Audit of Political Engagement 10* (2013), pp. 53–5.

[12] See, e.g., Committee on Standards in Public Life, *Survey of Public Attitudes towards Conduct in Public Life 2012* (2013), pp. 13–14; and Ipsos MORI, *Trust Poll*, 13 February 2013 (<http://www.ipsos-mori.com/Assets/Docs/Polls/Feb2013_Trust_Topline.PDF>, accessed 15 September 2014).

[13] Hansard Society, *Audit of Political Engagement 7* (2010), pp. 94–5.

parties take concerted action to select candidates who better reflect the social make-up of the country.

The sense of politicians being 'out of touch' also manifests itself in relation to the lack of civility on display in Parliament. The behaviour that the public witnesses, particularly at Prime Minister's Questions, is simply not like that seen in most other walks of life and is considered unprofessional. Only 12 per cent of the public say that Prime Minister's Questions makes them proud of Parliament and nearly a third of the public say it puts them off politics.[14] The public wants passion and commitment in debate, but not misbehaviour; it wants the issues that affect daily lives to be treated seriously and not as 'pantomime farce'; and it wants politicians to behave like grown-ups, not children.

But public attitudes to and expectations of MPs have to be seen in the context of a general lack of knowledge about politics and what being an MP entails. Most people can readily identify the role and function of a judge, a doctor, or a teacher, but many of us find it much more difficult to identify just what it is that MPs actually do. Consequently a number of myths persist in which current MPs – depicted as slavish, ineffectual lobby fodder for their party whips – compare unfavourably to their predecessors. But in truth there has never been a golden age of independently minded backbenchers and today's MPs are far from supine. In the past decade we have witnessed the largest rebellion since the repeal of the Corn Laws over Iraq and a backbench revolt that stymied government intervention in Syria. There have been historically large rebellions on the government backbench over issues such as Trident, Europe, tuition fees and foundation hospitals.

---

[14] Hansard Society, *Tuned in or Turned Off? Public Attitudes to Prime Minister's Questions* (2014), pp. 45–8.

A golden age decline thesis also extends to Parliament. But as with MPs, there was never a 1950s parliamentary nirvana of rigorous scrutiny and superior law making to which we should aspire today. On any objective test, Parliament in 2015 is a stronger institution than it was in decades past. The work of select committees has vastly improved scrutiny of government and other bodies, such as the media, bankers and the BBC. Public Bill Committees now facilitate public engagement in the legislative process, backbench business debates allow discussion of topical issues that the frontbenches might prefer to avoid, and the Liaison Committee can question the Prime Minister directly several times a year. And the House of Lords, emboldened by a mix of elected hereditary peers and appointed members, is a more rigorous scrutiny body than ever before.

Parliament is far from perfect and substantial reforms are still required but, seen in historical context, it is immeasurably better than in times past. But whether the public's critique is accurate or fair is now largely irrelevant. The reputation of our politicians is rooted in public perceptions built on past experiences as well as anticipated future behaviour and the public don't expect much to change.

So if that is the diagnosis, what of the prescription?

Successive governments have pursued a smorgasbord of constitutional and institutional reforms designed to restore public trust, enhance opportunities for citizen participation in decision-making, and provide greater transparency and openness. But few, if any, of these initiatives – devolution, referendums, direct election of local mayors and police and crime commissioners, e-petitions, citizens' juries, a tightening of the regulations governing party funding and the setting up of new oversight bodies such as the Committee on Standards in Public Life – have had any marked impact on public attitudes to date.

In part this is because politicians persist in introducing reforms that do nothing really to address the underlying reasons why people don't want to vote or to get involved in politics in other ways. And too often their responses smack of short-term political calculation rather than cogent adherence to principle, leading to unforeseen and unintended consequences that undermine their position still further.

The political focus on changes designed to engender trust is almost doomed to failure from the start; how can politicians regain what they have never really possessed in the first place? Reforms to provide for greater openness and transparency, while providing a restraint against abuse, have also had a detrimental impact by fostering a culture of suspicion with knock-on effects for the public's perception of the system of governance, the relevance of institutions and the influence which they, as one individual, can exercise in the system. The creation of new posts – for example, directly elected mayors and police and crime commissioners – has been met with a great yawn by a public that simply anticipates more buck-passing when things go wrong. And the drive for greater public participation in the political process is anathema to many citizens who hold a narrow view of what politics is, and who rarely make the connection between their most pressing interests and the seemingly remote and esoteric world of Westminster or town hall politics.

So what should be done? The solution may lie in the pursuit of change in five key areas. First, there is now a case for less democracy but more accountability. A never-ending cycle of elections in which fewer and fewer people participate is not benefiting citizens, elected representatives or political parties. Second, politicians need to change the way in which they conduct politics, adopting a more values-based approach. All professions depend for their public standing on the strength of their values and ethical base as well as on demonstrations of their competence. Politics is no exception. Third, we have to stop the continual denigration of politics, reminding ourselves of the underlying benefits of representative democracy. That will require an end to the de-politicisation of public life, an end to ritualised public disagreement, and the creation of a more open, honest discourse about the important role politics plays in our daily life. Fourth, we need to rejuvenate citizenship education in order to foster a better understanding of politics, to manage public expectations and to stimulate participation: in short, to remind ourselves why politics matters. And finally, as the parties conclude their manifestos for the 2015 general election, there needs to be a more strategic approach to political reform, rooted in clear principles to reshape cogently the future character of our democratic system in an age when technology makes direct citizen participation possible to a greater extent than ever before.

Less democracy, more accountability

It is somewhat heretical to call for less democracy but the sheer number of elections held each year in different parts of the country using five different electoral systems is detrimental to public engagement as well as to the health of our party system.

At the time of writing, since the 2010 general election depending on where you live in the country you will have had an opportunity to vote for a county councillor and your Member of the European Parliament. You may have voted for a district councillor once or three times depending on whether your council is elected all at once or by 'thirds'. You might have had the chance to choose a parish councillor or town councillor, perhaps even a mayor, and you will certainly have had a vote for a police and crime commissioner. If you live in London you will have had the option to vote for the Mayor as well as your representative in the London Assembly and if you live in Scotland, Wales or Northern Ireland you will have had a vote in the devolved Parliament and Assembly elections.

Given this patchwork quilt of elections and voting systems, it is not surprising that people are put off from voting, and confused about who does what and who they should therefore hold responsible for the decisions that affect their lives. In all the elections that have taken place since 2010, turnout rose above 40 per cent only in the national elections to the devolved legislatures.

The electoral system needs to be rationalised and the representative function strengthened to provide greater accountability to the public. This will require a rethink about the voting systems we use, MPs rather than independent bodies being given greater responsibility at the national level and the restructuring of local government. The aim should be to both empower national and local elected representatives and more clearly delineate the lines of responsibility, and therefore accountability, between them. Such radical reform is a once-in-a-generation step but the outcome of the Scottish independence referendum may provide the necessary impetus.

But if the representative function is to be strengthened, parties must become much more serious about political recruitment. At present the number of elections is turning local parties into little more than 'Get Out The Vote' machines servicing the annual round of democracy each May. With supporters confined to an electoral hamster wheel of leafleting and canvassing, important but often time-consuming functions necessary for the future health of a party – such as fostering in-depth relationships with local civic groups, political education and fund-raising – are side-lined and often non-existent. The most damaging manifestation of the problem can be seen in the recruitment of candidates who are increasingly drawn from a narrow social base, often with extensive political connections but limited 'life experience' and record of professional success in other fields. The criteria used to select candidates don't really reflect the needs of modern government or address public expectations, and insufficient effort is devoted by parties to reaching out in communities to find potential representatives with a broader range of experiences and skills. So a rethink is needed about the skill-set required of the modern representative nationally and locally. But much more radical measures, such as job sharing, child care support, improved access to training and time off for public service, may also be needed if people from a broader range of backgrounds are to be persuaded to stand for election.

A more values-based approach to politics

As a physical building the Palace of Westminster, more than most, carries profound ideological symbolism in relation to probity and integrity based on implicit understandings about the nature and morality of law. Yet the public do not believe that the politicians who inhabit it are generally men and women of probity and integrity. Members of Parliament are perceived to have enormous power and influence at their disposal and to make important decisions that affect the lives of ordinary people. But the public believes politicians consistently fail to set an example in doing so.

What the public wants are politicians who have a high moral outlook on their work, who regard service in Parliament as more of a vocation than a job, and who prioritise the public interest over private gain. Indeed, three-quarters of us believe politicians should be prepared to make personal sacrifices along the way if they want to play a role in running the country. As a calling, pursuing a career in politics should be done for its own sake; income or other material rewards should be peripheral.

More is expected of politicians than other people precisely because of their role at the apex of our democracy. But here there is a clear tension in public attitudes: is it realistic or fair to hold MPs to a higher standard than that to which we would hold ourselves and is it consistent to want MPs to be like us, to be 'ordinary', and yet to expect the extraordinary of them? The answer is no but the dilemma needs to be tackled and politicians need to work with the grain of public opinion.

One way of doing this would be to adopt the 'duty of care' approach being considered in relation to other sectors that have suffered an egregious loss of reputation in recent years, such as the banks and the media. Hitherto the concept has related entirely to the idea that a 'duty of care' obligation was owed to elements of civil society such as the armed forces or the elderly. But it is now being extended to other sectors. Lord Puttnam, for example, argues that a duty of care 'for our shared but fragile democratic values' should be developed in relation to the media, focusing on standards and values such as honesty, accuracy and impartiality.[15] A number of professions publicly demonstrate their commitment to a shared set of values and principles, to ethical behaviour and integrity. Police officers swear an oath when they join the police service, doctors take the Hippocratic oath and lawyers also swear an oath to ethical conduct. Members of Parliament do swear an oath at the start of a Parliament but this is one of loyalty to the Crown and

---

[15] See, e.g., Lord Puttnam, *Speech at the Institute of International and European Affairs*, Dublin, 22 March 2013; and David Puttnam, 'Does the media have a "duty of care"?' TedXHouses ofParliament, June 2013, (<http://www.ted.com/talks/david_puttnam_what_happens_when_the_media_s_priority_is_profit>, accessed 15 September 2014).

there is little if no discussion, at least in public view in the Chamber, of their ethical obligations and need to observe the House's Code of Conduct.

The starting point for adopting a 'duty of care' to our democracy should therefore be an augmenting of the current oaths to incorporate a public declaration by MPs and Peers of commitment to ethical conduct, integrity and their mutual obligations to uphold the reputation of Parliament. This would act as a powerful public reminder to all new Members of their responsibilities at the start of each Parliament, and reinforce the fact that it is a duty which cuts across partisan differences and which it is in their mutual self-interest to uphold. This then needs to be buttressed by a rigorous and transparent sanctions process for when they bring the institution into disrepute, up to and including expulsion in the absence of any power of public recall.

A new standards framework should be buttressed by the adoption of a job description that defines the roles, responsibilities and expectations of MPs. Such a measure may seem cosmetic but is symbolically important in the context of narrowing the perceived gulf between representatives and citizens ('them' and 'us'). Defining the role will not curb poor behaviour on its own but it would at least remove a 'difference' that currently exists between politicians and the public which, when constituents are confronted with the knowledge that MPs do not have a job description (usually when cases of misbehaviour hit the headlines), tends to be a source of some dismay.

Beyond issues of personal probity, there is a further dimension to a more values-based approach that is worth considering. In an age of issue- rather than interest-driven politics, policy choices are more fragmented. Reflecting our consumerist culture the public take a broad-church approach, a form of 'pick and mix' politics that our current party system is not suited to deliver. So political parties that can adapt to a more 'values'-based politics, stressing moral choices in pursuit of a distinct vision for the organisation of society rather than decisions rooted in 'interests' and old ideological divisions predicated on outdated social class differences, may prosper. The managerial, technocratic politics of recent decades has proven dreary and uninspiring, leaving politicians at sea when 'what works' actually doesn't. What's missing from our politics is any sense of overarching vision of the kind that inspired the collective political action of the post-war settlement that delivered so much social progress despite the nation being almost bankrupted by six years of global war. It's also worth remembering that the core planks of that settlement emerged across the parties: the welfare state of the Liberal William Beveridge; the education reforms of the Conservative R. A. Butler; and the NHS brought into being by Labour's Nye Bevan.

Adopting a value-driven approach to politics also requires us to rethink our approach to political engagement itself. Two-thirds of the public continue to have a strong sense of a 'duty' to vote and it is the biggest driver of participation at successive elections.[16] Different age groups see the concept of a 'duty' to vote in different ways; young people, for example, conceive of it in very different ways to older voters. Nonetheless, voting is increasingly discussed in the context of being contingent on an issue or a specific benefit rather than on it being an unambiguously good thing to do. Rather than predicating participation on instrumental, often personal outcomes, we need a renewed emphasis on the broader community good derived from activities undertaken through a sense of social duty and civic responsibility.

---

[16] Hansard Society, *Audit of Political Engagement 11* (2014), pp. 25–6.

Defending politics

If politicians are not continually to disappoint the public then they need to become better at managing public expectations by being clearer about what they promise, by engaging the public in a debate about what is realistically possible and about the inevitable trade-offs and consequences that one political decision may have on another. It means an end to ritualised disagreement and a shift to communicating in a way that better reflects the underlying purpose of representative democracy and its capacity to deliver in the public interest. But for this to happen they need to operate in a political and media environment that is more conducive to an open, honest discourse about policy, parties and the merit of politics itself. Here institutions of civic society – including churches – have an important role to play in addressing the de-politicisation of public life that began in the early 1990s, a consequence of which is that any form of political party activity and association is too often stigmatised and treated as an object of suspicion rather than admiration.

Renewed emphasis on the value and role of active citizenship in politics offers a way forward. Those active in wider society as well as politicians themselves must explain why politics matters: politics and politicians need advocates who will stress the value of representative politics and talk up its importance rather than constantly knock it down. Our political system needs community leaders to be ambassadors for it, demonstrating a faith in and commitment to democracy in spite of its imperfections, prepared to speak out and defend the underlying nobility of the endeavour. They need to become visible and active participants in grass-roots politics and elite politics, not suspicious spectators.

Take the example of party funding. It is not in the public interest that parties should have an over-reliance on institutional sources of funding and/or high value, wealthy donors. But if political parties do not have enough money to carry out their activities, democracy cannot function efficiently. Conversely, nor can democracy work fairly if the sources of party finance lead to the over-representation of some interests and the under-representation of others. The ability of political parties to perform their role and functions in full is compromised by the current ebb and flow of funding and the impact of the political pendulum. The present funding system also handicaps smaller parties who cannot command institutional finance. Reforms to cap national expenditure and thereby curtail undue influence in the political system are needed. But donations to political parties will still remain the preserve of a small minority of wealthy people as long as donating to political parties is not encouraged, valued and respected by wider society. Donations to political parties should rank alongside charitable philanthropy in importance but at present, rather than being seen as an honourable act of citizenship, the reverse is the dominant view.

Rejuvenating citizenship education

To support this process we need to rejuvenate citizenship education – specifically political literacy – for all age groups, but particularly for young people, in order to foster a better understanding of politics, manage public expectations and stimulate participation.

People's perception of what 'politics' is remains narrow and their knowledge and understanding of the basic tenets of our system of parliamentary democracy is worryingly low. As tested in the Hansard Society's annual *Audit of Political Engagement*, two-thirds of the public don't recognise that most of the money that local councils spend is not raised locally through council tax. Despite the level of political debate about Europe, nearly six in ten members of the public (57 per cent) don't know that

British members of the European Parliament are directly elected by British voters. Although the future of the House of Lords was debated extensively between 2010 and 2012 as the coalition considered new legislation to reform the upper chamber, a third of the public (33 per cent) could not correctly identify that members of the House of Lords are not elected. Thirty-nine per cent either answer incorrectly or don't know that government and Parliament are not the same thing and nearly three in 10 (29 per cent) think that 16 is already the minimum age for voting.[17]

High-quality citizenship education, delivered by well-trained and motivated teachers, can improve young people's knowledge, participation levels and the efficacy of their involvement in the political process. Sir Bernard Crick described political literacy as 'a compound of knowledge, skills and attitudes' to enable citizens to navigate their way through the complex nature of politics and decision-making.[18] In the light of the importance of politics in all our lives, it should be considered a basic social skill and treated accordingly.

A more strategic, principled approach to political reform

And finally, with the political parties considering the policy priorities for their election manifestos, it is a relatively safe bet that a plethora of political and constitutional reforms will be unveiled, some new and some a rehash of old commitments that they have previously failed to deliver. Reducing the voting age to 16 will appear in some manifestos, House of Lords reform may be resurrected in others, and a referendum on our continuing membership of the European Union will certainly feature.

---

[17] Hansard Society, *Audit of Political Engagement 10* (2013), pp. 32–5.

[18] B. Crick, *Essays on Citizenship* (London: Continuum, 2000), p. 61.

A constituent's right to recall their MP may be revisited if the legislation promised in this last Parliament is not delivered by the election. Some parties will pledge support for electoral reform, reducing the number of MPs in the House of Commons and equalising the size of all constituencies, and party funding reform may also be resurrected. Much work remains to be done to resolve the future of the devolved nations settlement in the aftermath of the Scottish independence referendum.

Each reform, in isolation, has genuine merit, but as a collective group they lack any animating principle to shape cogently the direction of democratic reform and address the causes and consequences of 'anti-politics' in the long term. And they singularly fail to address the central question now facing the political parties: how is representative politics going to adjust to the challenges posed by the growth in enthusiasm for direct and deliberative democracy – seen most popularly in recent years in the form of petitions and referendums – arising from public disenchantment with party politics and MPs?

This is a challenge that is only likely to grow in the future given that technology now makes citizen participation possible in new ways and on a greater scale than ever before. By lowering the barrier of entry, technology offers new opportunities for a more plural, participative form of politics. Online campaigns can now facilitate quick, cheap, organic initiatives by individuals or loosely aligned groups on single issues, uniting citizens in ways that are now beyond political parties. The 38 Degrees campaign,[19] for example, uses the internet to link up its 2.5 million supporters – numbers that the political parties can only dream of – to discuss and decide on the issues they should campaign on together. Its campaign was instrumental in persuading the coalition government not to go ahead with the proposed sell-off

---

[19] <www.38degrees.org.uk>, accessed 15 September 2014.

of our national forests. And other efforts, blending traditional campaigning methods with the viral power and reach of social media, have led to policy changes in this Parliament concerning the reorganisation of the NHS and the lobbying Bill. Thus technology combined with public disaffection with traditional representative politics is reshaping relations between the public and the political class in favour of more direct forms of democratic engagement.

But there are dangers here. Whereas representative democracy is able to mediate between and balance competing interests, it is likely that some forms of direct democracy – particularly the politics of petition or referendum – rather than increasing involvement, engagement and participation, may simply entrench the views and attitudes of those members of the public who want to be involved – those prepared to shout the loudest – to the detriment of the rest of the population who do not. One only has to look at the situation in California to see the dangers of governing by direct democracy. Rather than empowering more people in the political process citizens have become mere consumers of television advertising in favour of or against ballot initiatives. It is a form of 'audience' rather than 'participative' democracy that, in the absence of real debate, negotiation and compromise, left the state bankrupt and almost ungovernable.

When thinking about the shape of democratic reform in an age of anti-politics, our political leaders thus have to answer several important questions. How will our democratic arrangements be revised to address changing public expectations and behaviours? What principles and criteria will command public support in bridging the gap between representative and direct or deliberative forms of democracy? Unless and until these questions are answered, all other political reforms will lack coherence and the unsatisfactory nature of the patchwork quilt of reform we have experienced for the past quarter century will continue. Politicians should therefore not be surprised if the public response also remains the same.

Conclusion

Public disillusionment with and disengagement from politics are not new phenomena but we are experiencing them today in heightened form. 'Crisis' is a much overused word but certainly, at the current rate of progress, we face the prospect of a crisis of legitimacy in our politics at some point in the near future if electoral turnout and public engagement levels continue to deteriorate. The problem is not going to be rolled back by more piece-meal constitutional and institutional initiatives: reducing the voting age to 16 or enabling constituents to recall their MP, for example, may be useful measures in their own right but they fall woefully short of representing a coherent agenda to tackle the true scale of the anti-politics problem. Indeed, they demonstrate that in many respects the politicians continue to misunderstand the nature of the problem.

It's not possible in one short essay fully to encapsulate the range of change that needs to happen to address the vexed questions facing our democracy. In painting a 'big picture' about the state of representative politics and how it needs to change there are inevitably important details left out. But doing so helps focus on the core priorities. A greater focus on accountability, an expansion of political education, a new emphasis on the duties as well as rights of citizenship and an understanding and valuing of the important contribution that politics and politicians make to our daily lives and national progress are vital in the long term. But ultimately nothing will change unless politicians themselves change, in terms of both their approach to the values and ethics that should underpin politics and their own personal conduct in the future, and how they go about politics itself, adopting a more values-based approach, stressing moral choices in pursuit of a more distinct vision for the organisation of our society. Everyone in Parliament – which is a far more effective body than many of its critics acknowledge – as well as in the political parties, civic society and the media has to recognise that they face a shared challenge to educate and inform the public about the nature and complexities of politics and what can be achieved.

Together, this is a demanding and ambitious prospectus. And the challenge for those of us who care about the state of our democracy is that such changes – requiring a radical transformation in our attitudinal, behavioural, and cultural approach to politics – are often the most difficult to bring about.

10

Building our future

PHILIP MAWER

Faith, Hope and Charity – these are the three anchors which hold fast the ship of the mind amidst the dangers of the waves.[1]

Introduction

It is a brave archbishop who at any point produces, or who contributes to a book about, the values that should underpin our future society, and especially so in the year of a general election. Brave because such a project immediately invites criticism from secularists who object to faith occupying anything other than the private part of our life and from politicians and commentators who sense in what is written support for the views of their opponents.

But an election is a defining moment in a democratic society. It is about more than personalities and individual policies: it is also an opportunity to take stock in a fundamental way of the direction of our society and of the values that are informing its development. It is on the common ground of debate about

---

[1] Alfred the Great, 'Augustine's Soliloquies', in S. Keynes and M. Lapidge (trans.), *Alfred the Great: Asser's Life of King Alfred and Other Contemporary Sources*, p. 142, quoted in Justin Pollard, *Alfred the Great: The Man Who Made England* (London: John Murray, 2005).

those values that secularists and people of faith should be able to meet. And if archbishops cannot write, and encourage others to write, about such matters, one might reasonably ask, 'What are they for?'

This is a book about Faith, Hope and Love (or Charity):[2] Faith – in politics; Hope – for justice; and Love – of neighbour, as expressed in the search for the common good. In chapter 13 of his first letter to the church in Corinth – read at so many church weddings – St Paul identifies these three qualities as hallmarks of the Christian calling. They are a pattern not just for a happy marriage but for a fulfilled life. And, this book suggests, they can also provide a means of ordering the foundations of a healthy politics in a healthy society.

As I write that, I can already detect the sceptics reaching for their pens. But bear with me for a moment. In our darkest moments of despair about the direction of our society, isn't it precisely then that we articulate our fear that we have become, or at least are becoming, a society which has lost faith in the political process and politicians; can see no hope of justice; and has lost a shared understanding of what the common good might be and what values should underpin it?

The contributors to this book do not share that despair. They believe strongly in the value of each and every individual in society, at each and every stage of life. They believe strongly that we can only achieve our full potential in relationship with each other (and, the believers among them would add, with God). They see the aim of political, economic and social action as being to foster and enable solidarity and, through it, human flourishing. And they believe strongly in the possibility, indeed the necessity, of political action to that end.

---

[2] In the King James Version of the Bible, St Paul talks of 'faith, hope and charity' (1 Cor. 13.13).

This book is not, on the one hand, a justification of the role of the market, nor, on the other, a call for a cosy and crushing collectivism. It is certainly not an attempt to impose the values of one religion on the politics of all. It is emphatically a call for a new style of politics, one which is marked by policies which are based on the clear and confident assertion of the values that are essential for our society to be healthy and successful and by personal and collective behaviour that is ethical, transparent and accountable.

Faith in politics

The importance of politics

At a time when politics and politicians are generally derided, this book is an affirmation of the value, indeed the central importance, of politics in our national life.

Politics is both an activity and a set of outcomes. It is, of course, about the distribution and use of power on behalf of us all to achieve socially important ends – including the rule of law, the maintenance of order, and economic and social justice. Too often, contemporary coverage of and discussion about politics focuses on the activity of politics (particularly the ebb and flow of party political debate) rather than on the ends to which political activity should be, or is being directed.

This focus on the tactics of politics rather than on its strategic ends is one of the factors which have undermined public confidence in politics and politicians. This has been compounded by the media's concern with personalities rather than policies; with soundbites rather than with mature and extended discussion of the complex issues with which all politicians have to wrestle; with the clash of opposites rather than the search for the common ground. These are all factors which contribute

to the public view that politics is predominantly about gladia-
torial combat of the sort exemplified by the weekly clashes at
Prime Minister's Questions.

Yet, as Ruth Fox amply illustrates, the loss of trust in politics
and politicians cannot all be blamed on reporting by the media.
In their search for the oxygen of publicity for their views, and their
desire to differentiate those views from the offerings of others
in the political marketplace, many politicians have colluded
with the media in presenting a one-dimensional view of what
politics is about. The well-publicised and repeated failure of
some politicians to act with integrity over their expenses claims
or when lobbying on behalf of others – coupled with the failure
of political leaders to grip the issues which underlie (though
they do not excuse) some of those failings[3] – have confirmed
the age-old view that politics is about feathering my nest at
the expense of yours, a view which centuries ago led Aesop to
protest: 'We hang the petty thieves and appoint the great ones
to public office.'

As I know from over forty years' contact with UK politicians –
almost twenty of them in Whitehall and another ten helping
to regulate the conduct of politicians in both Parliament and
government – the tragedy is that many, indeed most of those
active in political life in Britain, in all the political parties,
are not in it for themselves but because they are inspired by
an ideal of public service and a desire to set the country on a
better course (although often their views as to what that course
should be differ). The work of an MP – especially one serving
on the backbenches – *is* demanding; the hours *are* long; the
pressure of leading your life totally in the public sphere *is*
considerable; and the monetary reward *is* (when compared

---

[3] Issues which include the funding of political parties and the proper remuneration
of MPs.

with jobs of similar responsibility and complexity) relatively modest. The chances of this being recognised by well-paid news-paper editors or financially hard-pressed constituents may be slim but the point needs making.

More fundamentally, in our consumer-driven society, faith in politics has suffered from the sense that, for the great majority, political involvement is just another form of consumption, in which political leaders and parties compete for our attention in the political marketplace. Ignorance of the nature of the political process combined with lessened attachment to political parties and voluntary associations such as trade unions mean that there is less engagement in politics (local and national) and with politicians as people rather than as media personalities.

What can be done to rescue the art and science of politics from the atmosphere of distrust and disengagement in which it currently languishes? In her perceptive contribution to this book, Ruth Fox argues that 'anti-politics' will not be eradicated by piecemeal tinkering with changes to the voting age or other one-off institutional changes. If the public is to be re-engaged with politics and our system of representative democracy is to adapt and survive, sustained attention is required to the develop-ment of a politics with 'less democracy but more accountability',[4] and to a politics based on values and ethical behaviour, 'stressing moral choices in pursuit of a distinct vision for the organisation of society rather than decisions rooted in "interests" and old ideological divisions predicated on outdated social class dif-ferences'.[5] Attention is required also to the defence of politics, with a 'renewed emphasis on the value and role of active citizen-ship in politics';[6] to educating not only our children but people

---

[4] See p. 199.
[5] See p. 204.
[6] See p. 206.

of all ages to the purposes and processes of politics; and to a strategic and principled rather than a piecemeal approach to institutional reform.

I have a sense that what is required as well is a sustained change not only in substance but also in style and behaviour. The current appeal of the United Kingdom Independence Party (UKIP), for example, does not only depend on the distinct nature of its policies but also on the apparently no-nonsense manner in which they are presented. Whether that no-nonsense style covers a lack of deep thinking which oversimplifies complex political and economic realities is the stuff of party political debate which I do not propose to get into. But that a significant part of the public finds it attractive cannot be denied. The message here for politicians of all parties is to find ways of communicating with the public which achieve clarity and avoid fudge. That does not mean covering over the complexities of life. It does mean speaking plainly and from the heart about what you stand for.

The contribution of faith to political discussion

If the required transformation in the nature and style of our representative democracy is to be achieved, the voice of those who speak from a position of religious faith cannot sensibly be excluded from the discussion. This is not only for the pragmatic reason that religious belief (sometimes more, sometimes less, coherently articulated) is still an important component in the lives of many citizens and that faith communities fulfil important functions within our society. It is also because one of the core components of the life of faith is the attempt to model that life on clear ethical values. There are many examples of people of faith who have made or continue to make a profound contribution to public life, inspired by (in part at least) their understanding of what their faith requires. Historical examples include William Wilberforce, Elizabeth Fry and William Beveridge, and there are many others in our contemporary society. Discussion of the values which should underpin our politics is one area in which no faith has a monopoly of wisdom but all, certainly, have much to contribute.

Politics is about more than tactics. It is, or should be, about vision and leadership. It is not merely instrumental, about the means to an end (obtaining and then holding on to political power), but about the ends we desire for our society itself.

Secular ideologies – communism, fascism, inward-looking forms of nationalism – seek to fill the void left by the retreat of faith from the political space. But they are controlling rather than informing, projecting a world-view with which everything and everyone has to be made to conform. The values of the Christian faith inform political debate; they do not dictate political outcomes.

Nevertheless they provide a set of broad objectives and an ethical framework within which political action can be developed. It is natural therefore that religious leaders should contribute to debate on political and social issues, although they are wise if they avoid doing so in ways which appear simply to involve taking sides in a partisan manner. However, pronouncements about public policy by religious leaders are commonly criticised, for example if they are about matters of economic policy on lines that they are invariably 'left-wing' (or, if about matters of sexuality, that they are 'conservative'), or that faith leaders lack expertise or understanding of the real nature of the problems under discussion.

Such criticisms often reveal more about the motives and failings of their critics than they do about the adequacy of the contribution made by faith leaders to political debate. Of course, faith leaders cannot be given special treatment. If they enter debate about public policy, they must expect to have their views challenged and, if they are to be recognised as competent and worth discussing, those views must be seen to be based on evidence as well as the testimony of either Scripture or claimed religious authority. No one can expect to be respected, let alone trusted, without acquiring the authority that comes from proven competence in addition to the authority of office. But simply to dismiss the comments of faith leaders as 'unworldly' and therefore not worth engaging with is both arrogant and intellectually flabby.

A *values-based politics*

If we are to achieve a politics in which policies are based on a clear and confident assertion of underlying values or ethical principles, what do the contributors to this book suggest those might be? Four core principles are reflected in the different contributions:

1 The equal value of each of us, at every stage of our life, not only in the sight of God but in the eyes of society. So, in relation to education, Andrew Adonis speaks of 'an equal care for all, across the whole spectrum of social class and ability' as one of the keys to getting our educational system right.[7]
2 Acceptance of this fundamental equality of individual worth calls for a commitment to offer opportunities to every citizen to maximise their capability, contribution and ultimate satisfaction, at each stage and in every sphere of life. Julia Unwin talks of the need for 'a commitment to value each individual, maximise their capability and contribution, and so secure a greater, more sustainable prosperity',[8] and Ruth Fox of the importance of equipping all citizens with the political

---

[7] See p. 91.
[8] See p. 110.

literacy skills necessary 'to navigate their way through the complex nature of politics and decision-making'.[9]

3 My well-being is inextricably linked with your well-being. We are essentially social animals and can only achieve our highest expression of happiness in and through relationship with one another. Thus Kersten England identifies the importance of vibrant communities in promoting the health and well-being of all.[10]

4 Along with a responsibility to others comes a responsibility to oneself. So, in relation to health and care, Kersten England calls for 'a renewed debate about the rights of individuals and how those are exercised. It is a debate that must include discussion of responsibilities and citizenship, because the debate is fundamentally about our connections with each other, our "social contract" and about the type of society we want in the UK.'[11] And James Woodward identifies the need for us to be realistic about how far the State can meet our needs and expectations about care as we age.[12]

From these four principles flows a concern to shape political policies around fostering hope for justice and what contributes to the common good. Hope for justice because (as I go on to argue) both individual fulfilment and social stability require a sense of confidence that things can be better and that it is worth striving for this. A focus on the common good as the precondition for a society which is not dominated by sectional interest but in which there is opportunity for all to flourish, none are abandoned and, in taking responsibility for myself, I also accept my responsibility towards you.

---

[9] See p. 208.
[10] See pp. 150ff.
[11] See p. 155.
[12] See pp. 173 and 183.

How do the principles which are embodied in what contributors to this book have written translate into values that should shape the behaviour of individual politicians, if faith in politics is to be restored? At the end of the day, they are about individual and institutional integrity, moral courage and social vision. Successful political leadership depends upon:

1 presenting a clear account of the challenges facing the country or your community, and giving an honest account of the issues, in which you treat the public as intelligent;
2 setting out a convincing vision of the kind of society you seek and of the values and principles which underlie it;
3 taking and accepting responsibility for leadership, and doing what you say you will do – and if you fail to deliver, honestly admitting it and explaining clearly why failure has occurred;
4 in your public (and, some would add, your private) life, behaving with demonstrable ethical probity – and more than a touch of humility.

The public does not expect its politicians to be saints, any more than it thinks of itself as saintly. It does expect plain dealing and that when people say they will do something, they either do it or explain convincingly why they have not. The same approach matters in respect of individual conduct. As Parliamentary Commissioner for Standards, I would always advise anyone who had acted contrary to the rules to own up at the earliest opportunity – as long as it was in a way which indicated genuine contrition and full acceptance of responsibility for what they had done.

Hope for justice

Sustaining hope for justice

The most important task of any political leader is to sustain hope – hope for justice including the possibility of a better life –

and, so far as lies within their power (an important and, in my experience, under-rated proviso), to encourage the conditions which will enable that hope to be realised. The Christian vision of society is of a group of individuals, each one of great worth, who recognise their interdependence and band together in order to realise (under God) the conditions which will enable the greatest flourishing (moral, material and spiritual) of each one of them.

In the concept of the common good, the Christian Church has sought to articulate that idea of the good which reaches to the fullest possible extent beyond *somebody's* good to become *everybody's* good, that is, the good of the human community as a whole. This is not an immutable vision of the kind of society to which we should all aspire – nor a set of plans which every politician should have in his or her back pocket. Rather the challenge for each and every political leader is to define, in terms appropriate to the times in which they live, what would constitute that common good and how it might best be realised. In making that assessment, they can be guided by the principles I have set out earlier.

Justice is a key component of a society which is marked by the common good. Achieving justice – whether in terms of social outcomes or individual disputes – involves reflective assessment on issues, within the context of a clear moral framework. In Western societies, that framework is still largely derived from the Judaeo-Christian tradition.[13] In a democracy, the pursuit of justice is a task for all of us, but particularly for those who, as community leaders, are especially so authorised by the people whom they serve. It is a task which should always

---

[13] As found in the Old and New Testaments, notably in the Ten Commandments and in the sayings of Jesus, e.g. in his summary of the Law (Matt. 22.34–40) and in the Sermon on the Mount (Matt. 5—7). Today it is variously made effective in the statute law and in codes of conduct and other non-legislative instruments.

be directed towards building up rather than undermining the community – one which should invite understanding and where possible agreement – and never be undertaken arbitrarily. Its aim should be to establish and to secure a condition of *right* – an order of social relations which is publicly understood and accepted because it privately corresponds to the understanding of the desired nature of social relationships held by each member of the community.

The hallmarks of a just society

How might we recognise a just society? Drawing on the contributions to this book, it is a society marked by:

- acceptance and valuing of the unique worth of each individual citizen, and by fair access to the means of individual fulfilment;
- recognition of the importance of social solidarity (togetherness and mutuality), not just as a bulwark against social instability but as a precondition for all to flourish, and of relationships which reflect cooperation and trust across the generations as well as between different social groups;
- commitment to the principal aim of political and social action as being to achieve a just society (as previously defined) through the pursuit of the common good;
- manifestation by political leaders of the wisdom which comes from deep, informed and balanced reflection on fundamental economic, social and political issues.

All the contributors to this book are looking for a politics which is based on mutual respect and an empathetic understanding of the position of those less advantaged in society; for policies that are based on sound evidence and a full consideration of their risks and consequences; and for solutions to policy problems which are sustainable and applied in both a consistent and a sustained way.[14] The policy approaches they suggest assume a political process in which government (central or local) is not regarded as having a monopoly of wisdom but is valued as a leader, enabler and partner in achieving solutions alongside voluntary and community groups, and in which there is full community engagement as policies are developed. In working out the correct policy solutions, taxation is regarded not as anathema but simply as one useful tool among many for bringing about social improvement. And policies which are adopted should encourage participation, along with individual and institutional responsibility and accountability, in helping to build the common good.

The contemporary challenge to building a just society

The conditions which help to constitute a just society based on right relationships are challenged and require constant re-addressing because of economic, social and political change. The economic crisis of 2008–9 constituted one such major challenge. In his masterly review of the way ahead for the British economy, Andrew Sentance describes the emergence of the 'New Normal' UK economy, in which lower growth and/or greater economic volatility may be the norm.[15] The challenge which he identifies from rising inequality and higher levels of youth unemployment is also reflected in the contributions to this book of Andrew Adonis, Oliver O'Donovan, Julia Unwin and Kersten England.

Together, these contributions underline the need for an honest account, and a facing up to by political leaders, of the nature and consequences of deep-seated social and economic

---

[14] One of Andrew Sentance's key principles for shaping our economic future, e.g., is that of 'sustainable growth'.

[15] See pp. 56ff.

changes which are driving a potentially growing gap between the haves and the have-nots in our society, and which have meant that, for an increasing number of people, honest work is no longer a guaranteed route out of poverty.

The scope for increased social tension revealed in the analysis of the contributors is not purely a result of economic factors but of other differences – among them educational, regional and generational disparities in skills, learning and employment. Like Andrew Sentance, Andrew Adonis draws attention to the predominance of unemployment, and under-employment, among the young. This has social and ethical as well as economic consequences and its effects are long term. Raising skill levels among young people – and among the long-term unemployed of any age – is crucial. Both writers point to the need to raise educational standards in schools, in terms of the number and quality of apprenticeships and in terms of early opportunities for gaining work-place experience.

In his 'Reflections on work', Oliver O'Donovan reminds us how central work is to our God-given nature and how its three dimensions – material, social and spiritual – are bound up together. If we focus purely on the material dimension of work, we tend to think of it simply in terms of 'employed work' (i.e., work we are paid to do), ignoring forms of work or occupation which, although unpaid, have huge social as well as personal benefit. Even in respect of employed work, such a limited focus can drain the work we are paid for of its capacity to give us an experience of social cooperation and community and a sense of personal fulfilment and of self-worth – in short, of all that we sum up in the phrase 'job satisfaction'.

His essay is a timely reminder that statistics of new jobs created tell only half the story. They inform us about quantity but tell us little or nothing about the quality of the work involved:

[A]s employment is not the only work there is, and unemployment not the only unmet need there is, our policies need to look beyond quantitative measures of unemployment to qualitative problems of underemployment, mismatches between work and workers, failures in education and training for work, unsatisfying or degrading work, exploitation and so on.[16]

In fighting the risk that our work (paid or unpaid) will be hollowed out, deprived of all its positive features, Oliver reminds us, the onus is not just on government but on leadership in business and all of us as individual workers to insist not only on opportunities to work but also that they should involve 'good' work, and that we should be continually given to such work, 'since good works are a cultural gift of vast importance, too easily lost by forgetfulness and negligence'.[17]

The implication of these and other contributions is that our society faces a moment of enormous challenge, a challenge which if unaddressed could see it fracture. The challenge is not the result of the failings of politicians – although some of their actions or failures to act may well have exacerbated it. It is not about how to restore steady growth or rebuild our economy – although these are very relevant to a solution. It is not about unregulated immigration or the bureaucracy of the European Union, although these may have exacerbated feelings of alienation and powerlessness in some sections of our community.

It is a challenge of social solidarity brought about by deep-seated economic, demographic and technological changes, one in which the forces of globalisation are driving wedges between a smaller group of the well-off who possess the skills required to prosper in a technologically advanced society and a larger

---

[16] See p. 123.
[17] See p. 131.

group of those who lack such skills and for whom finding 'good' and rewarding work is increasingly difficult. It is a challenge which is also created by the forces of demographic change in an increasingly mobile and rapidly ageing population, which threaten to drive wedges between different national and racial groups and between the generations. It is a challenge in which the differences are reflected geographically, notably in an increasing divide between London and the South East and the rest of the country. And it is a challenge which is made more difficult to handle because of the widespread disillusionment with and disengagement from representative politics itself.

This leads a number of contributors to this book to call for a contemporary restatement of the social contract, our understanding of the relationship of reciprocal rights and obligations between the individual and the State. The idea of the social contract is not of course new: its roots can be traced back in British political thought at least as far as the writings of Thomas Hobbes and John Locke. In Judaeo-Christian thinking, the notion of the covenant – between God and humanity, between God and the People of Israel, and as found in the New Covenant embodied in the life, death and resurrection of Jesus – is also highly relevant. The theme of this book is that the values which should underpin such a restatement of the social contract can all be found in Christian teaching. They are reflected in the principles which I set out earlier.

1 All people are of equal individual and social worth in the sight of God – the equality principle.
2 This equality of value is not expressed, in political, economic and social terms, in equality of income and possessions but in equal access to certain rights, including equal treatment under the law, equal opportunity to access and to

influence the holders of public office and equal opportunity to acquire the skills necessary to economic success – the equity principle.

3 It is also embodied in an equal acceptance of certain individual and social obligations, for example, my obligation to have regard to the consequences of my actions for you and for the maintenance of the social fabric in general, for the attainment of their rights by others and for building the common good – the solidarity principle.

4 And in an acceptance of my responsibility for myself and my own physical, spiritual and moral well-being – the autonomy principle (based on the concept of individual free will).

On this understanding of the contemporary social contract, the common good is not just or mainly about how we distribute or redistribute goods among ourselves but about how we envision the good which is of and for us all and how we best contribute to its achievement. It is to the concept of the common good that I now turn.

Love of neighbour

Love of neighbour and the common good

All the world's great religions embody what is often referred to as the Golden Rule – the notion that each of us should hold the interests of our fellow human beings as dear to us as our own. Christians are enjoined to love God and to love our neighbour as ourselves.[18] And to the question 'Who is my neighbour?' Jesus responds with one of his most powerful stories, about the Good Samaritan who comes across the badly beaten victim of a robbery and, although he is from a different, indeed

---

[18] Matt. 22.37–39; see also Matt. 7.12.

an outcast, social group, binds the wounds of the victim and makes provision for his continued care.[19]

This principle, of love of neighbour, is of great importance to individual action and also has huge social value. And if it is the case that, as Justin Welby powerfully suggests, 'Society today displays a crisis of solidarity',[20] it is one which is particularly important at the present time.

What does it mean when we speak of the common good – of the good which reaches beyond the good of the individual to embrace that of the whole community?[21] First, that we can live a common life together, reciprocating one another's contributions and being dependent on one another in receiving the good gifts of God (*mutuality*). But since living together is not a state but an activity, the mutuality takes form in what we undertake to do as *cooperation*. This implies that roles and functions are distributed among us and that we each need, and are ready to rely on, the performance of their allotted role by others. We place *trust* in each other. Trust is at the heart of all human relationships not based entirely on coercion, that is, of all worthwhile relationships, and in a democracy is at the basis of community life. It is not, as some would argue, simply a quality to be earned but it also has to be given. Indeed it cannot be earned without also being given. It then grows firmer on the basis of proven reliability. But *reliability* too grows mutually, each partner to the cooperation becoming more trustworthy as the others are trustworthy. Trust is, in short, a quality which marks and inhabits a mutuality of relationship.

---

[19] Luke 10.25–37.

[20] See p. 40.

[21] I am indebted to Professor Oliver O'Donovan for a number of the thoughts which follow.

This mutuality of relationship lies at the heart of the Christian vision of society. It is embodied in the Christian concept of 'solidarity' which, Justin Welby reminds us, 'is concerned with how we value people and communities. That is, it values people not according to their economic output or capacity but in and of themselves.'[22]

Solidarity entails a commitment to enable human flourishing through promoting the common good. It draws on a grace-filled approach to others which manifests itself in generous giving (gratuity). Such an approach to social relationships brings with it, Welby argues, the possibility for each one of us of a sense of stability (rootedness) and of hope. The stability it offers is not static, nor is it 'found in arrival at the end of the journey' but comes 'through the journey itself, a journey that is taken together'.[23]

Discerning the common good in our own time

'Yes, but what does pursuing the common good mean for us?' I hear some ask. 'Never mind all these nice, platitudinous and vague phrases. What would policies that seek the common good look like today?'

The contributors to this book have not sought to set out an alternative election manifesto. That is a job for those seeking political office. However, they cannot be accused of failing to say what adopting the approach each urges to their subject would mean in practice.

On the economy, Andrew Sentance argues for an approach based on three key principles – sustainable growth, shared prosperity and responsible business. These principles, he suggests, point to the need to develop policies which provide skills,

---

[22] See p. 37.
[23] See p. 51.

education and employment opportunities for all; involve a comprehensive review of the effectiveness, efficiency and fairness of the UK tax system; re-establish confidence in the financial system and in business more generally; and manage the necessary transition to a low carbon economy in order to achieve environmental sustainability.[24]

On regeneration, Justin Welby calls on politicians to articulate an economic programme based on four building blocks.[25] These are the adoption of the Living Wage; the provision of good and affordable housing; improvement in the quality of education and training opportunities; and access to financial services that can help everyone integrate into the economy and provide for a more stable life. On work, employment and training, Andrew Adonis, Oliver O'Donovan and Julia Unwin identify one of the key threats to social solidarity as the growing gap between those countries and individuals with the skills to compete in today's labour market and those who lack them. Andrew Adonis speaks of the crucial need to skill up young people, thereby improving the chances of preventing extended periods of unemployment. To achieve this requires insistence on higher standards in our schools, more apprenticeships, and opportunities to gain early work experience; and on the need to remunerate those in employment appropriately.[26]

Julia Unwin calls for a concerted attack on poverty in today's society. This is not a simplistic call for action by government alone but rather one for concerted action by the State, markets, communities and individuals. Indeed one consistent theme across all the contributors is that it is not simply a matter of blaming the government, or the banks, or 'benefit cheats' or

---

[24] See pp. 73ff.
[25] See pp. 45ff.
[26] See pp. 82ff.

East European immigrants but of recognising that to deliver policies which promote the common good requires action by all of us – government, central and local; markets; organisations; the Church and other community groups; and individuals.

So, in urging action to tackle fundamental inequalities in health and well-being, Kersten England calls for a re-energised debate about the responsibilities of the State, individuals, communities and healthcare professionals in relation to the attainment of personal health and well-being.[27] And James Woodward, in acknowledging the resource consequences of our rapidly ageing population – for pensions, for the NHS and for the provision of social care – suggests that action is needed on the basis of a fresh understanding of the respective responsibilities of the State, communities and individuals, coupled with an empathetic understanding of what it is like both to be young and to be elderly in today's society.[28]

The contributions in this book suggest that policies to support the common good need to be based on an empathetic understanding of the issues; sound evidence and analysis; full consideration of the risks and consequences of action; ensuring full community engagement; encouraging individual and institutional responsibility and accountability; being sustained and sustainable; and fostering shared prosperity. Policy-making in such a context cannot adopt a narrow perspective but calls for a comprehensive and integrated approach, one which is not collectivist but which fully recognises the complexity and interconnectedness of our lives. For, as Justin Welby argues: 'We really are all in it together',[29] and 'Unless all are building, what is constructed will not stand.'[30]

---

[27] See p. 157.

[28] See p. 173.

[29] See p. 42.

[30] See p. 45.

Conclusion

This is a book about more than policies, however. It is about the values which should guide us as we seek to develop our society so that all may flourish, about the firm basis on which economic, political and social policies should be constructed.

I have suggested that running through the contributions to this book we may discern three themes: Faith – in politics; Hope – for justice; and Love – of neighbour as expressed in the continuing search for the common good. Drawing on all the contributions, I have suggested that what our society needs in order to regain faith in politics and politicians, to sustain hope for justice and to fashion policies which deliver the common good is to develop a new, values-based politics reflecting four core principles:

1 recognition of the equal value of all in society;
2 commitment to offer everyone the opportunity to flourish;
3 appreciation of our essential human inter-relatedness;
4 acceptance of our responsibility towards ourselves as well as towards others.

From these principles, we can identify the hallmarks of a just society as one which is based on equality, equity, solidarity and autonomy. To give such a society expression, we need not only politicians but also leaders in other walks of life who are committed to action, in whatever sphere they occupy, which aims to deliver the common good, and are also committed to behaving in ways which are ethical, transparent and accountable.

At the beginning of this chapter, I quoted from the translation by King Alfred the Great of the *Soliloquies* of St Augustine. Alfred – the only English leader ever to be called Great – is the subject of much myth and legend, a lot of it generated by the

Victorians and not necessarily for the best of motives.[31] What is clear, however, is that he lived through times of great danger and turmoil, constantly unwell himself and often uncertain of the future. Strengthened by a great faith and inspired by a strong love of learning, he succeeded not only in maintaining his kingdom but also in laying the foundations for the emergence of a country united under the rule of law. Of course, his world was very different from our own but in the eternal human challenge – the challenge we all face, in every society and at all times, of undertaking the journey of life in company with others whom we would not necessarily choose as companions yet in a way which contributes to their well-being as well as to our own – perhaps it was not.

> Faith, Hope and Charity – these are the three anchors which hold fast the ship of the mind amidst the dangers of the waves

and, we may add, the ship of State too.

---

[31] For a short, popular history of the life and times of King Alfred, read Pollard, *Alfred the Great*.

11

Conclusion: Firm foundations for Britain's future

JOHN SENTAMU

——•••——

Any community, church, nation, that forgets its memory becomes
senile.

> (Adapted from Professor Henry Chadwick,
> General Synod, February 1988)[1]

The task we set ourselves in our symposia, and in this book, was
to consider the foundations, the values and the virtues, which
support our society and the hope and vision we can have for
a sustainable future. How do we make the Christian virtue of
hope communicate with the people who are in the rough and
tumble of decisions in a globalised and more secularised Britain?

Within the context of the Church's God-given calling to love
and care for our neighbours and to share the Good News of
God's kingdom with all, we have examined what it means to
contribute to the common good.

The Establishment of the Church of England may have its
detractors including some contemporary religious progressives

---

[1] My adaptation of Professor Henry Chadwick's epigram on memory loss and our past
inheritance, during the Debate on the Report on the Crockford Preface, in which he
said, 'No, we do not want to get stuck in our past . . . But nothing is sadder than
someone who has lost his memory, and the Church that has lost its memory is
in the same state of senility – and it can be very tragic' (*General Synod Report of
Proceedings February Group of Sessions 1988*, Volume 19 No. 1, p. 85).

and secularists, but it does bear witness to two essential and enduring gospel truths. One is the fact that the love of God extends to all, rich and poor, saint and sinner, believer and unbeliever. A second is that everyone, and every institution in society including the Church itself, sits under the judgement of God.

These truths have informed the development of all our social institutions. Of course, the Church of England was born out of political as well as religious motives and to our shame we have not always behaved as we should have done towards those whose theological views differ from our own.

In addition, as the influential social and political thinker Phillip Blond has argued, the established nature of the Church of England, as it has evolved over the centuries, has helped to create conditions favourable to the development of 'a more diverse political and social life, prevented religious extremism and helped to minimise partisan conflict and secular violence'.[2]

So, within the context of asserting the contribution that all faith communities can make to the common good, the specific or unique contribution the Church of England can make to that good is confidently and vigorously to exploit all the opportunities it has been given to proclaim and to demonstrate the Good News of the kingdom of God to all communities in England, and then offer it as gift to the Church in the rest of Great Britain – reciprocating and mutually resourcing and enriching our four nations.

Robert Kennedy, the younger brother of John F. Kennedy, and onetime Democratic Presidential Candidate, until his assassination, used to keep in his desk drawer a copy of a letter sent by the poet John Keats to his brother and sister-in-law,

---

[2] *Blond on Britain*, BBC Radio 4 (22 December 2010).

George and Georgiana Keats, in 1819. The letter said this: 'While we are laughing the seed of some trouble is put into the wide arable land of events. While we are laughing it grows and suddenly bears a poison fruit which we must pluck.'[3] The poison fruit that has sprouted within our democratic system is that of apathy, disempowerment and forgetfulness of our history, culture, and tradition. It is a lack of interest, or boredom, born not only of material excess, where consciences have grown so fat on consumption that they have ceased to function, but also of the lack of a shared vision of what our society should aim to be.

Ruth Fox, in her contribution to this collection, explores the apathy and lack of trust in the electorate and what we can do to make the situation better.

Wilkinson and Pickett, summarising the ineffectiveness of inspiration by piecemeal politics, write:

> For several decades progressive politics have been seriously weakened by the loss of any concept of a better society. People have argued for piecemeal improvements in different areas of life, campaigned against new environmental threats or for better treatment of asylum seekers, and have demonstrated against military interventions. But nowhere is there a popular movement capable of inspiring people with a vision of how to make society a substantially better place to live for the vast majority. Without that vision politics will rarely provoke more than a yawn.[4]

As I pointed out in the Introduction,[5] Jim Wallis's diagnosis of this explains why.

---

[3] John Keats (1820), *The Complete Works of John Keats Volume V: Letters, 1819 and 1820*, ed. Harry Buxton Forman (New York: Thomas Y. Crowell and Co., 1895), p. 37.

[4] Richard Wilkinson and Kate Pickett, *The Spirit Level: Why Equality Is Better for Everyone* (London: Allen Lane, 2009/London: Penguin, 2010), p. 248.

[5] See pp. 3–4.

He says, in his book *On God's Side*:

> It's time to find a better vision for our life together. Politics is failing to solve most of the biggest problems our world now faces – and the disillusionment with elections and politicians has gone global. Politicians continue to focus on blame instead of solutions, winning instead of governing, ideology instead of civility.[6]

Today things have become more complicated. Communities have become far weaker in our country than they were sixty years ago. There is far less sense of fraternity, a weaker commitment to neighbours or to playing a role in our local communities.

We have become a society which is increasingly ill at ease with itself. But this, I believe, is due to losing the sense of a common vision.

So, what are we then to do?

The role of the Church

The Church is charged by its foundation and mission to provide a voice which continues to bring challenge as well as hope, because we know that it's not a question of what governments can do for us but what we can *all* do for each other.

As Rabbi Abraham Heschel aptly said, 'We must continue to remind ourselves that in a free society, all are involved in what some are doing. *Some are guilty, all are responsible.*'[7]

The challenges and opportunities we faced five years ago as we embarked on the symposia meetings and the challenges and opportunities we face now are not without precedent. We

---

6 Jim Wallis, *On God's Side: What Religion Forgets and Politics Hasn't Learned about Serving the Common Good* (Oxford: Lion Books, 2013), p. xi.

7 Robert McAfee Brown, Abraham Heschel and Michael Novak, *Vietnam: Crisis of Conscience* (New York: Association Press, 1967); also Evelyn Wilcock, *Pacifism and the Jews* (Stroud, Gloucestershire: Hawthorn Press, 1994), p. 169.

need to build on the wisdom and experience of those who have gone before us, to consider and build on the work of Christian pioneers of social justice in our country's history and indeed across the world.

'Any community which forgets its memory becomes senile.'[8] As the United Kingdom of Great Britain and Northern Ireland, we are in danger of suffering from collective amnesia when it comes to considering the work of those who have uncovered the truth of the kingdom of God in our history. In particular, we seem to have airbrushed out the motivation of these social pioneers who have been inspired to act by a passionate and vivid faith in the God 'who has shone in our hearts to give the light of the knowledge of the glory of God in the face of Jesus Christ.'[9]

I have spoken in the Introduction about the work of Archbishop Temple and his contemporaries, Richard Tawney and William Beveridge, who recognised that the transforming power of trust in and worship of a loving God, of love of neighbour and of caring for creation are public duties not limited in their application to individual lives and circumstances. It is quite possible for the State to adopt these principles in establishing a vision of what it is to govern. 'The art of government in fact', wrote William Temple, 'is the art of so ordering life that self-interest prompts what justice demands.'[10]

This marrying of justice and self-interest is deeply unfashionable in a political scene where parties rush to outdo each other in enticing and beguiling the swing vote of middle England not with a vision of justice but with appeals to individual preference, interest and consumer choice. But if we are to build

[8] *General Synod Report of Proceedings February Group of Sessions 1988*, Volume 19 No. 1, p. 236.

[9] 2 Cor. 4.6 (NRSV).

[10] William Temple, *Christianity and Social Order* (Harmondsworth: Penguin Books, 1942; London: Shepheard-Walwyn/SPCK, 1976).

firmly for the future, we need to embrace the kind of wide and generous vision which Temple and Beveridge conceived.

As an archbishop, I know that I am called to follow in the footsteps of Jesus Christ – 'The Way, the Truth, and the Life', and in the old paths trodden by the giants of faith.

The Venerable Bede, in his *Ecclesiastical History*, tells not only of how the English were converted, but how, through its corporate discipleship, the Church played a major socialising and civilising role by uniting the English and conferring nation-hood on them.

The villages, hills and forests of northern England had rarely been visited by a Christian minister. The first three archbishops there were driven out – because of war and revolution. But the small band of Christians courageously stood their ground, bringing the Good News of freedom and hope to the North of England, an area which is now full of a lively faith and warm fellowship.

It is very clear that the socialising and transforming power of the gospel, lived out in corporate discipleship, wasn't only evident in the Church in seventh-century England, but has been evident in our own lifetime too, for example, in the reports *Faith in the City*[11] and *Faithful Cities*,[12] studies commissioned by the Church to speak out, on behalf of people in Urban Priority Areas, against injustice and oppressive conditions. Namely, *fabric decay, social disintegration* and *economic decline.*

This was a real and courageous witness of Christians in stand-ing up and proclaiming the virtues and rights of those who are weakest in our society.

---

[11] Archbishop of Canterbury's Commission on Urban Priority Areas, *Faith in the City: A Call to Action by Church and Nation* (1985).

[12] Church of England Urban Commission on Life and Faith, *Faithful Cities – A Call for Celebration, Vision and Justice* (London: Church House Publishing/Methodist Publishing House, 2006).

But, on facing savage attack not only by those in the government of the day but also by other powerful figures in society, the Church leadership then lost its nerve and moved on to internal 'churchy' matters. It did not consistently act prophetically. Instead, it focused on pastoral and social projects, albeit well delivered by the Church Urban Fund. My mantra was 'I do not believe in salvation by projects.' And the response was . . . ?

By showing fear and reluctance to act prophetically, the Church has failed to maintain a big vision. By acting prophetically, I do not mean being the voice of 'a vested interest' among other interest groups, but instead a body which can stand back and be a voice for the powerless, the weak and the dispossessed. In my mind, it is more important than ever that churches of all denominations fulfil this role today.

Rediscovering a vision for Britain

We cannot stand by and do nothing. We must rediscover a big vision for the Church and for our country. Moreover, everyone needs to be involved, or it won't work.

We have a great cloud of witnesses urging us on, the pioneers of Christian social action and political involvement over recent centuries.

William Wilberforce, rather than becoming ordained, found an expression of his faith through politics. His election as a Member of Parliament, at the age of 21, marked the beginning of a parliamentary career during which he fought tirelessly for numerous causes, not least for the abolition of the Transatlantic Slave Trade.

That same era saw Elizabeth Fry, a Quaker and an evangelistic preacher of great repute, beginning a lifetime of service to the imprisoned and the homeless. The appalling state of prisons and the particular ill-treatment of women prisoners led Fry to devote much of her time to the welfare and well-being of prisoners as well as setting up one of London's first night shelters for the homeless in 1820.

Then there are those wonderful Quaker industrialists whom I like to call 'The Chocolate Trinity': George Cadbury, Joseph Rowntree and Joseph Storrs Fry.[13]

George Cadbury (1839–1922), whose faith was his primary motivation in improving the living conditions of thousands, influenced legislation, created models for future industry and became a catalyst for social change.

Joseph Rowntree (1836–1925) was both an active Quaker and also a hugely successful businessman. His legacy includes not only two charitable trusts which continue today but also, with a vision for tackling the root causes of social problems rather than treating their symptoms, the establishment in 1904 of what was to become the Joseph Rowntree Foundation. The Foundation's research programme continues to provide challenging data on poverty, housing and health, some of which its current Director, Julia Unwin, has outlined in this collection of essays.

The third of the Chocolate Trinity was Joseph Storrs Fry II (1826–1913). Born into a Quaker household, Fry continued the family concern which had developed a reputation for innovation, quality and honesty, all hallmarks of Quaker industrial practice which was distinctive during this era. He too was a generous man, with the heart of a giver and a desire to serve God.

In their own ways, and with varying success, each of the Chocolate Trinity sought to enable those who worked for them by giving dignity and meaning to their work and life and leisure.

---

[13] I am grateful for the articles by Kris Coppock in Transformational Business Network – using business to bring spiritual and physical transformation to the world – at <www.tbnetwork.org>, accessed 10 October 2014.

Their desire to serve God as their motivation was unapologetic and unashamed.

Fifty years after Wilberforce, Josephine Butler, married to an Anglican priest, was campaigning on behalf of the hundreds of destitute and poverty stricken women she had met who had turned to prostitution as the only way out of desperate poverty.

From 1869 until 1883 Butler dedicated herself to this work, campaigning for the repeal of the Contagious Diseases Act which criminalised prostitutes rather than those who paid them. For Butler, uncovering the truth of the kingdom of God translated into letting the oppressed go free.

I could cite many other examples of great lives lived in the service of others, men and women who have taken seriously Christ's beseeching and urging and have through their work reflected God's will being done on earth.

In Britain alone in the past century there was Bruce Kenrick, the first Chairman of Shelter and one of its founding fathers; Chad Varah, the London vicar who founded the Samaritans who now receive over 14,000 calls a day; Peter Benenson, the young Christian lawyer who founded Amnesty International; Dame Cicely Saunders, the founder of the Hospice movement, who declared that, without the inspiration of Jesus' teaching and the strength given her by his Spirit, the problems she faced would have overwhelmed her.

Of course this selection is far from exhaustive and does not begin to take account of the work of all those Christians from these shores and beyond who have lived the will of God in their own countries and the countries of others.

The names of Mother Teresa, Martin Luther King Jr. and Archbishop Desmond Tutu are familiar to all, while the martyrs of the Church such as Oscar Romero, Janani Luwum and the martyred Melanesian Brothers show us that following the teachings of Christ in the serving of others can be as costly as to demand your life.

How far away do such figures seem from those Christians ridiculed by psychologists and sociologists for using their faith as a crutch. Faith is not a crutch to lean on. It is the very act of leaning.

In my inauguration sermon as the ninety-seventh Archbishop of York I said that the Church in England must once again be a beacon by which the people of England can orient themselves in an unknown ocean, by offering them the Good News of God in Jesus Christ in a way which is practical and relevant to their daily lives.

Have we lost that vision? My sense is that there is a real desire for this vision to return.

Over the past four years I have been involved in two initiatives which have striven to combat the evil of inequality and unfairness. As Sponsor of The Fairness Commission in York, I was encouraged by the collaboration we saw between all sections of the city's society, and their willingness to address injustice and inequalities among our citizens.

More recently, from 2013 to 2014, I chaired the Living Wage Commission, whose report, published in July 2014, uncovered not only the misery suffered by those who were poor and in work but also a clear business case, a clear economic case, a clear social case and a clear moral case for paying our workers a Living Wage. There is no justification, in our society, for leaving people in poverty.

As Winston Churchill, then President of the Board of Trade, told the House of Commons in 1909, 'It is a serious national evil that any class of His Majesty's subjects should receive less than a living wage in return for their utmost exertions.'[14]

---

[14] Hansard, House of Commons Debates, col. 388, 28 April 1909.

The response to this from all sectors of our communities, secular and religious, has shown that the wellsprings of solidarity are not extinct but are rising steadily.

Temple's three social principles

I now return to the social principles which Temple formulated in his *Christianity and Social Order* to provide a moral compass for our time just as they did for his, the principles of *freedom*, *fellowship* and *service*.

But these principles must be understood in a particular way.

Freedom

Temple's account of *freedom* is worth quoting in full.

> The primary principle of Christian Ethics and Christian Politics must be respect for every person simply as a person. If each man and woman is a child of God, whom God loves and for whom Christ died, then there is in each a worth absolutely independent of all usefulness to society. The person is primary, not the society; the State exists for the citizen, not the citizen for the State.
>
> The first aim of social progress must be to give the fullest possible scope for the exercise of all powers and qualities which are distinctly personal; and of these the most fundamental is deliberate choice.
>
> Consequently society must be so arranged as to give every citizen the maximum opportunity for making deliberate choices and the best possible training for use of that opportunity. In other words, one of the first considerations will be the widest possible extension of personal responsibility; it is the responsible exercise of deliberate choice which most fully expresses personality and best deserves the great name of freedom.

> Freedom is the goal of politics. To establish secure true freedom
> is the primary object of all right political action. For it is in and
> through freedom that a man makes fully real his personality –
> the quality of one made in the image of God.[15]

What is noteworthy about Temple's understanding of *freedom*
is that, to put it in modern terms, it encompasses not only
freedom from interference (negative freedom) but also freedom
from domination. For Temple says:

> Freedom, in short, is self-control, self-determination, self-direction.
> To train citizens in the capacity for freedom and to give them
> scope for free action is the supreme end of all true politics.[16]

You cannot love someone as your neighbour if you dominate
them. So, if you love someone as your neighbour, then you
will work to set them free. Thus, freedom, in the sense not only
of non-interference but also of non-domination, entails social
justice.

And we need to distinguish, perhaps, what it is for someone
to *exercise* freedom from what the State can do to *enable and
enhance* freedom. To exercise freedom is simply to take responsibility for the ways in which we live, our policies, decisions
and actions. We cannot be made to do it, and nor can we be
stopped from doing it. But we can be helped to do it or dis-
couraged from doing it.

It is important that the State should help, not hinder our
exercise of freedom, which it can do (1) by enforcing laws
that secure basic liberties, (2) by overseeing an economic
system that gives opportunities to earn a decent living to
all who can work, and (3) by ensuring that the social infrastructure is in place to afford healthcare, education, housing

---

[15] Temple, *Christianity and Social Order*, p. 39.
[16] Temple, *Christianity and Social Order*, p. 68.

and well-being support, as they are needed and can be made good use of.

If a person lacks any of these basic, public goods, they are dominated; dominated by the 'Five Giant Evils' that Beveridge identified in his report: Squalor, Ignorance, Want, Idleness, and Disease.

As Nelson Mandela said concerning poverty, 'Overcoming poverty is not a gesture of charity. It is an act of justice. It is the protection of a fundamental human right, the right to dignity and a decent life. While poverty persists, there is no true freedom.'[17]

When Temple, Tawney, and Beveridge tackled the Five Giant Evils in the 1940s they had a clear vision as to how things could be different. In part, they were also tapping into the spirit of the immediate post-war years in which there was a great hunger to build a more equitable, more caring world.

It is that vision which we need to recapture today but remoulded in a way which is realistic for the circumstances we face now. We can do it, but we need the political will as well as moral and religious conviction.

And if one person is not free, none of us is free, for freedom is a public good. For no one is free if anyone is oppressed; just as, in Martin Luther King's words, 'injustice anywhere is a threat to justice everywhere.'[18] We need to hear this principle of freedom afresh, not least regarding our treatment of the elderly, those refused asylum, young people in the care system and the severely disabled.

[17] Nelson Mandela, 'Speech on Poverty' (2005) <http://news.bbc.co.uk/1/hi/uk_politics/4232603.stm>, accessed 22 August 2014.

[18] Martin Luther King, Jr., 'Letter from a Birmingham Jail', *I Have a Dream: Writings and Speeches That Changed the World*, ed. James M. Washington (New York: HarperOne, 1992).

These voiceless members of our society, without votes canvassed and without political advocacy, remain of equal worth in the eyes of God and should not be victims of our social denigration and economic decline. They, too, should be free.

Given that freedom, in Temple's sense, entails social justice as I have argued above, it entails a kind of equality of citizens – in particular, a more equal economic distribution of wealth.[19]

Without this freedom and equality, we run the danger outlined by Percy Bysshe Shelley (1792–1822) when he said. 'The rich have become richer, and the poor have become poorer; and the vessel of the state is driven between the Scylla and Charybdis of anarchy and despotism.'[20]

But with this freedom and equality, what a vision of Britain there could be! And we can do it. All it takes is a commitment to loving our neighbours as ourselves, from which follows freedom, social justice and equality for all.

Fellowship

Which leads me to Temple's next principle.

Fellowship is the recognition that we are all mutually dependent on one another. It is a rejection of the consumerism and individualism that has dominated Britain for the past thirty years. Fellowship is rooted in the sentiment behind John Donne's 'No Man is an Island':

> No man is an island entire of itself; every man
> is a piece of the continent, a part of the main;
> if a clod be washed away by the sea, Europe
> is the less, as well as if a promontory were, as
> well as any manor of thy friends or of thine

---

[19] Here, I side with Tawney in his disagreement with Temple over whether equality should be included in the social principles for ordering a just society.

[20] W. S. Landor, *Imaginary Conversations, Southey and Landor ii.*

own were; any man's death diminishes me,
because I am involved in mankind.

And therefore never send to know for whom
the bell tolls; it tolls for thee.[21]

We may live on an island, but no one is an island. We all need
one another.

Temple makes this clear in his explanation of the principle
of fellowship:

> No man is fitted for an isolated life; everyone has needs which
> he cannot supply for himself; but he needs not only what his
> neighbours contribute to the equipment of his life but their
> actual selves as complement of his own. Man is naturally and
> incurably social.[22]

That we are social beings is a thought by no means unique
to Temple. As we say in Africa, 'I am because we are. I am because
I belong. I am because I participate.'

Social fellowship teaches responsibility and interdependence.
It demonstrates the fallacy that people can live disconnected
lives, isolated and individualised or atomised one from another.
This social fellowship is expressed through family life, school,
college, trade union, professional association, city, county, nation,
church, synagogue, temple and mosque. It is an understanding
that we sink or swim together. That we are bonded together by
our common humanity. That we are members of the one race:
the human race.

The State needs to recognise that all these groups spring
up of right where people live together, and must be treated with

---

[21] John Donne, 'Meditation XVII', *John Donne: Selections from Divine Poems, Sermons, Devotions, and Prayers*, Classics of Western Spirituality 69, ed. and intro. John E. Booty (Mahwah, NJ: Paulist Press, 1990).

[22] Temple, *Christianity and Social Order*, p. 69.

respect. This includes 'fostering' where there is some threat to be countered, but may often mean simply leaving well alone.

Service

Freedom and fellowship operate best when we seek not our own well-being and wholeness first but the general well-being of all people. This is Temple's principle of *service*. Having learnt the infinite worth of each individual, and the value of interdependence, it is through service to both family and community that society as a whole benefits. Our wider loyalties can be used to check the narrower. We can and should check these keener loyalties, to family, career, and home, by recognising the prior claim of wider humankind, nation, and our global village.

As Temple writes,

> So a man rightly does his best for the welfare of his own family, but must never serve his family in ways that injure the nation. A man rightly does his best for his country, but must never serve his country in ways that injure mankind.[23]

Arguments will continue to rage about the causes and origins behind the most recent economic crisis. The answers will be important in terms of learning lessons for the future, but more important still will be how we deal as a nation with the situation in which we find ourselves. For me, the road to recovery is a path not to riches but to service.

It is rooted in the rediscovery of a vision to rebuild community in recognition of our common humanity. Of standing ready to help our neighbour not only because they may be a victim of the recession but also because they are created in the image and likeness of God and are an individual of infinite worth for whom Christ died and whom the Spirit calls to a purposeful life.

---

[23] Temple, *Christianity and Social Order*, p. 75.

The Well-being State

Beveridge called the system he developed a system of 'Social Insurance'. Soon after, Temple called it 'the Welfare State', and it is Temple's phrase that has stuck. However, in this present context I would prefer to talk less in terms of 'welfare' and more in terms of 'well-being' to illustrate how I think Temple's principles should be put into practice.

To begin with, Hugh Montefiore provides a marvellous summary of the moral foundation of the Welfare State:

> Whatever be the place of private charity, most of the necessary provisions can only be made adequately on a national scale and therefore there need to be national social services. Since most of our social benefits come from general taxation, and the rich pay more absolutely and proportionately than the poor, they are therefore making (as indeed they should do) a greater contribution to the social services of the country . . . However . . . it is the responsibility of the state to provide the great majority of our social services, especially in education, health, housing, family allowances, social security and in schemes of national insurance.
>
> This is the principle underlying our provision. And a very noble ethical principle it is! We have a duty to help our neighbours. This duty is best carried out at a national level, in many of the most important sectors of provision. From each, according to his resources, to each, according to his need. This is part of what it means to love our neighbour as ourselves. What could be better?[24]

What is most helpful about Hugh Montefiore's summary is how he traces the Welfare State to the concept of neighbourly love,

---

[24] Hugh Montefiore, *Taking Our Past into Our Future* (London: Fount Paperbacks, 1978), pp. 273–4.

something which I have argued both in the Introduction and in this concluding chapter.

This is why I suggested that we should think in terms of a Well-being State, for well-being has to do with *eudaimonia*, which I discussed in my introductory chapter. *Eudaimonia* refers to the flourishing, happiness, and well-being of human persons. Temple's three principles produce the *eudaimonia*, the flourishing, blessedness, and well-being, of persons in community.

Human life, the kind of life Jesus speaks about when he says, 'I came that they may have life, and have it abundantly',[25] goes beyond welfare. It is about well-being. In an age of austerity, we need a vision of abundance, and only a vision of a Well-Being State can provide that.

Jesus' prescription of the priorities of God's kingdom in which all these qualities can flourish is set out in the Beatitudes. This is Jesus' radical approach to the conflicts and pressures, the oppression and the self-seeking of the world.

It describes God's summons to us to respond to his invitation and become agents of his movement of transforming love and outreach through the power of the Holy Spirit.

This year, 2015, is the eight-hundredth Anniversary of the Magna Carta: the *Magna Carta Libertatum* or The Great Charter of the Liberties of England, in which the power of the temporal king of this nation was limited.

The Sermon on the Mount/Plain has always been recognised as the most important part of the New Testament. It is Jesus' Mission Statement and may be regarded as the Magna Carta of the kingdom of God which Jesus came to proclaim and demonstrate in his life and death, for it outlines the great and radical freedom we gain through overthrowing the oppressive, grasping, worldly powers of greed and selfishness, and

---

[25] John 10.10.

instead adhering to a new world order of love, compassion and mutual care.

In Jesus' Mission Statement, we see the divine qualities and the outcomes of belonging to God's reign, whose blessedness is modesty, compassion with sorrow, gentleness, an eager desire for justice, purity and singleness of purpose, kindness to all creation, bridge-building and not peace-breaking, and perseverance in spite of all difficulties and life-threatening challenges.

The Beatitudes are declarative statements. Jesus does not say, 'Be poor' or 'Be pure in heart' or 'Be merciful' or 'Be a peacemaker'. He says, 'Blessed are the poor', 'Blessed are the pure in heart', 'Blessed are the merciful', 'Blessed are the peace-makers', etc. These are divine qualities and are pure gift, freely offered to all citizens of the kingdom of God.

They give to all the great goal or end which will resolve the many difficulties in the battle of life which humankind faces, setting out an order for life which assumes the Ten Commandments and goes beyond them. They also exemplify the paradoxical character of Jesus Christ and his gospel.

Our present individualistic society may struggle to imagine the benefits of belonging to a society where personal satisfaction and acquisition are not the main motives for action.

In the Beatitudes, happiness, blessedness, is the paradox, which Christ promises if we live and behave in a way which humanly speaking is the very opposite of what our inclinations tell us would give us pleasure.

The resulting joy or blessedness is not a reward given for good behaviour, but the result of walking into the freedom which comes from responding to God's invitation to participate in a new way of living, acting, thinking and imagining.

The Beatitudes open up a new world of spiritual character and holy beauty and consequent joy, beyond humanity's perceiving.

They show us that blessedness lies, not in outward circumstances but in inward life. So, 'Blessed are the poor in spirit', that is, blessed are the unselfish – those who live for others, and not for themselves, leaving a large margin of their life for the awareness which comes from the Spirit of God, and also from what is in the world.

My father, preaching on this text, told the story of a Muganda king, who, on arriving with his guards from my clan, the Buffalo Clan, at the River Nile, fifty miles away from his Palace, said, 'Anyone who wants to be a king must first make himself a bridge.' And he carried his ten guards (who were terrified, because they didn't know how to swim), one after another, on his back, until they reached the other bank of the river.

That is what the Magna Carta of the kingdom of God is calling us to be. Bridges that enable others to get to the place of safety; working co-operatively together in unity of purpose; becoming servants of others; and serving the public good, not by doing their bidding, not by defending their interests, not by listening to their follies, but by seeking their well-being and good.

Jesus Christ's vision for a new world order goes beyond simple adherence to the detail of God's law, his rule of life. He calls us into a deeper understanding of the *purpose* of the rules, for guiding not just our actions but our attitudes and our relationships with one another.

That is why he concludes his Sermon on the Mount by expanding on the deep layers of meaning in the Law.

We are not to murder; neither are we to look with anger, bitterness, hatred, contempt, vengeance on our brothers and sisters. For it is attitudes such as these that lead to the dehumanising of others and the devaluing of their life.

We are not to commit adultery; neither are we to look on each other primarily as objects for the satisfaction of our sexual or physical needs. For this too leads to the debasing of all our relationships.

We are to approach one another with simplicity, openness, truth, generosity, love and forgiveness – respecting and honouring each person as having equal worth and showing the same kindness and forgiveness with which God our Father treats us.

In this book, we draw together a number of themes which have recurred in our discussions, and form a chain of thought about the good of the community.

At its head stand two terms: the kingdom of God and the common good. These terms are linked, not because they are synonymous, but because in Christian understanding they are inseparable. On the one hand, the rule of God over his creation; on the other hand the good which reaches to the fullest extent, beyond *somebody's* good, to become *everybody's* good – that is, for the human community as a whole.

Augustine, in his writings on the nature of Angels, declares that God alone and himself is our common good, meaning that to live under his rule is to participate in the good that he is and to share that good with others.[26]

As citizens of the kingdom of God we live a common life together, reciprocating one another's contributions and being dependent on one another in our reception of the good gifts of God. But since living together is not a state but an activity,

---

[26] Augustine of Hippo, *The City of God*, on the Nature of Angels says, 'That the contrary propensities in good and bad angels have arisen, not from a difference in their nature and origin, since God, the good Author and Creator of all essences, created them both, but from a difference in their wills and desires, it is impossible to doubt. While some steadfastly continued in that which was the common good of all, namely, in God Himself, and in His eternity, truth, and love; others, being enamoured rather of their own power, as if they could be their own good, lapsed to this private good of their own, from that higher and beatific good which was common to all, and, bartering the lofty dignity of eternity for the inflation of pride, the most assured verity for the slyness of vanity, uniting love for factious partisanship, they became proud, deceived, envious' (Book XII, Chapter 1) (trans. M. Dods, NPNF).

this mutuality and sharing takes form in what we undertake to do – our co-operation. The fruit of our shared life is the human flourishing, the state of well-being, which God has promised us – life in all its fullness.

This Well-being State – justified by our recognition of one another's common humanity, expressed in neighbourly love and guided by the principles of Freedom, Fellowship, Service, and the Rule of Law – are the firm foundation, the rock, we need for Britain's future. Only when we help one another perceive and imagine this vision together will we be like the wise builder of Jesus' parable:

> 'Everyone then who hears these words of mine and acts on them will be like a wise man who built his house on rock. The rain fell, the floods came, and the winds blew and beat on that house, but it did not fall, because it had been founded on rock. And everyone who hears these words of mine and does not act on them will be like a foolish man who built his house on sand. The rain fell, and the floods came, and the winds blew and beat against that house, and it fell – and great was its fall!'
>
> Now when Jesus had finished saying these things, the crowds were astounded at his teaching, for he taught them as one having authority, and not as their scribes.[27]

> 'Why do you call me "Lord, Lord", and do not do what I tell you? I will show you what someone is like who comes to me, hears my words, and acts on them. That one is like a man building a house, who dug deeply and laid the foundation on rock; when a flood arose, the river burst against that house but could not shake it, because it had been well built. But the one who hears and does not act is like a man who built a house on the ground without a foundation. When the river burst against it, immediately it fell, and great was the ruin of that house.'[28]

---

[27] Matt. 7.24–27 (NRSV).

[28] Luke 6.46–49 (NRSV).

Strong actions based on the foundation of the teaching of Jesus reveal that the doer, and not the mere hearer, will withstand the vicissitudes of life.

Total devotion to God and love of neighbour, as Jesus Christ has shown us by giving up himself to suffering and death on the Cross, are the only foundation rock we are to build on as individuals and as Great Britain. True religion, goodness and the well-being of a nation may be likened to a house built on solid foundations. Religions, people and nations are unwise when they build not on the Sermon on the Mount but on the shifting sands of self-serving and transitory desire. They are left naked and shelterless to the fury of the storm, as the entire fabric totters to its fall, since it has no firm foundation.

Individualism and consumerism are sand. Freedom, Fellowship, Service for God and neighbour, and the Rule of Law are rock. These are the firm foundations for Britain's future.